BULLYING

BULLYING

Responsibility Lies with the Parents

Evelyn Ekhator

© 2015 Evelyn Ekhator
All rights reserved.
Evelyn Publisher
The Netherlands

ISBN: 1514821001
ISBN 13: 9781514821008
Library of Congress Control Number: 2015910961
Createspace Independent Publishing Platform
North Charleston, South Carolina

What comes to mind when you hear the word *bullying*?
Oppression
Isolation Harass Unbearable
Low self-esteem Heartache Torment Sad story
Cyberbullying Affect kids Verbal abuse Wrong association
Pushing Stress Child Crying Sleeplessness Elementary school
High school Followers Children Upbringing Bystanders Sadness
Television programs Internet Victim Peer pressure Not nice
Bad people Jealousy Pain Bully Payback Persecution Headache
Depression School Aggression Terrible Miserable Angry
Annoying Egocentric Gossip Disability Work floor
Digital war Attack on self-confidence
Fighting Dishearten
Nightmare

Contents

	Introduction	ix
Part 1		1
Chapter 1	Bullying	3
Chapter 2	Types of Bullies	11
Chapter 3	Types of Victims	39
Chapter 4	Followers, Bystanders, and the Voice	57
Part 2		71
Chapter 5	The Fundamentals of Parenting	73
Chapter 6	Parents are the Antidote for Bullying	83
Chapter 7	Bullying in School	110
Chapter 8	Cyberbullying and Cloud Homes	125
Chapter 9	Workplace or War Floor	139
Part 3		153
Chapter 10	Bullies (You) are Better than Bullying	155
Chapter 11	Be the Victor and Not the Victim	172
Chapter 12	Love Versus Hate	190
Chapter 13	The Gift of Life	200
Chapter 14	Appeal to Parents and Society	209
Part 4		221
Chapter 15	Dreams and Purpose	223
Chapter 16	You Have a Role to Play	236
Chapter 17	The Keys—Observations and Guidance	252
Chapter 18	It is in Your Hands	261

Introduction

STORMS COME IN life to either make or break you, and so does the storm of bullying. Bullying is a storm that comes to hurt and destroy its victims. Unfortunately, the storm is raging in the homes of both the rich and poor, cutting across all races. Some people have been destroyed by the bullying storm, while few others have conquered it by using it to climb on the wings of another to fly higher in life.

There are different definitions for bullying, and they all depend on one's interpretation of the situation and the circumstances surrounding the bullying attack. In the past, there were only acts of physical and verbal bullying, but today there is cyberbullying. The effects of cyberbullying are much more devastating because innocent children can be bullied even within the safety of their homes, while homes ought to be safe havens for children to grow and develop their potential.

One of the obstacles in eradicating bullying in our society is the error of treating bullies as a group or entity instead of handling each case of bullying individually. There are factors that come into play in making a person a bully, and these factors differentiate one bully from another; hence, there are different types of bullies. Bullying is about taking and maintaining territory, because all a bully wants is to dominate others by playing god and boss over his or her victim, especially when a bully finds a weak link in a group, whom he or she targets as prey. A bully cannot operate without having a person susceptible to an attack, and this leads to victimization of that individual.

There are also different types of victims. Victims need to change their mentalities; otherwise, they will always be victims. Defeat is the outcome when you make yourself subordinate or inferior to others. Remember, how you see yourself will determine what you attract to your life. Do not allow any bully to make you his or her victim. Whatever power the bully is using against the victim is the power allocated to the bully by the victim. Thus, the victim must decide to be a victor, not a victim.

No one is born a bully or a victim, but environment can turn a person into either one. Both parents of a bully and a victim have a major role to play, as the support of each is crucial. Parents should also listen more to their children—especially to the victim, to help the victim find the right resources.

Schools have become a breeding ground for bullies to operate and recruit followers. School authorities have become firefighters trying to put out the bullying fire that is raging in their schools. Schools cannot solve the problem on their own; we all—especially parents—have a role to play in helping schools to stop bullying and make our school environment conducive for learning. Mothers and fathers are the first teachers a child will ever encounter; as such, it is vital for parents to teach their children the language of love. Wherever there is love, there is kindness, compassion, devotion, respect, and regard for others.

Teaching love to children should be a joint venture between parents and guardians. When there is love in a person's heart, there is no room for bullying. A heart that is filled with love sees what is invisible to the eyes. It is crucial to contain bullying behavior in a child when it is discovered at a tender age; otherwise, it will spill over to adulthood. The rules and principles that parents teach their children will reflect in the lives of their children as they grow older. It either lets them shine like the sun and sparkle like a diamond or be the bad ones in their generation.

As for the followers of a bully, they are accomplices that empower, strengthen, and enforce the agenda of the bully. A bully sometimes cannot operate alone. A bully needs followers to execute, promote, or support his or her agenda.

Meanwhile, bystanders are the majority in any environment where there is bullying. Most times, bystanders refuse to utilize their power as a

INTRODUCTION

majority because they believe it is not their business. What they fail to realize is that if you are not bullied today, it does not exempt you from being bullied tomorrow.

Bullying is a worldwide problem that requires a united effort to tackle. Several organizations are already doing a lot individually, but there is an urgent need for a global, unified body to coordinate the eradication of bullying tendencies in our society, and this is one of the aims of this book.

PART 1

Bullying is an agenda that is being carried out by bullies in their words and physical actions.

1

Bullying

Bullying is a word that rings different bells in people's ears and minds. To some it brings mixed feelings; to others it's terrifying, opening unhealed wounds and bringing up sad memories of loved ones they've lost. It might remind some of what incapacitated them or of what they conquered. Perhaps it reminds them of their strengths. To others it is a strange word that has no meaning because it has not affected them or someone close to them. Thus, they remain nonchalant when they hear about the havoc bullying is causing in the lives of victims and their families. Whatever group you might belong to, remember this:

Any violence that occurs as a result of bullying is one too many.

Bullying is the mechanism a bully uses to attack his or her victims. An attack on the victim's self-confidence is usually the bully's first point of entry in fulfilling his or her agenda. This attack on the victim's self-confidence drastically affects every area of the victim's life. Attacking the victim's self-esteem is the only way a bully can verify the self-effacing of the victim. The bully's findings will determine whether he or she will launch subsequent attacks on the victim because a bully will never attack anyone who is stronger than him or her, or who poses a threat.

When bullies conquer the self-confidence of their victims, they also indirectly conquer every area of their victims' lives. This automatically puts the bully in charge and in control of the victim, hence empowering the bully to control the belief system of the victim by determining what the victim thinks or believes about his or her self-worth, capabilities, and capacity.

It becomes a dilemma when victims believe the lies and negative pictures the bullies are painting about them. This will further deteriorate the self-confidence and self-esteem of the victim. Once this happens, the victims take this mentality into everything they do, which limits their performance.

Bullying is an agenda that is being carried out by a bully in words and physical actions.

To understand bullying, first of all, is to identify the motivation behind the bully's actions. When one understands bullying, one gains insight into what prompts bullies to use a bullying trigger. Likewise, the definition of bullying varies from one situation to another because the channels and modes of operation of bullies differ from one bullying case to another. That is why it is very important to handle each case of bullying individually, in order to understand the action or reason behind bullying, which will pave a way into the root of the issues. This will eventually help to address those triggers responsible for it, because to kill or destroy a tree permanently, you have to go to the root; going to the root in order to stop bullying facilitates understanding bullying.

Bullying Occurs in Levels

Bullying occurs in every facet of life: in homes, schools, offices, streets, hospitals, shopping malls, media houses, organizations, sports communities, and so on. Bullying eats deep into the fabric of society every day. It has become a problem people shy away from; in fact, some people choose to remain silent about it and even deny that it is happening.

Bullying is spreading rapidly in schools and in workplace. Schools and work floors have become recruitment grounds for bullies — bullying has become a plague that is contagious. The effect of bullying on the victims differs because bullying occurs in levels; thus, the level in which bullying occurs differs from place to place and victim to victim. Since the level of bullying differs, the havoc it creates and the response it gets differs, too. The level in which bullying occurs, then, will determine the results and the type of publicity it generates.

The truth about bullying is that most people have experienced bullying in one way or another. It is happening every day, whether directly or indirectly, but the response it gets depends on the interpretation. Some people might not see or call it bullying until they sit down to analyze the situation and the circumstances surrounding it. In each situation, the bully has an agenda for the victim; in turn, the victim has his or her own interpretation of the incident.

Despite bullying happening at different levels and in different channels, it is a problem that should not be tolerated or accepted. Bullying is a two-faceted problem that has its repercussions on the victims, including their families and even the bully. In as much as the heat of bullying is being felt by the victims, the smoke of the bullying fire is suffocating the lives of the bullies—plus their followers—to their own detriment. The pathway of bullying is dangerous and slippery, propelling everyone to a cliff and a fatal fall.

Since the pathway of bullying is a highway of destruction, pain, heartache, and anarchy, it is crucial for bullies to deviate from that highway for the interest of humanity. Abjuring the pathway of bullying is beneficial to human existence.

Bullying is Deadly and it Creates a Vacuum

Bullying is like an earthquake; it shakes the lives of those who are affected. It shifts, moves, changes, destroys, and even influences the decisions of the victims. Bullying can result in either physical or emotional death—whether a bully kills someone with a physical attack or with his or her words, or pushes the victim into taking his or her own life. Either way, bullies are responsible for the outcome of the victim's actions. Before a bully decides to engage in bullying, he or she ought to realize it's not just about carrying out an action of harassment, control, or domination but an action that could be deadly.

In other words, bullying can become deadly when it is a battle for superiority, control, domination, and territory. Never in human history has dominating and acquiring territory not been bloody or deadly. Therefore, bullying another person can become deadly when a person's life is used as a springboard for bullies to gain selfish interest or popularity in spite of the havoc it might create in the life of the victim. Thus, a bully's quest for recognition or superiority or supremacy can lead to holding another person's life as ransom. Bullies use these tools to settle scores if quick and appropriate steps are not taken to intervene.

Most of the bullying happening today is terrible and heartbreaking; innocent people have been bullied to death as they were forced to make irrational decisions, which led to some of them committing suicide. To truly gain a glimpse of the complexity of bullying in the lives of the victims is to be sensitive to the pain and havoc bullying has created in the lives of the victims and their families.

Bullying is an intense and aggressive war; in spite of the atrocity and chaos bullying has created, little has been done to stop this deadly war that is so prominent in schools and even the workplace. Bullying tampers with people's dreams, vision, and focus. It is a valley of pain and rejection; it is a dark isle in the life of the victims, which is fraught with loneliness. Any form of bullying always takes something away from the victim, by killing the victim's dreams, focus, confidence, or aspirations.

In some cases, bullying results in the death of the victim; such cases affect the parents whose hopes and dreams for their children where shattered before they were even realized. These parents might be living, but part of them died when they lost their children to a bully. In this way, bullying creates a vacuum in the lives of parents who lost their children in the cross fire of bullies.

Whatever the reason bullies engage in bullying, the vacuum or space it creates in the lives of the victims' families and friends cannot be compensated. Some of these parents are still paralyzed with the agony of their loss. Indeed, bullying is a worldwide epidemic; the problem is that most countries lack a structured process of resolving the bullying behavior and subsequent damage.

Bullying is a Worldwide Epidemic

When you hear about war, disaster, or food shortages in the world today, you hear about the United Nations; when you hear about injustice or war crimes, you hear about the World Court; and when you hear about human rights, you hear about Amnesty International. But when it comes to bullying, which is spreading like a virus in schools and in the workplace, there is no unified body worldwide that is even attempting to eradicate it. Bullying has become acceptable culture among the youth today, especially when it comes to physical and cyberbullying.

The problem of bullying should be addressed from homes to local, national, and international levels. There should be a joint effort at all levels to destroy this monster that affects so many innocent children. How far we succeed in eliminating any form of bullying will be determined by the cooperation of parents and all other organizations working together as one body. Therefore, one of the keys to finding a lasting solution begins by handling bullies as individuals in order to know the *why* behind their actions.

> *"And that's why the world is in such terrible danger right now. It's not dangerous so much because we have atomic bombs. It's dangerous because of the human hearts back of the bombs filled with envy and hate and strife and greed and lust and all the other things that can pull the trigger."*
> —Billy Graham

Bullying is Driven by Emotions

Bullying is a behavior that is driven by emotions, and emotions are at the mercy of thought. Thought, in turn, is being propelled by the bully's surroundings; hence, emotions are a major trigger that sponsors bullying. Negative emotions will incapacitate a bully from making a rational judgment. They hinder a bully's ability to make the right choice. Bullies can make a difference when they redirect their energy into a positive endeavor. Thus, a cure begins by filtering what surrounds the bully and what accesses his or her senses. Whatever accesses the senses of bullies controls their thoughts, which is the catalyst for their emotions and determines how they feel about and react to others. Accordingly, their emotions are the vanguard of their dealings with others because people, including bullies, consciously or subconsciously take their feelings into whatever they do with themselves and others.

Factors that Incite Bullying Behavior

There are factors that create a bully or a victim, such as parenting style or upbringing, society or environment, associations or medical issues, and so forth. Such factors contribute to promoting or enforcing bullying in an environment. But the role parents play is significant—crucial even—in promoting or stopping bullying. In every aspect of life, when people keep to the rules, there is always peace. Sometimes these rules are not easily followed; still, they need to be enforced. Thus, ending bullying in any environment begins with teaching children how to obey rules, especially when dealing with human lives.

This book cover is a message on its own. Just as there are rules guiding the game of chess, there are rules guiding human behavior. Whether we acknowledge them or not, these fundamental rules exist. Furthermore, our decision to accept or ignore the rules has consequences, just like the rules guiding the game of chess.

In the game of chess, there are opponents on opposite sides of a board, and the goal of the game is to checkmate the king. Checkmate happens when a king is in a position where it cannot escape from being captured. The movement of the pieces on the board determines if a piece will be captured or not. Generally, pieces move into positions where they can defend their own pieces, in order to protect them from being captured. The same is true in life: the positioning of parents in the lives of their children determines if their children will be labeled as a bully, victim, follower, or bystander.

In reality, life is played between two opponents on opposite sides (i.e., the good and the bad), but the end result of which side of the board you end up on is determined by the choices you make, and these choices are a result of the fundamental principles that guide your life and family. These rules and principles will reflect in the lives of your children—namely, whether they will choose the right path (the good side)—so that they can shine like the sun and sparkle like a diamond among their generation. On the flip side, if they choose the wrong path (the bad side), it's checkmate.

Acronym for BULLYING

- **B** Bad Behavior
- **U** Uselessness
- **L** Lawlessness
- **L** Lead
- **Y** You
- **I** Into
- **N** Negative
- **G** Group

A bully should avoid the pathway of bullying because it always leads to negative group associations as stated in the acronym above, which will result in consequences a bully is not willing to face.

A bully is an individual and not a group.

2

Types of Bullies

When it comes to bullying, bullies are always addressed and handled as a group or an entity, which has only amplified the problem. Until bullies are handled as individuals, one cannot know what drives their actions. Only when each bully is handled as an individual can one identify the reason behind a bully's actions, because there are factors that come into play in making a person a bully. These factors help us identify the type of bully we are dealing with and what kind of help or support to give them to bring about permanent, positive change.

Treating all bullying cases as an entity, with the tag *bully* or *bullies*, is an error that must be corrected and avoided in the future because what makes one bully get involved in bullying activities might be different from what makes another bully do the same. It is like going to the doctor when you are sick, and the doctor writes a prescription without examining you or asking you questions about your symptoms. Fortunately, this is not permitted within the medical field. But the reality today is that bullies have been handled or treated without full knowledge of the reasons behind their actions. We know that doctors always diagnose the sickness before administering treatment or prescribing drugs to patients. Bullies are no exception; identifying the type of bully will help eliminate bullying activity in schools. *Inquiring is the key to acquiring anything in life, including finding solutions to problems such as bullying.*

Bullying is a Symptom

For any victim or society, bullying is a problem. For a bully, however, bullying is a symptom of deficiencies in areas of the bully's life. Bullying can be a sign of hidden problems or issues that cause a volcanic eruption when there are pressures or mental deficiencies. This is a catapult for supremacy tendencies in bullies in their quest for power, leading to frustration, emotional imbalance, peer pressure, negative influences or associations, and so on. The lava of the bully's bottled-up issues burns the weaker link in the group.

Such issues need to be resolved before an effective change can take place in the bully's life. Suspending or expelling a bully from school does not solve his or her problem; it only covers up the wound without applying the necessary medicine to prevent infection. There cannot be a fight where there is no dispute or quarrel, and there cannot be a bully where there is no bad influence, hurt, and bitterness. Thus, when the different issues fueling a bully are tackled and addressed one person (bully) at a time, there will be a silver lining in the horizon.

The Concept of Bullies

Bullies are like sales reps that specialize in selling their good products, but in the case of bullies, they sell their negative ideas about a person to others, including their victims. Thus, the concept of bullies is the major sponsor for victim entrapment, which leads to a victim mentality. The picture the bullies paint for most of their targets has held these victims captive and has created in them a concept that becomes a baseline for who they are.

The picture is used by the bullies as a derivative to determine the worth of their victims, and the ability of bullies to entice victims to buy into their concept about them enables the bullies to create a web in which the victims become entangled. When the victim keeps on believing the bully's lies and negative propaganda, the possibility of the victim getting out of the bullying web becomes slimmer.

There cannot be a fight where there is no dispute or quarrel, and there cannot be a bully where there is no bad influence, hurt, and bitterness.

Types of Bullies

There are different types of bullies:

- Association bully
- Behavioral-disorders bully
- Blackmailing bully
- Camouflage bully
- Crisis bully
- Cyberbully
- Discrimination-mentality bully
- Drug bully
- Gossip bully
- Inherited bully
- Privileged-oppressive bully
- Racial bully
- Retaliating bully
- Second-class-citizen bully
- Word bully
- Physically aggressive bully

Association can influence a person positively or negatively; thus, the company you keep is a preview of your future. So parents beware of the friends your children associate with because a lot of children have been initiated into bullying due to fraternizing with bullies.

Association bully
Association bullies are influenced by the company they keep and as a result of the friends with whom they mingle; thereby, they have been initiated into bullying, which affects their decision-making process. As they exhibit the same behaviors as their associates, they are sometimes called the bandwagon bullies. These people became bullies as a result of fraternizing with bullies. They initially began as followers but then eventually graduated to

become accomplices by carrying out their bullying activities whenever they see the victims.

Sometimes they carry out their bullying by calling the victims names, making negative comments, making jokes, throwing things on the victims, or forcefully taking personal belongings of the victims. Most times these bullies were followers in the past, but they are now bullies and recruiters of new followers to carry out their instructions. As a result of the company they keep, they make unwise and negative decisions, which leads to tormenting and terrorizing others.

This group might come from nonbullying parents or environments, but their associations have influenced them, hence corrupting and undermining the work of the parents. As a result of their fraternity with bullies—and the "if you cannot beat them, join them" mentality—a lot of followers have become bullies themselves. Some have been caught in the cross fire, while others have eventually become casualties and end up paying the price for joining the bandwagon of bullies.

Behavioral-disorders bully

These are vulnerable group because they are both bullies and victims as a result of medical conditions of behavioral disorders. They bully others because they do not have any control over their actions and behaviors.

Most times their bullying behaviors are not intentional; hence, they snap and behave in an irrational manner. They usually do not play by the rules or follow instructions; some of them are extremely active and impulsive, and their actions are not meant to harm others. They do what they do as a result of their disorder. Mostly labeled as troublemakers or bullies, they end up being victimized, ridiculed, and isolated by others because of their medical issues.

Blackmailing bully

Blackmailing bullies use information they have about the victim to manipulate and oppress their victims to keep on dancing to their tune, especially if the information might have a detrimental effect on the victim; hence, the victim is forced to respond to the beck and call of the bully. These bullies are highly manipulative and hold the whip in taunting the victims to succumb to their requests and do their dirty work for them. They believe the victims owe them dues that need to be paid, without informing the victims prior about their demands.

They are found in all age demographics but more commonly within children and adolescents. Such groups of bullies are very active in schools. They will manipulate a child to commit crimes that he or she would not have done under normal circumstances and use all opportunities to get more weapons to enforce their domination over the victim.

Unless victims cry out or ask for help, they will keep on sinking into an endless pit; they will be locked in the grip of the blackmailing bully.

Camouflage bully

Camouflage bullies are also called the cover-up bullies. The major aim of their bullying is self-defense and protection. These bullies are involved in bullying activities out of fear of being victims due to issues in their lives that make them susceptible to attack.

Camouflage bullies have a secret in the form of a weakness that they don't want to be seen by others; they are afraid this weakness will make them vulnerable in a group. Hence, they use bullying as a camouflage to divert attention away from their weaknesses and shortcomings in order to avert the threat of being vulnerable in the group.

Since fear is an unpleasant emotion that might likely cause them pain or threat, camouflage bullies choose bullying as a cover-up in order not to be exposed to the attacks of others. Their vulnerability has made these bullies act in an irrational way; fear of their weaknesses has incapacitated them from making rational judgments. To protect themselves they choose the wrong pathway of bullying others. This group of bullies is not willing to be exposed to anything that will cause them pain or threaten their territory. They are like a lion that roars in order to safeguard whatever position they might be holding within a group. For this reason, they engage in bullying activities to protect themselves by being on both the offensive and defensive.

Crisis bully

Crisis bullies become bullies as a result of a sudden change in their lives, or at home, which can be traumatic and cause a change in their behaviors. This change can be the result of emotional stress, health issues, or financial stress. Maybe the parents are going through marital issues. Regardless, such changes have a negative impact on a crisis bully's life, which causes his or her bully behavior.

Crisis bullies blame others for their problems, and if there is no proper support system for the children to express their feelings or struggles or fears, they eventually seek out an avenue or a person they might blame for what they are experiencing.

Most times the only way they can express themselves or their sufferings/emotions is by bullying others. They want their victims to feel the pain they are going through. They believe no one else is permitted to be happy when they are not happy. By inflicting pain on others, they can release their own anger and pain. Thus, they gain some form of satisfaction or gratification in the process.

Cyberbully

This group carries out its bullying activities anonymously via the Internet. Under normal circumstances, they would not bully others, but because of the anonymity they have to some extent on the Internet, they are active in destroying the lives of innocent victims. Cyberbullies are the most dangerous group of bullies because they can penetrate the safety of a home to attack the victim without the parents' knowledge.

The cyberbully's activities vary from online grooming, trolling to sexting, to posting derogatory messages on the Internet in order to destroy the reputation of another person. The operation of this particular group of bullies has resulted in many deaths. The devastating part about these bullies is that they have more victims and, in some cases, more followers than any other group of bullies. Most times their followers are not even aware that they are followers of cyberbullying because they directly amplify the atrocities of the bullies without knowing the authenticity of the information they are spreading about the victims, or the effects such actions have on the victims.

Discrimination-mentality bully

There are two types of discrimination-mentality bullies: those who believe they are superior to others and those with a distorted mentality.

Superior discrimination-mentality bullies have been raised or groomed to believe they are superior to others and to see other human beings as inferior to them. When they come in contact with a group that they see as inferior, the tendency to bully ignites because they have been groomed to see others as inferior as a result of their privileges in life. They discriminate against others and, in the process, cause them harm. In some cases, bullies are not aware of the devastation that their behaviors and actions are causing in the lives of their victims or in their victims' families. There are other cases where the bullies are fully aware of the toil their actions cause the victims and their families, but they simply do not care because they have been groomed to be the way they are. Because their hearts have been hardened, they are not affected by their victims' pain.

Distorted discrimination-mentality bullies have a distorted mentality of being discriminated against as a result of their beliefs, religion, color, sex, and so on. They also believe that they are being prejudged as a result of being the minority in a group; hence, they develop the mentality of being aggressive and offensive as payback for the injustices they are still experiencing.

They have been programmed by their environment to believe that everybody is against them. They are always ready to attack, so they are always aggressive and offensive in their actions and communications with others. They are not willing to listen or try to reason with others but are always on the alert to launch an attack when necessary to protect themselves. This group in school always targets those who have been tagged as enemies.

To some extent, they might have a basis for their actions, but two wrongs don't make a right, even if there are legal, authentic reasons for these bullies' actions.

Drug bully

Drug bullies engage in the use of drugs. Some of these drug bullies come from environments where they are exposed to drugs early on, even in the womb of their mothers while others are influenced by their association with bad friends.

These bullies operate under the influence of the toxic materials they have ingested into their systems, and they come to school high on drugs; they are ticking bombs that are ready to explode at any given time. They are also involved in selling drugs to innocent and ignorant students in school. Their actions and behaviors are fully under the influence of drugs, and everyone is susceptible to their attacks, including the teachers. Some teachers are not even aware of what they are dealing with; whatever techniques they might want to deploy to bring order to their classes will certainly be wasted effort on a bully who is under the influence of drugs.

It becomes more interesting and challenging for teachers to handle a student who is under the influence of drugs, since teachers were not taught or trained to handle such cases; hence, no disciplinary actions or discussions will have any positive effect until the bully is no longer taking drugs.

Gossip bully

Gossip bullies use gossip as a weapon to bring down others in order to gain favor, especially in the workplace environment. They specialize in using their mouths as weapons, setting in motion rumors that will defame the victim. Subtle and manipulative in their operations, gossip bullies will go to any length to achieve their goals, even if it includes befriending the victim in order to gather information that they will use to smear the victim's reputation. They might backstab their victims with slander, for example. The difference between a gossip bully and a word bully is that gossipers consciously conceive and execute their plans when the atmosphere is conducive for them to operate. They always have intentions for their operations; their actions are mostly premeditated; and their modes of operation are well defined.

They are convincing in telling or selling their tales about others, but when inquiry begins to validate their tales, it is discovered that their words are not credible. Gossip has become a lifestyle for them; they might be nice in the presence of their victims, but they are backstabbing them with their words. Their actions and words do not usually align. These bullies are very active, especially in the workplace, and their words are like venom, which they use in character assassination of the victim, hence isolating the victim from the team at school or in a work environment.

Inherited bully

The law of creation says that everything should bring forth after its own kind, which is why a lion gives birth to a lion, and a bully gives birth to a bully. Similarly, a child from a bullying parent automatically inherits the characteristics of that parent and becomes an inherited bully.

Inherited bullies come out of bullying home environments; such bullies have inherited their desires and behaviors from their parents or their guardians. They were born into a bullying culture, and that is the culture they know. It has become a way of life for them.

These bullies tend to bully anywhere, anytime, whether the atmosphere is conducive to tolerate it or not. Their environments made an impression on them and molded them to become bullies. They are prompted in launching an attack because it is normal and acceptable to them. Just as the cub of a lion does not need special training to inherit the genes of its parents, neither does the cub need coaching to roar like its parents; such actions are automatically transferred to the cub. When a child grows up in an environment where bullying is accepted or seen as a way of life, the child automatically becomes a bully because that is all he or she knows. It becomes a tradition and a legacy.

Privileged-oppressive bully

Bullying is all about oppressing and intimidating others who are weaker in a group. All the different types of bullies have this common characteristic. But the privileged-oppressive-bully group uses its privileges in life as a weapon for oppressing others instead of using it to build up people. Privileged-oppressive bullies use their positions, statuses, privileges, and authority (invested in them as a result of the office they hold) to intimidate, molest, abuse, and sexually harass and oppress others around them. Although they are found in all facets and spheres of life, in this book we are addressing oppressive bullies from a workplace perspective.

Privileged-oppressive bullies use their privileges as weapons to oppress others in order to show their supremacy over their victims. In reality, their behavior only confirms their ignorance and insensibility. They fail to realize that no person can boast of what will happen in the next few seconds or predict the future.

In some cases they do not contribute to the workflow or success on the work floor—yet they take the glory, especially when operations are going smoothly and praises are being sung. But when things are not working well, they heap the blame on others. Their insensitivity to the needs of others has made them abused those working for them or with them, leading to nervous breakdowns for some victims, while others lose their jobs.

The irony of this group is that not all of the oppressive bullies are in a position of authority, but they use their connections to an authority figure; hence, their cordial relationship with an authority figure in an organization is being abused and used to oppress others. Either way, an oppressive bully always uses his or her position as a wild card in hurting and harassing people, both sexually and otherwise, and this eventually destroys the victims.

Racial bully

Racism is like a piercing sword that divides people to create segregation, where some become haters while others have been hurt and harmed by this sword.

TYPES OF BULLIES

Racial bullies are inoculated with hatred and prejudice for other races that are different from their race; they believe one race is superior to another. They are groomed by their environment to discriminate against others if they are not of the same race, eventually leading to racial conflict and segregation in schools and society.

Perhaps they did not have the opportunity to compare or try to know something about other races other than the information that were imputed to them at an early age. The impact of this influenced all their dealings and relationships with other people. It is all they know. Sadly, they even discriminate within the people of their own race with flimsy excuses such as the color of their eyes, hair, or skin, and whether they are rich or poor. What this group of bullies fails to realize is that there is no difference between human beings when it comes to the organs that make us human because our existence depends on these organs irrespective of who we are.

Retaliating bully

Retaliating bullies are victims who turned 360 degrees to become bullies. Bullied in the past, they did not get the support they needed from their parents or society when they were being victimized. In the process of trying to protect themselves from the continuous attacks from bullies, they became aggressive, and sometimes to the extreme. These bullies use the pain and experiences from their past to decide to aggressively hurt others in order not to be a victim again. Most times their aggression is motivated by fear because they are afraid of being a victim again or of history repeating itself. They have developed the payback mentality with the slogan *never again*. They are like a flood that washes away anything that stands to oppress or oppose them; they are the *never-again bullies*.

These people used the heat from bullies as an incubator to build and develop themselves to become bullies, thereby descending to the level of a bully by being on the attacking and aggressive side as protection from being victimized. They refuse to be beaten twice; hence, they launch an attack, and they are always on the offensive. This group fails to use the heat from the bully as an incubator to grow stronger and be a survivor in order to be a better person. Instead, they descend to the bully's level and become a bully themselves. But this group should realize that the best revenge is to rise above the level at which bullies operate; they should not descend to their level.

There are two types of retaliating bullies:

- Subtle-retaliating bully
- Aggressive-retaliating bully

A *subtle-retaliating bully* is a victim who was bullied in the past and who used the heat from the bullies as an incubator to build his or her muscles. These bullies are different from the aggressive-retaliating bully because they are only on the defensive. They do not go into fight mode quickly or unnecessarily, but they are target specific in their operations and responses. They will only respond to the bully when there is need for a response.

They are subtle in their operations within a well-defined boundary and project an aura that says "no trespassing." They are the never-again bullies who say bullying will not happen a second time, which is why they are defensive in order to maintain their territory. Their red-flag warning signs are well positioned so that a bully will see them from miles away. These are people you will not want to mess with; they are like the lion that roars in order to inform others that they are in charge of their domain. They know how to protect themselves without getting into trouble, and they only respond when the bully calls.

The *aggressive-retaliating bully* is a victim who was constantly bullied in the past and could not or did not get support from someone who could have helped to handle the bullying attack. Their parents failed to support them because the parents were either not listening or not sensitive enough to discern the trauma their child was going through. It could be that the parents were too busy providing for physical needs and so failed to see the emotional needs of their child.

TYPES OF BULLIES

This group was failed by the school system and society. The school failed by not providing a safe environment for learning; society failed because these bullies were prejudged even before they were being examined. For example where, social workers assigned to the cases of aggressive-retaliating bullies were biased in their assessment and were not able to see beyond the story or picture that was painted in the report they received about the child; hence, the triangle authority (parents, schools, and society) failed to execute their influence as authority figures in the life of the victim. As a result, the child decided to stand up for himself or herself by becoming aggressive in behavior and response.

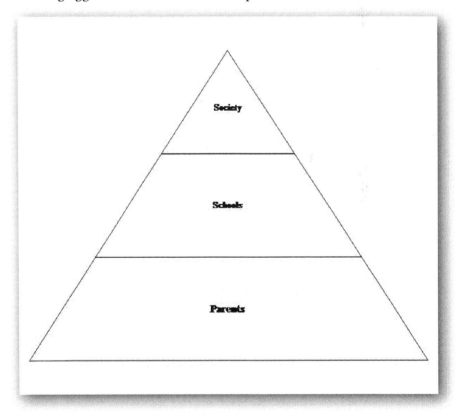

Figure 1. The triangle authority

The **triangle authority** comprises parents, schools, and society (institutions). As the triangle above shows, parents form the base in the child's life, and their role is crucial. They have a huge responsibility to recognizing bullying of their child before the school and society can avert a red-flag situation. There are sometimes red-flag signals in the behaviors of some retaliating bullies because of the bottled-up emotional pain and disappointment they have experienced or are still experiencing, making them aggressive and offensive in their dealings with people. They can be tagged as the troublemakers in the group, or the rotten eggs in a basket, and this has led to them being more victimized and blacklisted by schools and society. In some cases, they pay the price for the negligence of parents, schools, and society.

Below is a true-life story of an aggressive-retaliating bully.

Lara was a beautiful, young, intelligent girl full of dreams to study and go to university; she was a humble and nice little girl. At the age of six, when she was in elementary school, she was constantly bullied, without the knowledge of her parents. They were too busy providing for the physical needs of Lara and her siblings, failing to connect with her and provide for her emotional and mental needs.

The bullying continued in school, and there was no external help from the parents or the school. Lara was drowning in the sea of bullying, and in the process of continuous attacks from the bullies, Lara was facing the battle alone. Gradually she became aggressive in her responses and behaviors. She started exhibiting the red-flag symptoms. Meanwhile, there was no help coming forth, and the only way she could survive the attacks coming from the bullies and their followers was to fight back by becoming very aggressive, which led to her beating up anyone who tried to step on her.

Every day in school there was a fight between Lara and those bullying her; in the process she became too strong for the bullies and their followers. Lara was not only aggressive but also offensive, both at home and in school, because the authority figures in her life failed to take ownership of their duties. Eventually, the more the bullies tried to attack her, the more they were beaten up by Lara, and Lara became unbeatable by the bullies.

She was now the one beating up the bullies whenever they tried to attack her, and that was when the school noticed there was a problem. At that point, the school informed her parents, who'd had no idea of the battle Lara had been fighting. The school and her parents could not trace the sudden change in her behavior because they were not sensitive enough to discern what made her so angry or involved in constant fighting in school.

Lara was expelled from school, and the former school passed the information to her new school, which led to the new school refusing her admission. Social workers were involved, but the social workers failed in executing their duties because they could not see beyond the stories that were written to them by the school.

Lara was victimized not only by the bullies but also by the school because they were not well equipped to help, or they chose to be biased in their actions. The social workers failed because they couldn't see beyond what was written. The parents failed to find out or ask the right questions that would have led them to the core of the sudden change in her behavior. They also didn't stand up for her against the decision of the educational system.

As Lara fought for herself, the triangle authority failed her because she was kicked out of school. The bullies eventually won the battle against Lara.

Second-class-citizen bully

Second-class-citizen bullies are not accepted by the society to which they belong. This lack of acceptance and belittling by those who ought to be an anchor in their lives leads to these bullies believing the lies they were told growing up—lies that they are not worth their dreams or visions, or that such dreams and visions are not meant for people of their class. Some in this group had a dream as a child to be the next president, prime minister, first lady, best surgeon, best professor, or best entrepreneur, hoping to make an impact on their generation. They had a dream, but their dream was thwarted by those who were in a place of authority. Their peer groups may have convinced them that their dreams or visions were not achievable or meant for people of their class or demographic, thus sowing negative seeds to kill their dreams and visions. These bullies might be indigenous of their country or children of immigrant parents.

Second-class citizens are found everywhere, even with the children of immigrants. They are partially accepted in the land of their birth, which is the host country of their parents, and they are strangers to the land of origin of their parents; hence, they are forsaken between two worlds, becoming twice foreigners. Frustration ensues, and when the parents are not sensitive to their children's battles or do not have the capability to help them build a life that will give them influence and affluence, the children go through life plagued by a frustration that will overshadow their dreams and visions. When they grow older and realize that they are better than where they have found themselves in life, they become more frustrated, and so some become bullies. These bullies will seek revenge for the misfortune that befell them; they believe that others were responsible for their predicament. Thus, they become angry, offensive, and troublesome.

When you go deeper and scrutinize the lives of some (if not all) of the bullies in this group, you will discover that they yearn for something. There is a vacuum that needs to be filled, a missing link that will complete the circle of their lives. Wherever they find this missing piece, they will wholeheartedly embrace it, even if it is detrimental to others. That missing link is *acceptance*. Once these bullies find a place to call "home," they will gladly blend in, never realizing that this might be a pathway of destruction.

At this stage, if the necessary tools or resources are not available to help them, second-class-citizen bullies will become susceptible to any negative influences. Thus, these negative influences will come into their lives to fuel these bullies' anger, which makes them a time bomb waiting for an opportunity to explode. In this way, they become a danger to themselves and to society. In this group of bullies, acceptance or rejection is mostly the propellant for their actions.

Acceptance versus rejection comes from the way we receive and relate to others, which matters a lot; it communicates to those we are dealing with whether they are welcome. The truth is, we are either receiving people we come in contact with or we are rejecting them. There is no in-between. Even in a circle where people are being tolerated, there is still tension, which makes one feel the vibes of rejection.

One of the most crucial needs of any human being is to have a place or circle where he or she belongs—a place where he or she is truly accepted and welcomed for who he or she is; it is a desire that nothing else can replace. Regarding acceptance versus rejection, people have different ways of coping with their acceptance or rejection issues. When people are confronted with rejection, for example,

- some people bounce back;
- some will break through the wall of rejection and create a niche for themselves, where they become an authority;
- some will break down and weep; and
- some will form an alliance where they become a bully.

When people cannot meet these needs in the place where they thought they could, they will go searching for it elsewhere. During this search, they are exposed to any association, which can either build them up or destroy them. Some people have formed an alliance by aligning themselves with the wrong crowd because of rejection, which eventually results in them becoming a bully. Some bullies know that what they are doing is wrong, but they crave a place where they can belong, and they will keep on mingling because they feel they are welcomed.

Returning to acceptance versus rejection, some people have been groomed to walk away from a circle where they are not accepted with their head raised up high. When they are thrown against the walls of rejection, they bounce back on their feet. Others break through the walls of rejection by using their hidden potentials to build their own niche where others come to be positively influenced. There are some who do not have the capacity or strength to deal with rejection; hence, they break down by the walls of rejection and weep. With their experience of rejection, they end up becoming susceptible, where they are easily victimized by any roaming bully.

The effects of rejection are felt by all; rejection creates a red-flag situation where the heat and the smell of smoke indirectly or directly pervades society since a person can become a bully as a result of rejection and crave for acceptance by aligning with the wrong crowd. Others have become susceptible to victimization as a result of rejection.

In order to avert such happenings, it is crucial to stop judging others because of their background or inability to speak against any form of rejection in our schools and workplaces, especially with children. Let us come to a place where all children are treated equally with respect, irrespective of their backgrounds, in order not to create an atmosphere of "you are not welcome" or "you are not qualified to be in this school" or "you are not meant to go for such studies or programs."

When we all come to a place where people are treated appropriately, certain red-flag issues will be averted, and thus crises will be avoided. Remember, rejection creates barriers and sets limitations on people. Rejection is the birthplace for loneliness plus depression, triggering disunity and segregation, which disseminates into warfare that eventually generates crises where everyone feels the heat. Acceptance, on the other hand, is a place of unity; it makes room for positive tolerance, where people are welcome with open hands, and the hand of help is extended when necessary to help them work on their weaknesses without a selfish agenda. Acceptance is the trigger for welfare and funfair. It is our desire as human beings to have a place where we're all each other's keepers.

When asking the opinion of the general public about bullying, each and every one of us will always say that bullying behavior is unacceptable, but our actions are always contrary when a bullying attack is happening around us. Thus, whatever you do when someone is being bullied in your presence is a confirmation if bullying is truly unacceptable by you.

TYPES OF BULLIES

Word bully

Words are seeds sown into the lives of people; they can be positive or negative words, eventually impacting the lives of those where it was sown. A word bully is not an exemption; these bullies specialize in sowing evil words about their victims, which they use as weapons to hurt and hunt their victims. These bullies did not necessarily emerge from a bullying environment; rather, they became bullies because of their ignorance of the power of their words. Word bullies are children, teenagers, and even adults. These bullies dominate most schools and workplaces; they specialize in slander and calling others derogatory names. They were not taught the power and effect words can have on others. While they may not be violent or physically aggressive, they are aggressive with their mouths and the way they use their words.

Words are powerful…they have the power to put a smile on or wipe a smile off someone's face. Words can be used as a weapon of protection or destruction, to pacify or aggravate, to instill peace or affright people around you. Choose your words carefully today, and let your words give life to those that come in contact with you. Stop bullying people with your words.

Using their words as weapons in bullying others, some word bullies do not know the gravity of their words on their victims. They are not aware of the havoc and pain their words cause their victims, and neither do they understand that their words do not just evaporate but remain in the victim's memory, even when the word bullies are long gone. The effects of a word bully can be devastating if the victim does not have the ability to uproot those negative words that were sown into his or her life. The bully might not be with them physically, but the effect of the words will continuously play in the mind of the victim, hence setting a limitation on him or her. That is why a negative word spoken to a child can still haunt the person after many decades.

Word bullies live in the moment and say whatever fits or suits their emotions, without thinking beyond that given point in time. They believe words are merely to be used flippantly and facetiously, while failing to realize the power of their words. Words can destroy, but they can also defend, protect, or even encourage others.

Word bullies are mostly impromptu in their operations, and they use words to ridicule and belittle others, causing them to lose their self-esteem and self-confidence. These bullies talk flippantly and act ignorantly because they were not taught the power of their words on others and even on themselves, hence using their words as weapons of destruction. Words are powerful, and that is why word bullies use words as weapons to torment and alienate their victims. A child can be frightened when he or she hears stories that convey fear, and an adult who constantly hears he or she is useless or not good enough is automatically programmed to be a failure if the adult does not have the necessary tools to undo the effects of those negative words. Word bullies are always sowing negative word seeds into the lives of their victims, which eventually produces depression, misery, isolation, fear, and low self-esteem.

Physically aggressive bully

Physically aggressive bullies engage in physical combat with their victims for different reasons. The throwing of fists becomes a medium for some to communicate their dissatisfaction with the behavior and actions of the victim. Others are involved in physically aggressive bullying in order to maintain their territory or settle scores. Some bullies choose this pathway for survival purposes, especially amid continuous harassment. For others it is an avenue to expel their bottled negative emotions.

For some of these of bullies, their might be a legitimate reasons for their actions, but most times their actions or responses make them the bad ones—all because their method of expression has become a weapon that is used against them due to their inability to manage their anger or oppression.

Similarity in Their Actions

Bullies, as already mentioned, should not be treated or handled as a group but as individuals, because what drives a drug bully is different from what drives an inherited bully. Neither will the cure for a drug bully work for a retaliating bully or crisis bully. Thus, people or authorities should stop addressing bullies as a group and start addressing them as individuals because a medicine for headaches will not cure constipation or heal a broken heart.

There might be a similarity in their actions, but their reasons for bullying are different.

The intentions of bullies might be similar, but the reasons behind their actions are not. Whatever types of bullies you are dealing with, their end result is to cause pain and make the environment unsafe. A common link exists between most of the different types of bullies. Most of them use the same strategy to locate their victims, for example, the major tool they use to identify their victims is to find a weak link in a group or someone who looks different from them, which they call the *weird one*. Once they can identify the weak link in the group, the bullies will then feast on the vulnerability and personality of the victim, hence making the victim more susceptible to the attack. Most times they look for a person who is too quiet or extremely intelligent, dresses differently, has a low self-esteem, behaves differently from others, or has a unique physical appearance.

Based on all these factors, bullies make their judgments and decisions to alienate their victims from the group—except for the behavior disorder bully who, to some extent, has no control over his or her behavior, and the retaliating bully who became a bully because of what he or she went through in the past and wants to defend/protect him- or herself. While the drug bully might not necessarily have any target, the influence of the drugs makes everyone susceptible to his or her attack. Although there might be a common link in how bullies identify their victims, they all have a different mentality and reasoning that makes them do what they do. It is high time for authorities and schools to stop putting a square peg in a round hole; to bring about an effective change, each bully's case should be handled differently.

Below are the different groups of people in a bullying environment:

- The bully
- The followers
- The bystanders
- The victors or victims
- The voice

For any bullying attack to be executed, there are different groups of people who must be on the scene. These groups contribute in one way or another, either directly or indirectly, while the environment either amplifies or undermines the process of bullying. Bullying occurs sometimes as a result of a bully trying to take attention away from himself or herself because of his or her weakness, imperfection, or fear.

Bullying starts with one person but can be stopped with one person making the decision not to bully someone else, no matter the situation or circumstance. A bully can choose not to torment a person, even when the opportunity is there and the atmosphere is conducive to operate as a bully. Since bullying starts with one person, a bully can decide not to comply with any urge to bully another person, not even for a second; it will go a long way to minimize or even put an end to bullying in our society.

Who is a Bully?
Like every other human being, a bully has blood flowing through his or her veins. A bully is full of potential and energy but needs redirection in order to utilize his or her energy positively. Bullies are like ships that need

captains to steer them in the right direction. Bullies are easily known by their actions and their deeds, which are always destructive. There are different definitions, but there is one outstanding characteristic to identify bullies—that is, wherever bullies are in operation, they make the environment unsafe and unbearable for their victims.

A bully, then, is any person who uses force to get what he or she wants without the consent of the other party involved and uses manipulation to play on the vulnerability of a person. A bully acts irrespective of the emotional or physical effects the action might have on his or her targeted person, or uses words negatively in order to hurt or degrade a fellow human being.

Some bullies use words carelessly and fail to realize that words are like a sword—the sword pierces into areas of life that a physical sword cannot penetrate. The scars might not be seen physically but stay with the person for life if appropriate help is not given. It is high time we all learn how to choose our words more carefully, because our words can be weapons of destruction. Conversely, words can be used in defense or in love. If your words are weapons of destruction, then you are a bully. Bullies should seek help in order to be educated on the power of their words, whether they are spoken or expressed through social media.

It is vital for all bullies to know that their words, actions, decisions, or choices today carry weight. It's a weight that can be negative, and the impact of the weight might or will have a direct impact on them and those around them, especially in the future.

Am I a bully?

"Am I a bully?" is a question we all need to ask ourselves every day in order to weigh our actions, words, and behaviors while dealing with others. Some people are not even aware that they are bullies or that their actions are destructive. It is very important for us to always summarize our actions and dealings with others into one word in order to know if our behavior can be defined as harassing, intimidating, tormenting, or persecuting. Whenever you force others to succumb to your will for your own satisfaction to the detriment of another, or you derive pleasure from hurting and dominating others, you are a bully. There are questions that you need to ask yourself whenever you are dealing with other people because in every *why* there is an answer. Here are the questions:

- Do people feel safe around you?
- How do you react to the weaknesses of others?
- Do you use force to get what you want from people despite their objections?
- Do you derive pleasure from the trouble or pain of other people even when they deserve it?
- Are you easily manipulated into cooperating in bullying others?
- Are you willing to swap positions with the person you are dealing with?

Is bullying preplanned?

Sometimes bullying can be impulsive, but most of the time bullying is preplanned. The main bully in a bullying environment is the one who plans and strategizes the process while recruiting followers to execute the plan. The followers don't usually consider their actions, hence cooperating with the bully in executing his or her plans. Bullying is not always a spontaneous action but an action planned in advance which can be executed in a conducive environment.

Why do followers cooperate with bullies?

Bullying tendencies thrive more in atmospheres that tolerate it. For bullying to occur, the bullies have to identify their prey (the victims and sometimes the followers) before launching their attacks. Bullies always look for their prey in a weaker person, such as a well-cultured child who has been taught to respect and love others; when bullies can identify such an individual, then they look for a conducive atmosphere and launch their attack. Followers fail to ask themselves why they should cooperate with a bully in hurting another person because they do not understand the hidden agenda of the bully. Followers are neither part of the planning process, nor do they discuss their actions with their parents. Instead they carelessly cooperate with the bullies, later realizing they have made a great mistake because of their unwise decisions.

Is there a difference in bullying in boys and in girls?

There is no much difference between a female and a male bully because their intention is to hurt or cause someone pain. There might be some difference in their method of operation, but their end result is often the same—hurting a fellow human being.

The method of operation of a female bully is different from a male bully because male bullies' activities are more easily noticed. Male bullies engage in physical contact and power tussles, while female bullies are more subtle and manipulative in their bullying actions. Female bullies begin with gossip; they spread negative rumors about their targeted prey, which results in name calling. The victim, now the subject for ridicule, becomes uncomfortable within the group. Having nowhere to turn, the victim is now an outcast. There are some rare cases where male bullies indulge in manipulation and gossip in their bullying atrocities, but most male bullies start their bullying escapades with name calling, ridiculing, the throwing of objects, or forcefully taking the belongings of their victims.

Whether their method of operation differs or not but the impact on the victim is the same. Neither sex should engage in bullying because the little boys or girls of today will be the fathers and mothers of tomorrow. Therefore, there is an urgent need for parents (mothers and fathers, and even grandparents) to speak to their children or grandchildren and encourage them not to embark on the pathway of bullying.

For those girls who have been labeled as a queen bee in school, mothers need to take a stand to ensure that the queen bee mentality is not permitted to blossom. The refusal to address it now will result in breeding more queen bees tomorrow, since these girls might eventually become mothers themselves. If this is not corrected, there will be a loop hole that will serve as an avenue to raise more female bullies. Likewise, male bullies should not be left alone to continue in their bullying escapade; fathers should awaken to their duty by being there to correct and be a role model for their sons.

Are there medical reasons for bullying?

There are some behavioral conditions that might be responsible for bullying in children. These bullies are also victims due to behavioral conditions. As a result of these conditions, they have no control over their actions and behaviors. Take, for example, the attention deficit hyperactivity disorder (ADHD) group. They can snap and do what is least expected of them; some of them have difficulty following instructions no matter how clearly you present them; and they can blurt out inappropriate comments at inappropriate times. Most times these children are tagged as the troublemakers or the bullies in a group; however, it is important to know that not all bullies have these disorders.

Children with ADHD can have the following symptoms:

- Hyperactivity
- Impulsivity
- Inattention

When a child has any of the symptoms listed above, there is the tendency to be a bully or a victim. In such cases, these children are easily angered, and they react quickly, and when they are growing in a hostile environment they have a higher risk of being a bully. There are cases where some are victims; this occurs as a result of issues with self-esteem, anxiety, and peer relationships. Either way, these disorders impair the child's social functioning.

There are support systems out there with programs helping either the victims or the bullies in order to minimize the effects of these disorders. As for this group, we should be more tolerant instead of condemning them.

Questions:

- What comes to your mind when you hear the word bullying in the news or learn of the havoc it is causing in our society?
- What is your reaction to bullying in your environment today after reading this chapter?
- Are you a bystander or an inhibitor in a bullying environment?

Whatever your answers are, always remember that today, someone's life is depending on you speaking out against all forms of bullying in your environment.

Whatever you tolerate you cannot change. When you tolerate oppression, you become the oppressed, and when you tolerate a bully you become bullied.

3

Types of Victims

BULLIES ARE ADVANCING their channels of operation, enforcing their quest for power, territorial control, and supremacy, and many people have become victims during this advancement. Some victims are drowning in the sea of a bully's quest; others are suffocating or gasping for air. But few have refused to be a victim of any bully. The truth is, bullying is a reality in someone's life, a reality he or she is living every day, a reality that has become a turbulent storm in the life of the victim and his or her family. The reality of this storm has broken too many lives. While some have been incapacitated, only a few have soared like an eagle above the storm.

To those who have experienced bullying in the past or are being bullied now, know that life is a fight for territory, and nobody is willing to give you the peace and respect you deserve. Therefore, victims must change their mentality; otherwise, they will always be the victim. Victims need to know that they determine the game plan, not the bully, because of the power that lies within them, which is the power of choice. They decide whether they will be a victim or a victor, because whatever power the bully is using against them is the power they allocated to the bully, which determines execution.

They should always remember that they are not the victims but the victors. They were not born to be a victim or to be held incapacitated or to be at the mercy of any fellow human being. The power to conquer resides in each of us. Whatever a bully is doing or has done in the past does not have to control a victim's life and destiny. Victims must choose to take ownership of their life by making use of their will not to be anybody's victim. According to an African proverb, it is the way you position yourself in an event that will determine if you will be addressed as a guest or a servant; hence, your price tag determines the offer you get in life. The value you place on yourself will determine the responses you get from others.

Your price tag determines the offer you get in life. The value you place on yourself will determine the responses you get from others.

Tolerance is good when it is not at the expense of your life; tolerance becomes foolishness when it will cost you your right to exist as a human being. You were not created to be the victim of any bully because whatever you tolerate you cannot change. When you tolerate oppression, you become the oppressed, and when you tolerate a bully, you become bullied. Being a victim becomes a reality only when you refuse to take ownership of your life; only then are you the victim. However, there are many people who have experienced bullying in one way or another but refused to enhance the agenda of those bullies. Remember, the agenda of a bully is to take your focus away from your dreams and aspirations in order to cut you short in your journey.

    A bully is like an obstacle that is meant to stop or hinder your journey, and you have a choice to either be stopped or look for an alternative route that will bring you to your desired destination. Focusing on the obstacle will only rob you of your dreams and future. But your decision to keep your dream alive by focusing on your possibilities will make you a conqueror because in life you are either conquering or being conquered. Either way, your mentality and the choices you make are the propellers that will determine which side you will end up on in a bullying battle.

    It is crucial for you not to allow a bully to define your life because whatever defines you controls you and will eventually define your purpose and vision. Whenever a bully rises against you, it is in your own interest not to leave your post because your post is your purpose and vision in life. When you lose focus as a result of bullying, then you are susceptible to the control of bullies; it is only then you become a victim. You are not a victim until you cooperate with a bully to derail you from your purpose in life, whereby the bully is now defining your life's purpose.

A wise woman always tells me "that in every relationship there should be a measuring gauge to determine your position in that relationship in order to protect yourself from being hurt." I believe that anyone who has experienced bullying or will experience bullying should measure his or her relationship with the bully. A measuring gauge doesn't necessarily exempt you from being bullied or hurt by others, but it will help you reduce the density or gravity of the pain by acting as succor to minimize or avert the effects and damage that might have occurred without the measuring gauge. Thus, the measuring gauge is your life's airbag in case of an accident. It is your responsibility as an adult or as a parent of a child who is being bullied not to allow those who have nothing to do with your future to rob you of your dreams or all the beauty and opportunities that await you. Even those who have something to do with your future should not be given the opportunity to use their privileged access as a means to abuse or belittle you to a nonentity.

There is no guarantee that you will not be bullied in the future, but rest assured that your choice will determine if the bullies have won or will win or not. In all these instances, we can choose whether or not to be a victim or a victor. This is up to you to decide. In the process of you making choices lies your reaction, which will determine your action. Whatever action you take will reflect the choices you have made.

> *"You are not a victim of your biology or circumstances. You cannot control the events and circumstances of your life but you can control your reactions. You have free will you can choose. The Mind can change the brain."*
> —Dr. Caroline Leaf

However, there are children experiencing bullying at school who cannot stand up for themselves. It is the responsibility of the parents and school authorities to stand up for these young people. Parents, do not play politics or friendship with the welfare of your children. Your first responsibility is to your child and no other person; utilize all available resources to help your child. You are the one who needs to speak up for your children, especially when they are in a stage or situation where they cannot stand up or speak for themselves. It is up to you as the parents and society to speak up for them.

In the face of bullying, it takes courage to conquer and your courage streams from your self-confidence. How solidified your self-confidence is will determine how courageous you are. Thus, your self-confidence is the fertilizer that boosts your courage. It takes courage and boldness to confront a bully in a bullying environment, because courage is not bound to the present pain but focuses on the victory and not the defeat. It is vital, in the midst of bullying, that you stand strong and be secured in who you are. Don't allow a bully to define who you are or what becomes of you—not even for a second should you attribute to any bully any form of power to define your life. Bullies don't have such power, except the power that you give to them.

There are different types of victims but whatever category of victim you might be in, it is very important to realize that your mentality has a lot to do with the choices you make, which will determine your status as a victim or victor. Your mentality guides how you operate and your decision-making process. It is only your mentality that will prepare you for the unknown.

Types of Victims

There are several types of victims:

- Boomerang victim
- Fear victim
- Person-with-disability victim

TYPES OF VICTIMS

- Nurtured victim
- Second-class-citizen (or twice-foreign) victim
- Silenced victim
- Self-made victim
- Ignorant (or circumstantial) victim
- Behavioral-disorders victim
- Why-me victim
- Victors
- Inferiority-mentality victim

Boomerang victim

Boomerang victims are bullies who were previously active in bullying others; they have failed to realize that life is not static but dynamic. They have found out the hard way that human beings are interactive entities, and whatever a person sows is what he or she will eventually reap. Thus, they are the group that eventually got a taste of their own actions; they are forced to swallow the bitter pills that they have been serving others in their past bullying actions. They become the victims when their bullying behavior backfires on them, especially when others use their previous weapons to fight them, which they used in the past to torment and oppress their victims.

The irony is that these victims are hit the hardest when they experience a taste of their previous bullying actions, and most times, their crash has a devastating effect on them when the table of their negative behaviors eventually turns on them. They have learned the hard way that the things they do today do not disappear but can actually reappear, waiting to either haunt or help them into a new phase of their lives. They have learned that their deeds do not evaporate with the day but transcend into their future, waiting for their arrival. They are the group living, fulfilling, and confirming the reality of the law of gravity and the law that governs sowing and reaping; thus, they are the beneficiaries of their previous bullying actions by reexperiencing it.

Fear victim

Fear victims are perpetually afraid to speak in a group; they prefer to live in obscurity. Despite their desire not to be noticed or recognized in a group, they are the ones the bully easily fishes out within a group. Most times they are timid and have a low self-image. As a result of their low self-confidence, they believe that they have no worth and are afraid to be put in the spotlight.

But the irony of the victims in this group is that what they fear is what usually befalls them, and the spotlight they were afraid of is right where they will be put by the bullies. Unfortunately for these victims, they are thrust into the limelight for all the wrong, negative reasons, which is quite detrimental to them. Their fears might differ, but their fears envelop them, like an aura, which attracts the nostrils of bullies who, like predators, can track their scent.

Once bullies have succeeded in identifying these victims, the bullies will torture them and feast on them whenever the opportunity arises, especially when the bullies can identify what the victims are afraid of. For example, a child who is afraid of a spider will be tormented by bullies at any given opportunity with a spider. A child who is afraid to speak in a class will be ridiculed continuously in front of the class. At the end of the day, these victims will be pushed further into despair and angst while bullies continue daily to feast on them, especially when they are still in the same school; being pushed further into silence will eventually affect all areas of their lives if help is not rendered to them in time.

Person-with-disability victim

Person-with-disability victims are sometimes called disabled victims. Disabled victims are the vulnerable group of victims because bullies capitalize on their disabilities to bully them. Some of these victims are bullied even by their own family members. Others are victimized as a result of their disabilities by callous individuals in our society.

TYPES OF VICTIMS

Sometimes a victim's disabilities are used as a yardstick to measure their abilities and capacities, which some selfish individuals try to use to relegate them to the shadows. Some people with disabilities have stayed in the shadows that bullies have forced them into; some are fighting not to be swallowed up by the expectations of others and the desires of those who believe they have little to offer, while others are fortifying a wall of resistance against their bully's agenda.

It is crucial to note that it is offensive to treat someone as a victim just because that person is living with a disability. No reason can justify such actions. The pain and agony it produces in the lives of the victims must be considered.

Below is a true-life story of a person with a disability who was turned into a victim.

Bryant uses a wheelchair; he was bullied as a child, and he is still being bullied every day as a grown man because of his disability. He is one out of millions of people with disabilities being victimized every day in our world. Bryant was born able to walk, but he had some impairment to walking, which later led to his using a wheelchair.

The most disheartening part of Bryant's story is the role his family played in bullying him because of his disability. His brothers mocked him and called him names, such as chicken legs, and even his parents called him names that were to them funny. But to Bryant it was humiliating. While in school, Bryant was always confronted by the bullies in his class and laughed at because of his smallish stature, which was the result of his disability.

He experienced bullying both in school and at home. He was bullied in class under the watch of the teacher, and despite all the bullying attacks in school and in the streets, the bullying from his family was the most hurtful. Bryant said when he was experiencing all the bullying attacks from school and from his brothers, he told his parents about it. They told him they do not have the time to deal with his bullying complaints. His parents did not show any concern, and to Bryant his parents did not care if he was bullied in school or by his brothers because they were part of the bandwagon that wanted to make him the victim as a child.

Bryant thought the bullying would be over once he was a grown man. But today, he is experiencing bullying on a different level from the one he experienced as a child. About three years ago, Bryant went somewhere and was attacked by four children between the ages of five and nine. These children were throwing stones at him for no just cause while he was using his wheelchair. Another time, children called him names on the street, and their parents or the adults who were with the children joined in to laugh at him.

Every day Bryant still experiences one form of bullying or another. Despite all the odds against him, Bryant worked hard to develop himself and become stronger. Despite all this hard work in educating and investing in himself, society still does not accept him. Even in the workplace he is being marginalized and discriminated against outright by some of his colleagues. Some make him the object of their jokes, and sometimes he feels robbed of the benefits he deserves, in terms of performance, because of his disability. His children also experience bullying attacks every day because of who their father is. People always ask him questions, such as "Are you the father of these children or their uncle?"

Below is a question section with Bryant:

Question:	Was there any organization or body you could go to as a bullied child?
Answer Bryant:	No, there was no one or no organization to support me when I was being bullied in school and at home.
Question:	As an adult with a disability, is there any organization or body you can go to for help or support?
Answer Bryant:	I am not aware of any system or organization that is helping people with disabilities who are being bullied every day in our society.

According to Bryant, it feels so lonely to have no one to care or support you in the face of a bullying attack. During the time I spent with Bryant talking about his experiences with bullying, I saw in him the pain of being disappointed by his family and society. I saw the loneliness in him, which was so conspicuous to me when he talked about his experiences and hurt. I saw a vulnerability that was always covered up with a wide smile and enthusiasm. I saw a man who was crying and reaching out to people to tell him I care (what I refer to as iCare) and not iBully.

As a child, Bryant lived a life of bullying nightmares, and now as an adult, the nightmare of how cruel human beings can be to a fellow human being with a disability continues. The effect of bullying on victims is colossal and devastating. My eyes were opened to another dimension of bullying and to victims who are drowning in the sea of bullying every day.

A message from Bryant: Please note that Bryant said that he doesn't want the pity of anyone, and neither will any person with a disability want to be pitied by society. All he wants is for people to connect with him and others with disabilities as human beings and not to pity them because being a person with a disability does not mean he or she is different. Bryant appealed to parents not to stigmatize people with disabilities by their responses or remarks, especially when young children ask questions. Parents should not encourage children to make jokes about people as a result of their disabilities. He believes that children with disabilities should not be segregated from other children. Society should allow children to grow together in order to know each other, and at the end, children will realize that a child using a wheelchair is human just like they are. When this mentality is inculcated into a child at an early age, it will put an end to prejudice and the segregation of people with disabilities in the workplace.

According to one proverb, it is the person putting on a shoe who knows where it hurts most. Thus, if you are not a person with a disability, you might not know what it means to be bullied every day because of your disability or know what it takes to support or help people with disabilities. That is the reason I asked Bryant what he wants society to do to help or support people living with disabilities who are being bullied every day.

Nurtured victim

Nurtured victims usually have a good home upbringing. They were raised well to be respectful and kind, they have a heart to help people, and they have regard for other opinions and boundaries.

The problem with the victims in this group is that their upbringing sometimes works against them in the midst of abusive peers. Their upbringing teaches them to play nice and be respectful to others, but there is failure on the part of the parents to inculcate in their children the mentality of being humble but still tough. They are taught among others to keep their hands to themselves and not to speak negatively or rudely to others, which bullies notice and capitalize on. They are not taught to set and enforce boundaries that others need to respect in order for them not to be overshadowed by their peers. Therefore, in the midst of a bully's attack, they find it difficult to find balance or cope with the situation that is confronting them. Eventually they are drifted to be too nice, even to their own detriment, and find it hard to stand up for themselves to resist the bullies.

In this case, their upbringing has become a weapon, which bullies use to fight them. They will accept all forms of abuse and insults from bullies and refuse to stand up for themselves because of an omission from their upbringing of differentiating between an enemy and a friend, welfare and warfare. It's a failure not to educate them to realize that life is sometimes a battlefield, where the strong oppress the weak, and the fast swallow up the slow. These groups of victims were deployed into society ill equipped to handle bullying challenges, which makes them susceptible to roaming bullies.

Second-class-citizen victim

In as much as we have them in bullies, there are also second-class-citizen victims or twice-foreign victims. The difference between the second-class-citizen bullies and the second-class-citizen victims is their reception to people's treatment of them. They both have something in common: the lack of acceptance both in the land of their birth and homeland of their parents; thus, they are caught in the middle of both worlds, where they are treated as a stranger.

Not all of these groups of people have accepted this twice-foreign identity; some have used it to build themselves up by creating a niche for themselves, and those with whom they come in contact have no choice but to accept them for who they are. Others became stuck and victimized because of their inability to create their own niche as their base.

The danger is that the people can turn 360 degrees in a second, in any place where they find acceptance. But most of the victims in this group become susceptible to the attacks of bullies because of their insecurities. This is especially true if there is nobody in their lives to act as a booster and catalyst to propel them to discover their inner strength to create a niche for themselves, where they will be generally accepted in their life's endeavors, and where they have become an influencer and a voice impacting others positively.

Silenced victim

The silenced victims are ridiculed and hushed in class by the bullies and their followers whenever they want to make contributions or ask questions. The bullies make derogatory comments in order to silence the victims, while the followers applaud and enforce the effects of such actions. And once this happens, the victims lose their confidence and self-esteem; thus, they automatically lose their voice and become a shadow in the group. In this way, the victim is silenced by the bully.

As a result of a victim losing his or her voice and confidence in a group, the bully has succeeded in preventing him or her from speaking and has pushed the victim into a corner where the victim becomes irrelevant in the class. Without a voice, you cannot be heard or countered as existing in the group. The victims in this group withdraw into a shell of depression and self-pity. Their voices have been drowned in the sea of bullying. They lose their strength or power to fight for their right and waste away in the darkness of oppression. When appropriate help is not given to them on time, they develop into self-made victims, especially when they don't seek help or stand up for themselves in the process of their attack because their lives are being defined by bullies.

Self-made victim

Self-made victims suffer from bullying attacks. As a result of these attacks, the victims' lives are silenced by bullies; they exist but are not living their lives to the fullest. Even if the bullying happened years or decades ago, they are still stuck mentally and emotionally in that scene and environment where they were bullied. The reality of that incident is more real to them than the reality of their lives today. This group of people believes they have been apprehended by bullies, thus always reliving and replaying their pain, and these incidents eventually incapacitate them from reaching their potential.

Instead of getting help to come out of the bubble the bullies have placed them in, they end up building and living their lives in that bubble. Their progress stalls. The irony is that although the bullies are gone, the victims are still using their past experiences or pain in pegging their future successes.

A bully's actions stole their dreams, and after many years, they are still living the life of worthlessness some bully created for them, even if the bully is long gone or even dead. This particular group fights with their shadows, trying to beat the air, but they end up fighting themselves and sinking into an endless vacuum. They have grown from being silenced to being self-made victims. Sadly, some of them know that the torment they are going through has to stop, and they have to move on with their lives, but they don't know how or don't attempt to seek help.

They are desirous but not willing to take the steps to free themselves. Some are postponing their decision to seek help or do not have the capacity to face the reality they've been fighting, as they constantly place the picture of the past scene of the attack in front of them instead of the picture of their bright future. Some are afraid to wake up from the dream and find out they don't have any dream or vision of their own because they have been preoccupied by the dream the bully gave to them. They are afraid of the unknown that lies on the other side; indeed, living in the cage where the bully has placed them is easier than fighting for a tomorrow full of great potential and opportunities.

Ignorant victim

Ignorance is deadly, and it has sent a lot of people to an early grave. The ignorant victims are those victims who lack a knowledge and awareness of the gravity of their actions. They act foolishly and are confronted with the consequences of their actions and decisions later. Ignorance is a fertile ground for bullies to victimize people. The bully lures the victim to a position in which the victim has no option or power to choose; that is, they are in a place where what the bully says goes and is final.

To harm him or her, the bully capitalizes on the ignorance and inability of the victim to choose. People are easily destroyed by lack of knowledge, and they become a fertile ground for the bullies to cultivate their bullying activities.

These groups of victims are not dumb or foolish in general, but they make foolish decisions that turn around and bite them later. They are not fully educated on the implication of providing identifying information or pictures on social media or online. They inadvertently provide weapons the bully uses to hurt them.

Ignorant victims arm the bully and the followers with ammunition to use against them in battle. These victims of cyberbullying are even victimized within the four walls of their homes. They are being swept away by the disruptive side of social media and the Internet. These are the victims of strange bullets that are flying every day on social media. The number of casualties in this group of victims is significant. The families of some of these victims have never or will never recover from the devastation and vacuum these attacks have created in their lives.

Behavioral-disorders victim

The behavioral disorder of this particular victim makes them disruptive in their actions and conduct with others. Some of them are tagged as bullies because of their reactions and responses to others, while others within this group are extremely quiet and withdraw into their own world. But in reality, they are experiencing a disorder that is beyond their control, and other children tend to disassociate themselves from them, pushing them into a corner. These victims are mostly ignored in a group. The results could be that no one wants to be their friend, and they are left behind to be ridiculed and bullied.

Why-me victim

The majority of those who have ever been bullied went through this stage, but the issue with this group of victims is that some of them are trapped in the *why-me* question. They find it difficult to leave the why-me stage to find solutions or help as a result of wallowing in self-pity. The why-me victims started asking the right questions but refused or failed to advance in their questioning in order to find the answers that might help them to conquer the battle of bullying. The why-me questions has led to indulging in self-pity, so they are stuck in the same corner where the bully has succeeded in putting them.

They are not progressing in their search for an answer to all the questions that might lead them in the right direction to get help and find solutions, which will empower them to become victors and not victims. They might have made an attempt to ask questions but did not have the capacity to ask the right questions—except for why me?—or the capability to go through the full process in seeking help. Hence, they are unable to make progress in escaping the snares of bullies. Until these victims start asking the right questions, they will not arrive at the right answers, because solutions are found when the right questions are asked rather than wallowing in self-pity.

Victors

Victors were bullied in the past, and despite all the atrocities, they escaped the hands of bullies. They rose above all the wicked plots of bullies to

TYPES OF VICTIMS

conquer whatever obstacles were put in their way. The victors have learned what to do when the storms of bullies hit them but choose not to succumb to the agenda of bullies. The victors say to themselves, "No matter how dark the night might be, it always gives way to the day." Hence, they choose to resist the bullies instead of assisting them by giving up in the midst of battle. Victors have made up their minds to pay the price by resisting the bullies, in order not to succumb to the bullies' agendas. Although their journey in conquering the bullies is not easy, they choose to fight for their right.

No matter how dark the night might be, it always gives way to the day...no matter how terrible bullies are, they always flee from those that resist them. So remember, your victory over bullies is guaranteed when you do not succumb to their agenda.

In spite of the schemes, pressures, pains, and heartaches they went through at the hands of the bullies and their followers, they rose above the tyrants. They know that injustice is real but decided ahead of time not to be victims of injustice; they believe that injustice can occur when they allow their validation of who they are or their worth to depend on the opinions and comments of others, especially bullies. They do not allow their history to destroy or interfere with their future or lay embargo on them but use their potentials, opportunities, possibilities, and prospects to propel them into the future. The victors have confirmed the quote of Winston Churchill:

> *"Victory at all cost, victory in spite of all terror, victory however long and hard the road may be; for without victory there is no survival."*
> *— Winston Churchill*

Rather than whine in the midst of battle, victors use what they went through as an incubator to discover inner strengths that were lying dormant in them. Refusing to condone the expectations bullies had for them, they choose to keep on swimming in bully-infested waters in order not to be drown. The way of the victors to victory is not easy or pain-free, but they paid the price, which eventually empowered them to conquer the bullies. Some of them have battle scars; nevertheless, they refuse to allow those scars to hold them back or put them in bondage. In fact, they use their scars as souvenirs of what they have conquered.

> *"A man only begins to be a man when he ceases to whine and revile, and commences to search for the hidden justice, which regulates his life. And as he adapts his mind to that regulating factor, he ceases to accuse others as the cause of his condition, and he builds himself up in strong and noble thoughts. He ceases to kick against circumstances but begins to use them as aids to his more rapid progress and as a means of discovering the hidden powers and possibilities within himself."*
> —James Allen

Inferiority-mentality victim

Inferiority-mentality victims allow their circumstances, their family background, and their financial status to cripple them even before the bully launches an attack. They believe that because they are from a poor background, it is OK for anybody to trample or look down on them. Due to their less privileged status in society, they have a low self-esteem, and they are an easy target for a bully to prey on. In class, they are being orchestrated in a group to suit the agenda of the bully.

The bully uses the circumstances and unique features of his or her victims as a weapon to degrade them, such as the color of their hair or skin, the shape of their nose or ears, the freckles on their face, the types of clothes or shoes they wear, or their family's financial status. These victims allow the bully to control their focus in order for them to see themselves and their uniqueness as a problem or limitation, and once the bully has succeeded in controlling their mental pictures of themselves, they end up believing what the bully says about them, instead of realizing who they really are. They choose to believe their uniqueness is a problem, failing to see the opportunities and the greatness in their uniqueness; hence, they are indirectly and subconsciously empowering the bully to advance an agenda. But what these victims fail to realize is that where you were born, who you are, the family you came from, the color of your skin, or what you wear does not have to define who you are. What define you is your content, ability, and mentality.

> *"Your background does not mean that your back has to be on the ground."*
> *—Pastor (Dr.) Paul Enenche*

Whenever a person decides to use his or her background as a yardstick for defining his or her self-worth, especially when the person is from a poor background, he or she places an embargo on himself or herself, which the bully will only come to enforce because the person sees himself or herself as subordinate or inferior to another person. In such situations, this group has already lost the battle even before the war began because the bully does not need to exercise much supremacy to conquer the victims. Until these victims make up their minds that their backgrounds are not legal grounds for their backs to be on the ground for bullies to trample on, they will remain victims for life. Do not seek affirmation from bullies. Refuse to believe the negative validations of bullies about yourself because bullies are like sales reps who specialize in selling and promoting their negative agenda. It is vital for the people in this group to work on their mental pictures of themselves in order to build their self-confidence. Remember that self-confidence and the level of satisfaction in yourself will determine what you conquer or what conquers you. The ball is in your court to help you fight any victim mentality because as they say, as a man thinketh, so he is.

Defeat is the outcome when you make yourself subordinate or inferior to others, because how you see yourself will determine what you attract into your life...hence do not allow any bully to make you a victim.

Most of the time a bully cannot operate alone without followers and bystanders who directly or indirectly endorse bullying operations.

4

Followers, Bystanders, and the Voice

LIFE IS A compilation of scripts that are being engaged at different phases in one's life journey, and when a person misplaces his or her script in a particular phase of life, he or she goes out of line. As we become susceptible to the influence of others, the possibility of acting and borrowing the scripts of others becomes a reality.

Followers

Followers of bullies have abandoned their scripts and have chosen to use a bully's script to live their lives; hence, they go out of line and start living the life of another person. This lifestyle of using other scripts to live your life is quite dangerous, and many have been caught in the cross fire while using the scripts of bullies to shape their lives, becoming an accomplice in doing evil.

A follower is any person who was enticed or tempted by a bully into indulging in any bullying activities in order to fulfill the evil desires of the bully. When a follower assists in bullying another person, the follower is an apprentice of bullies who eventually becomes an accomplice who joins the bandwagon of bullies to hurt others, to his or her own detriment, and that of innocent victims.

Followers of bullies who have allowed a bully to entice them into bullying others have relinquished their power of choice to the bully at the place where they agreed to comply with the bully's agenda. Followers or accomplices should never forget that when a bully instructs them to carry out a plan to bully an innocent person, they are not under pressure or compulsion to do what bullies expect of them. At this stage, they still have their power of choice. Whatever a person decides to do with his or her power of choice will determine the side of the bullying ring on which he or she stands.

The key is whether the follower chooses to aid and abet a bully in hurting or harming a fellow human being. But the moment a person chooses to become a follower or accomplice by aligning with bullies to hurt or harm another person, the follower has lost his or her right to choose for himself or herself. In short, by assisting in bullying another person, followers have transferred their power of choice to the bully.

Being a follower of a bully can be dangerous. If followers can be easily influenced by bullies to wash their dirty linen, it is likely followers will be easily influenced into more dangerous crimes as a result of association. The reason is that when followers are exposed accidentally or otherwise to wrong associations, they will be easily initiated because they have no vision or purpose of their own. Due to their lack of vision and purpose in life, followers form alliances with bullies and become partners in crime, and such alliances never go unpunished.

This should send a strong message to all followers (accomplices) collaborating with bullies to bully another person. Their actions and behaviors are not acceptable and will not be tolerated at any level. The consequences for cooperating with a bully do not only affect the victim, but the followers too, because when one decides to be a follower of a bully, that person chooses to be like the rest instead of being the best. By this decision, one can never rise to the top because he or she is existing under the shadow of a bully. The followers will go no further than the bully as a result of the bully being their mentor.

Followers, do not be like the crab that has its teeth in its stomach—stand up for who you are and not for what a bully wants you to be. Refuse to live the bully's vision; instead, have your own vision and pursue it.

Lack of Vision

Every one of us was created for a purpose, and until we all know the purpose for our existence, there is the tendency to live a life with no vision. We might be bound to live the vision of others, which will eventually derail us from the purpose of our existence. A lack of vision is the main reason why a bully has followers who assist him or her in carrying out bullying. When a person does not have a vision, he or she is living a life without purpose and a life inside a vacuum—a life that can be easily influenced by the ideology of others. Such a person is living the life of another, mortgaging his or her own life to fulfill the vision of a bully.

Whenever you cooperate with or assist a bully in bullying another person, you are like the person without vision and purpose who is living the life of someone else. Due to their lack of vision and purpose, these people's lives are like a vacuum that is being taken over by a bully to carry out his or her evil plans and actions.

Where there is no vision, there is no choice; anything that comes your way is acceptable; even being coaxed into bullying becomes acceptable to a follower. Put another way, where there is no choice, there is no chance of making a rational decision or judgment. The choice you make determines the chance you have, and the chance you have reflects the choice you made. Because followers of bullies do not have their own visions, they have no power of choice. Hence, they will accept any assignment given to them by a bully, thereby fulfilling the vision of the bully to make the life of another person miserable. They have sold their power to a bully as a result of their lack of vision.

"Be sure you put your feet in the right place, then stand firm."
—Abraham Lincoln

When you lack your own vision, how can you know the right place to put your feet? You will always think anywhere you put your feet is the right place. This is the result of having no vision and purpose in life, which makes a follower an accomplice.

Vision will guide your actions and give you direction, enabling you to know the right place to put your feet. It also helps you to activate and develop the potential that is in you. Vision determines where you end up, and when there is no vision, others will give you theirs. You will end up living their lives instead of your own. A vision clarifies your future, your potential, and the possibilities ahead. But followers are visionless; their lack of vision leads them to become accomplices to bullying in our society, and they are eventually swallowed up by the immediate agenda of the bully, losing sight of the ultimate purpose of their existence and the vision that would have propelled them toward the reason for their existence; hence, they end up living the life and the dream of another.

The company or association you mingle with can either brand you positively or negatively, but certainly you are being branded by the company you keep.

Power of Association

The company you keep determines what flows into your life and what eventually comes out of you in the form of your behavior and attitude. Associations affect behavior, and it is very important to know that not all associations are profitable. The association your child keeps can pollute and affect all the good fundamental principles you inculcate in your child, if the roots of those principles are not deeply embedded in the child. Who a person spends time with will certainly rub off on that person. This is true for children as well, especially when they continuously hang out with bullies; they will attract the bullying behavior and mentality because evil communication corrupts good manners. It is imperative to know that some bullies might not have come out of a bullying parent's home but might become a bully as a result of his or her association and continuous fraternization with bullies.

"One thousand friends are not too much, but one bad friend is too much."
—Archbishop Benson Idahosa

The company you keep determines what you become because iron sharpens iron. In other words, you cannot be different from the association you keep. As a result, your behavior is programmed by the company you keep. When you keep on associating with bullies, you will end up being their followers and eventually a bully. The reason is that the quality of a person's life cannot be higher than the quality of people around him or her. Water is profitable for survival, but salty water is of no value to a thirsty person. Also in life, not all associations are profitable.

That is why you, as parents, have to put all of your children's contacts under observation in order to know which associations are profitable and which need to be sieved out of their lives. It is very important to sieve the associations of your children, especially when they are still young, in order for them to choose the right friends in the future. The contacts or associations made can either make or break your child. In order for your child's destiny not to be destroyed by associations, tell your child that it is better for him or her to take advantage of positive associations and not negative associations because his or her associations paint the picture that will eventually influence his or her destiny.

Fraternizing with bullies causes others to go astray.

Peer Pressure

We, as human beings, crave acceptance and a niche we can belong to, which is normal. But our hunger for acceptance and a niche to call our own can become dangerous when the craving is not well defined. Thus, a person without any aspirations can be easily inspired by others, and followers are not exempted. They have been inspired by bullies to join them in doing their dirty work.

Peer pressure is the place of initiation into questionable behavior and activities. When a child continuously fraternizes with bullies, the child goes astray because of his or her desire to belong to the so-called reigning group in school. It certainly attracts a price, which the followers need to pay in order to belong to the caucus of bullies, and the price is for the followers to aid and abet them in carrying out their atrocities.

Most of these followers know that their actions and activities are wrong because of their desire to belong or feel accepted; they are being pressured to comply with the manifesto of bullying for the day. Despite their victims' pain, followers will still stifle their conscience to prevent being an outcast within a group; hence, the reputation of followers is more important to them than their character, and when this issue is not quickly addressed in a child, it will reflect in his or her adult life, which leads to bullying other adults at work.

Peer pressure will make people do things without thinking about the impact or the consequences. People follow bullies blindly while placing their loyalty in a wrong endeavor to their own detriment. Thus, when followers align with bullies, it is an alignment for disaster.

Misplaced Loyalty

When a bully becomes a mentor, automatically the mentee becomes his or her follower, and the outcome is a misplaced loyalty because the source determines the outcome.

Misplaced loyalty makes a follower support a bully in bullying another person. When you collaborate with a bully as a follower, it shows that your loyalty is being placed in the wrong pursuit—it only confirms how worthless the relationship is and the value you've placed on yourself. A follower exhibits a misplaced loyalty as a result of his or her inability to have a word or opinion of his or her own. A true loyalty is elusive due to his or her lack of self-worth and self-confidence. A true loyalty will not permit or support any form of bullying. You will only gain honor in life when you appropriate your loyalty to a just course.

Collaboration with a bully is a useless investment that will only produce a seed of enmity. Misplaced loyalty only creates enemies, enmity, and blocks good opportunities that a follower would have had if his or her loyalty was not placed on a wrong endeavor. When you know, recognize, and understand the effects and the power of loyalty to another person and to yourself for a just course, then you decide not to be a puppy that a bully commands. Any collaboration with a bully is a wrong investment. So, you will decide by choosing where you place your loyalty because your investment will determine your reward and worth. Your worth reflects your capability and rating in life.

Bystanders

Bystanders are the onlookers in any bullying environment; they see the atrocities bullies are committing but decide to look away. But the truth is, there are no onlookers, no neutral ground. Either you swim or drown in the middle of turbulent waters. In a bullying environment, the role of an onlooker is even more disheartening than that of a follower because we have established that followers have sold their power of choice to a bully. A bystander, on the other hand, still has the power of choice to make the right decision to act against any form of bullying in whatever level it might be occurring. Choosing not to use your power of choice is an abomination to humanity.

Whatever is your stand regarding bullying, we all are signing our signatures, consciously or subconsciously, to either stop bullying or promote bullying activities.

Bystanders play a major role by not saying or doing anything about bullying in their environment. They fail to realize that they've been passive to any form of bullying that occurs around them; they are indirectly enhancing the bullies and their followers to take their bullying escapades to higher levels. This is a big issue because in any bullying situation, the bystanders are mostly the majority; their failing to utilize their power as a majority has compounded the issue. Bystanders must acknowledge this in order to stop the suffering of those being bullied.

All bystanders should remember that they are more powerful than the bully and their followers. In any environment where bullying is taking place, the bystanders outnumber the bullies or their followers. When bystanders unite as a team, their power and authority cannot be underestimated by bullies. In unity they will stand to conquer the bully and their followers. With such actions they are saving lives and impacting their generation.

Moreover, bystanders should know that there is a dark, heavy storm of bullying hovering over someone in their school, office, or neighborhood today. It is crucial for them to be an inhibitor to protect others from the storms of bullying and the web of bullies.

It is high time for bystanders to get off the fence and stand up for what is right by speaking out against all bullying activities. Refuse to be a bystander in the midst of bullying atrocities, and choose to be the stabilizer in the midst of any bullying battle. It is a choice to be a bystander or a stabilizer, but remember, any bystander who thinks it is not his or her business to speak for another person today might be the target of a bully tomorrow; that is, whosoever runs away from a fight today will need to fight another day. So, in any bullying environment, refuse to be an onlooker; instead, be a source of hope to those victimized by bullies. It is not enough to be aware of the bullying battle around you, so be sensitive to what is happening to those being bullied and plug in to find solutions. Take it upon yourself to make a difference by being a source of encouragement and hope to those being bullied.

Be a Source of Hope and Not a Bystander

At each point in life's journey, the weak, strong, timid, intelligent, brave, rich, and poor need a hand of support, fellowship, encouragement, motivation, appreciation, and applause in their victory through the difficult moments in life, especially in their dark hours.

In each hour in life's journey, any person that is facing a difficult situation will yearn for someone to come to his or her rescue, and that is why people are positioned around us. They are a support system and a rescue squad in a difficult situation, including bullying attacks. Those who have been or are being bullied are hoping and praying that bystanders will come to their rescue. Yet, bystanders ignore the cries of the bullied, allowing them to drown in the sea of bullies and their followers.

It is crucial for bystanders to refuse to be on the sideline watching another person be ripped to pieces by bullies. Bystanders do not know what lies ahead of them and thus they might be in the same situation as the victim tomorrow. When you extend a helping hand to support those facing challenging situations, you are sowing seeds for your future.

We all need someone who will extend a helping hand, caring enough to give us hope and not despair by being an onlooker—a bystander. When bystanders decide to support and care for those being bullied, the voices of those fighting against bullying will finally be heard. A hand of hope extended to a bullying victim is a hand of security and safety, because in life people feel secure when they have hope.

Bystanders, will you extend a helping hand to a victim today by giving him or her hope? *Your hand of hope will amplify the victim's voice.*

The Voice

The voice is the group of people who speak for others who are being victimized and bullied in any bullying environment. They are the stabilizers in the midst of human conflict, to ensure peace and justice prevails for the weak. They are usually just a few, but their voices cannot be silenced when they witness any form of abuse or injustice. These people reach out to protect others who are being bullied, and they stop the rule and reign of bullies in their environment. Acting as inhibitors in a bullying environment — they are the anticatalyst of bullies. While they might be like a drop of water in an ocean of bullies, their effect on bullies' operations cannot be underestimated. In the midst of a high-density bullying attack, this group steps in and acts as the voltage stabilizer in order to save a life and make the atmospheric current in the environment more peaceful and conducive for all parties present.

Not only do they have the power to stop the operations of bullies in their environment, but they also have the ability to influence the decision-making process of bystanders, because where they are, bystanders are easily converted to stand up and speak for those being bullied. The voices are the inhibitors in any bullying environment; they can prevent, stop, or reduce bullying. They are like the sun that generates light and warmth wherever bullying darkness is prevailing and dominating. Their presence energizes bystanders to become active and not dormant in their environment.

Their relationship with bystanders is like that of the sun and the moon. Their light reflects on the bystanders to empower them to speak against bullying in their schools or offices, while their presence in the lives of the victims is like a warm blanket that gives comfort on a cold, freezing day. They are the first trace of light that breaks through the dark cloud of bullies; they are the rainbow that gives hope to the victims. They might be few in number or like a drop of water in an ocean, but their impact is tremendous and lifesaving. Wherever they are found, they are the core and will not allow things to fall apart; thus, they are the stabilizers who bring people together so that no one is left behind, isolated, or abandoned on the sidelines. They are the transmitter of strength and unity wherever they are present.

Refuse to Assist but Choose to Resist

A bully is thirsty for power and authority but cannot succeed in his or her quest for power without followers and bystanders aiding him or her. Remember that if you are not resisting, you are assisting. In life, whatever you resist will eventually flee. Whether you are a victim, a follower, or a bystander, it is your responsibility not to aid and assist any bully who aims to hurt or harm. Do not look away as a bystander, and do not become a follower who has chosen to be an accomplice in hurting another person.

It is crucial for each person—whether a victim or victor, bystander or follower—to consciously choose to refuse to empower a bully in launching and carrying out his or her bullying agenda. Sometimes a bully does not have the capacity to operate alone, especially when the environment does not applaud it. Since you are part of the element that constitutes your environment, choose to resist and not assist bullies to succeed in their quest to make another human being miserable. You have a role to play in any bullying battle directly or indirectly. This responsibility should not be taken lightly.

Your responsibility is the catapult for your results in life's endeavors.

Everyone Needs a Friend

It is such a powerful thing for people to know that you are not only there for them, but you are with them no matter what they are going through. Let the person know that he or she has found a friend in you, despite the plans and attacks of some bully. The person should be able to have the confidence in you that you care and will stand with him or her when the winds of bullies are blowing.

Our lives tell stories to those with whom we come into contact, but whatever story a person's life is telling, please let his or her life tell a story of love and support to someone being bullied. The person's actions should tell a victim being attacked by a bully that he or she is not alone, despite his or her challenges. It's like saying, "I care for you, and together we can win the war of bullying."

Supporting someone today who is under the attack of bullying will be a lifesaving stand that can prevent emotional abuse and maybe even death. If we all know that we can save a life by taking a stand against any form of bullying, then that is a good purpose for living. When you help save someone from the jaws of a bully, you will experience a sense of satisfaction and fulfillment in your life, just as you enrich theirs.

Anyone who waters others will be watered in time of need. Therefore, when you decide to be a friend to someone today, a time will come when you will also need a friend because each of us needs a friend. Helping someone today who is being bullied is an investment in the life of the person and yours. Thus, extend a hand to those being bullied, and remind them that they are not going down, they have found a friend in you, and they can rely on you in the midst of a bullying tussle.

These are the questions we should ask ourselves:

1. Can you be a trusted friend in a bully-dominated environment?
2. Are you loyal enough to stand up for someone who is being bullied and tell that person, "I am here for you, and I am with you"?
3. Can you defend another person who is being persecuted by a bully?
4. Can you be that friend who sticks closer than a brother?
5. Are you devoted enough to be a refuge to someone being bullied?

Change starts with one person, and that person is you. Can *you* answer this great calling to bring change to an environment where bullying has been ruling and reigning? It is in everyone's power to make the right choice by standing against any form of bullying in his or her environment. Now is the time to make that choice because at this very moment, the choice can save or destroy a life.

This is your moment, and it might be the only opportunity to make a change and an impact on a generation. This very second can change a person's life and destiny. Why not use it wisely by not collaborating with any form of bullying in the environment? Be a treasure to someone today who is being bullied, and be there for him or her.

Questions for followers and bystanders:

- Are you assisting or resisting bullies in your environment?
- Are you a champion? You decide.

Champions are those who speak against any form of bullying.

Food for thought

- People might not recognize your face or remember your name, but they will never forget your good or evil deed. Your deed in the lives of those around you is always remembered even when you are long gone…Stop bullying so that you will be remembered for your good works as you know your deed is your legacy.
- The best way to help someone off a slippery path of bullies is to extend a hand of support. Your hands of support, friendship, and care will empower them to prevail in the midst of a bullying battle.
- Opportunities are thrown at us every day…They come in different forms and places, especially where you least expect it. Treasure every moment, and do not allow circumstances of life to deprive you of these opportunities.
- Any situation in your life you refuse to address today will consciously or subconsciously address your future. Refusing to take your stand against bullying in your life will make you the victim for life. Thus, address bullying in your life in order to avoid being a victim.
- Life throws curve balls at people, but encouragement and kindness from those around soften the landing of the ball on the individual; therefore, be a source of encouragement. Stop bullying.
- Injustice is real, but it becomes a real problem when your validation of who you are depends on the opinions and comments of others, especially negative people.
- Bystanders: refuse to be a spectator in any bullying environment by choosing to be the participant who goes home with the trophy for making a positive impact in someone's life—by standing for and with someone who is being bullied today.

PART 2

Each and every one of us was born blank, and none was born a bully, a follower, or a victim.

5

The Fundamentals of Parenting

THE WORLD IS changing, but certain aspects of life will never change, such as the fundamental principles governing parenting. These principles serve as a baseline for parents to build, develop, and carry out their responsibilities as parents. Once these principles are respected and implemented in the upbringing of children, they attract positive consequences. Conversely, when these principles are violated, they attract inevitable negative consequences. No matter the changes and developments in the world, these core principles of parenting remain the same, and any attempt to alter these principles will result in meddling, which will lead to malfunctioning in parenting.

These principles are nonnegotiable nor subject to change. Either you comply with these principles in order to succeed, or you decide to ignore/rebel against them to the detriment of your duty as parents. Certainly these principles are inflexible. They might seem challenging at times to apply or fulfill faithfully, but the reward is priceless, and the principles will work for anyone who chooses to apply them in the upbringing of their children. Parents' knowledge and understanding of these principles will empower and strengthen them to fulfill their parenting duties faithfully.

> *"Important principles may, and must, be inflexible."*
> *—Abraham Lincoln*

Some of the principles of parenting are as follows:

- Principle of responsibility (ownership, commitment to duty)
- Principle of parental lifestyle (behavior, response)
- Principle of authority (respect, honor)
- Principle of love (care, stability)
- Principle of discipline (rules, accountability, boundaries)
- Principle of time investment (consistence)
- Principle of communication (listening, connectivity)
- Principle of words (speech, conversation, communication)

The principles listed above are self-explanatory; however, they are equally addressed in other chapters of the book. Failure in implementing these parenting principles can result in poor parenting and can promote bullying in children. Because most parents are busy and distracted, schools have seen an increase in bullying. Parents are no longer there to parent their children; thus, external factors such as the invasion of technology into homes and the abuse of technology by teenagers are increasing bullying in schools today. Until parents identify, understand, and activate these principles in the upbringing of their children, there are bound to be lapses in the nurturing of their children, and children capitalize on such oversights or omissions on the part of the parents.

Parenting is all about the children, which attracts a series of responsibilities and activities for the parents. But some parents are not aware of these responsibilities, while others choose to ignore or modify or overlook them; either way, the principles of parenting are in force whether you believe in them or not. These principles are nonnegotiable and must be implemented in order to be successful as a parent. It is an obligation that is nontransferable. Many parents want to transfer their responsibilities to the school, which has led to escalated bullying in children and has made schools a recruiting ground for bullies to coax other children into bullying activities.

Oversight in parenting is the major sponsor of most bullying behavior in children, which leads to deficiency in the conduct and attitude of children and the victimization of innocent children. One of the core responsibilities of parents is to educate or teach their children the practicality of life and the reality of human existence, hence counseling them to make the right choices by watching and guiding them to ensure that these choices are respected and implemented in their daily activities. This is possible only if parents take seriously their responsibilities as parents and leading their children by example. Children learn faster that way, copying what they see more than what they are told. That is why parents should groom their children by living a life that impacts their children positively, even when external influences seek to derail them.

It is vital for parents to be alert and observant of what goes on around their children while keeping watch over the company they are keeping. It takes vigilance from parents to be able to sieve out the negative associations in their children's lives so that they are not corrupted by the external factors that are trying to infiltrate the good foundation laid by the parents. In life, it is responsibility that always sponsors possibility in whatever endeavor you find yourself, including raising a child; parents are responsible for raising their children to live a life that impacts their world positively.

"It is one thing to be a father or a mother, but it's another thing to be a parent. While any normal human being can be a father or mother, parenting requires responsibility."
—*Pastor E. A. Adeboye*

Different Seasons in Parenting

There are different seasons or stages in the journey of parenting, and each stage is crucial for the development and general welfare of the children. Any vital teaching parents give to their children has its rewards. Just the same, if at any stage the parents fail to nurture their children, there will be consequences. It is easier to groom a child than to correct an adult, which is why no stage of parenting should be ignored. There are specific seasons and turns in life where parents need to make decisions on behalf of their children, for the betterment of their children, and to say no to the decisions of the children. These days, because parents are too busy, some of the core principles of parenting are being neglected; thus, children are using it to bully others, and in some cases, the children are the ones running the homes.

Parenting is all about raising children with love and giving guidance that will establish children in the realm of good conduct for life. However, there is no perfect parent or parents who know it all. All parents are students in the parenting university and do not have a graduation date; parenting is for life. Your willingness as a parent to learn and study the fundamental principles of parenting will help you in carrying out your parenting duty. Parenting is an occupation that attracts a responsibility that doesn't permit going on holiday or retirement, even when the children are all grown; parents are still there making an impact directly or indirectly. It is the most rewarding investment that any parent can ever be involved in, especially when you put the core principles governing parenting and the best resources available into the upbringing of your children.

I believe every parent wants his or her children to be great and successful in life, and no parent wants to fail in his or her parenting responsibilities. In order for this desire to become a reality, parents need to be actively present in their children's lives, as their teacher, instructor, coach, and educator. There is no successful person today who was not under the tutelage of a good instructor or parent at some point. Although there might be some wild weeds that want to corrupt your child, parents can be observant and sensitive in averting damages. Therefore, a parent being actively present in the life of their child is the birthplace of distinction and excellence in any child. In a situation where parents are partially active or present in their children's lives, however, destructive behavior—such as bullying and disrespect for others—will be predominate.

In the end it is the positive involvement and impartation of parents in the lives of their children that will stand the test of time.

Until parents return to the core principles of investing time in nurturing, disciplining, and instructing their children in loving themselves and others, there will be a continuous, disheartening occurrence in society. As stated earlier, children learn by precept and through example; they learn to love people or bully people from the deposition of those who have constant influence over them. It is the duty of parents, especially mothers, to teach their children to love, respect, and honor people, because mothers are not just making or creating homes, they *are* the homes. In situations where mothers are not performing their duty as the home, there will be no home.

Parents' Responsibility to Stop Bullying

Responsibility is commitment to duty. As a parent, you are responsible for the upbringing of your children. How seriously you take this responsibility will determine how you will conquer the challenges that come with this responsibility. The ability to succeed in your duty as a parent is equivalent to how committed you are to parenthood responsibilities and the challenges that it attracts. When parents become distracted by the needs and supplies for the home, other areas of responsibility suffer. Meanwhile, children are bound to capitalize on their parents' weaknesses by misbehaving and, to some extent, becoming a bully at home or in school. Any parent who wants to be content has to find balance so that he or she is not drifting to one extreme of providing for the children while ignoring the other areas of parenting.

One of the assignments of parents is to implement these fundamental principles of life into the lives of their children, but some parents try to shift their responsibility to the school. What most parents fail to realize is that it takes commitment in order to be able to adhere to and implement these principles, especially after a hard day at work, given other issues demanding their attention. It is a commitment to parenthood that will make a parent say, despite all the issues demanding their attention, that it is necessary to make the upbringing of their children their number one priority, and not to transfer it to others.

Educating and training a child in certain areas is the responsibility of the parents, and it is vital for the upbringing of the child. Different aspects of life require different methods of upbringing. In other words, there are areas that you need to educate your child in, and there are areas you need to train your child in. Educating a child might not be enough to inculcate the right mentality while, on the other hand, it might be the best option.

For example, you cannot educate a pilot to fly an aircraft because a pilot needs training to fly an aircraft. In the same way, parents will not give their children sex training, but children need sex education. These are the dicing areas, where parents need to know when to train a child and when to educate a child. Your ability to discern where to appropriate training and educating in the upbringing of your child holds the power to succeed, which is only possible when parents are committed to their responsibility because nothing becomes glorious until you become committed to what you do.

Acceptance of responsibility and being committed to responsibility is the birthplace for possibilities, and therein lies the power to find solutions to tackle problems—including bullying issues in schools. Transferring the responsibility to school authorities to put an end to bullying activities in schools is a short-term solution that will have no lasting effect in making an impactful change. Parents must work with the schools. Thus, a short-term solution with a long-term solution in the pipeline will circuit a lasting impact. Abolishing bullying in schools starts at home, and until parents accept their responsibilities to stop bullying, there will be no lasting solution. Responsibility is doing what is expected of you at the right time, no matter how difficult it might be. It takes diligent work to make anything count in life. Thus, parents accepting responsibility to abolish bullying in schools is the start of lifesaving solutions.

Time Investment is Life Investment

The day a parent made the decision to become a parent, or the day you became pregnant or impregnated a woman, you made a subconscious agreement that the welfare of the child—whether emotional, material, social, or financial—will be your number one priority, even above yourself. The priority of parenting can affect the performance of the children, and that is why being too busy to have time with your child is not an option, and neither is shifting your responsibility to others, which cannot compensate for you being there to love your child. The love of a parent is not replaceable.

> *"When you hold your baby in your arms the first time, and you think of all the things you can say and do to influence him, it's a tremendous responsibility. What you do with him can influence not only him, but everyone he meets, and not for a day or a month or a year, but for time and eternity."*
> *—Rose Kennedy*

Investing time in nurturing children is not about you or your child alone; it is about humanity and grooming your child to be a treasure to his or her world. Such an investment will help parents to be more involved in the lives of their children, which will enable parents to know about issues or problems concerning their children. In this way, parents make it a priority to ensure that solutions are found to problems in order to avert red-flag situations that can be detrimental to the child and society. Spending time with a child who is being bullied will help the parents to know the depth and gravity that the bully's actions are having on a child because in the midst of their busy lives, parents can miss the signs that a child is at the constant torment of a bully. Some parents are not aware that their children are actively involved in bullying activities or being initiated into bullying activities in school; such behavior can be made known to the parents only if they are spending time with their children. That is when such behavior can be brought to light.

Only when parents are constantly involved in their children's lives by spending time with them can they know what is actually going on. That is when parents can fully support their children in order to restore peace and stability in their children's lives. Time spent with your children to either educate or train them is learning time, which builds confidence in your children. It is a lifelong investment that will make all the difference in the lives of children, because time is the currency of care.

Parents are Fountains

Water is a major source for human survival, and it is needed for our existence. Parents are like water fountains in the lives of their children, where they constantly get irrigated to help develop their child's personality and get refreshed when necessary. They are the water that irrigates the soil in which the life seed of their children's characters are germinated and cultivated. Although water is vital for the existence of humanity, not all water is profitable; thus, the process of watering and the type of water used is crucial for the harvest. Whatever fruit that is produced will reflect the soil type, the seed that was sown, and the quantity/quality of water the seed received.

The upbringing of children is a process of watering them, and the type of water used is vital because not all water is useful or profitable. Thus, the behavior, attitude, and mentality of parents are like an aura that rubs off on their children to build their personality. Parents, beware, because almost everything you do is being transmitted into your children's lives. Parents are the fountain that their children plug themselves into to develop their personality. Remember that whatever flows out of you as the fountain in their lives will be seen and absorbed by them. When the content of the parents is love and respect, it flows into the children, and it will be revealed in the children's behavior; but when the content of the parents is hate and bullying, it also flows into the children, and the effects are exhibited by the children wherever they go. Thus, these children take on this bullying behavior, which they have absorbed from their environment, into whatever they do. Either way, there is an emotional transmission flowing from the parental fountain, whether it is love or hatred; one type of this flow is beneficial to humanity, while the other emotion is destructive, which leads to bullying behavior in schools.

Whether you as a parent of the bully or victim accept it or not, your children are indirectly or directly absorbing what is flowing out of you. It will be of great benefit to you, your children, and society for all parents to evaluate themselves, and it will be surprising how we as parents have been the major sponsors of certain behaviors in our children because of what is flowing from us into them. Assessing ourselves as a parent will help us to discover areas that need to be addressed in our parenting assignment. In other areas of life, such as our job or profession, people go through assessments on a regular basis in their offices in order to rate their performances. The most important profession, however, is parenting; yet, we always refuse or forget to assess ourselves, and this has led to a lot of oversights. It is vital for parents to know that the process of assessing themselves will only lead to the truth (i.e., if you are ready to accept the truth because the truth is incontrovertible).

Transgenerational Parenting

Transgenerational parenting is a parenting style that has been transferred from one generation to another. It is a tradition that has been passed down from one generation to another. There are families with parenting styles based on bullying and hatred; these transgenerational parenting skills have been transferred from generation to generation and have become a norm, which defines a family's parenting pattern, thus making bullying an acceptable norm. It is a tradition inherited that has influenced their parenting styles. Such transgenerational parenting does not see anything wrong with bullying or making an environment unsafe for people because it has become a way of life, which parents implement daily. It has become a vicious cycle that must be broken in order to put an end to this family custom. This will be possible only when parents are educated about their contribution in enforcing bullying or the victim mentality in their children.

Parents need to find balance so that they are not drifting to extremes. This will be possible only when parents have the knowledge and understanding of these principles and learn how to implement them while executing their parental duties. This group of parents can only change through the process of enlightenment and awareness, because no matter the level of help a bully might get from any organization or system, until the mentality of his or her parents is renewed and transformed, it will be a wasted effort. Thus, eradicating bullying in our society starts at home. When families at home are willing to improve their way of living, change is inevitable. A continued improvement at home will lead to a continuous change in the behavior of bullies, which will eventually be reflected in our schools and in our workplace.

Naturally, when you hear about the reading of a will or an inheritance, your mind goes to properties and in some cases money after the death of the testator. But what most parents fail to realize is that their behaviors and actions are inheritance, too, which are being read to their children on a daily basis by the parents, and they are passing it over to their children while they are still alive.

6

Parents are the Antidote for Bullying

Parents are the sun and the rain that children need to grow and shape their lives and destinies. Parents hold and control the future of their children by the power of their spoken words and the foundation they lay for their children. The strength of the foundation of a child determines the destiny of that child, and the strength of this foundation depends on the positioning of parents in their children's lives.

Types of Parents

In any bullying incident, there are different types of parents represented. The positioning of each parent always determines the end result because no child was born a bully, victim, bystander, or follower. But a child's environment, associations, and upbringing created or made the child who he or she is. Just as the Japanese koi fish depends on its environment to grow because the growth of the koi fish is proportional to its environment, so are we as humans. That is why parents need to come together as a team and not as opponents; the role parents play is the major sponsor of bullying behavior or victim mentality in a child, whether directly or indirectly.

The different types of parents represented in a bullying incident are as follows:

- Parents of the bully
- Parents of the followers
- Parents of the victim (or victor)
- Parents of the bystanders

Parents of the bully

Among the parents of bullies, there are different categories. There are parents who applaud and support the bullying behavior of their children. This group will go to any length to shovel any form of blame from their children. Taking a closer look, you will also find the trace of bullying characteristics in the parents; hence, they are bullies themselves. Another group are the parents who might not necessarily be bullies, but their decision to see no wrong in their children has empowered their children in bullying others and getting away with it; put another way, they indirectly or unknowingly promote and support their children's actions because of their inability to see no wrong in their children. These parents will take it as a personal vendetta and will go to any length to influence the decisions of those in their network to join them in their propaganda.

The last category comprises parents who do not support or applaud the bullying behavior of their children; they are deeply troubled and sorry for the behavior of their children. For these parents, their children have been influenced by the company they keep. Most times these parents are shocked when complaints come from school about their children's bullying behaviors. They willingly cooperate with the school to stop such behavior in their children and are willing to cooperate where necessary with the victim and his or her family.

Parents of the followers

Among the parents of followers, there are two groups. The first is the group of parents who are aware of their children's mentalities as followers, and have already identified this weakness in their children. When complaints come from schools about their children's follower behaviors in a bullying incident, they are not surprised because they are aware of the strengths and weaknesses of their children. These parents will not only cooperate with schools but even go the extra mile to mend bridges with the parents of the victim (victor) in order for peace to reign.

The second group comprises parents who are offended by any form of complaint from the school or the parents of the victim. As a group on the offensive, they are aggressive in their reactions to the behaviors of their children. They believe that the parents of the victim (victor) have no right to complain when their child is an accomplice to bullying. They will go to any length to make enmity within children, and most times it is the mothers who exhibit this behavior.

Parents of the victim (or victor)

There are four major types of parents of victims.

The first group comprises parents who will go to any length to support their children in order to conquer any form of bullying attack. These parents are willing and open to any input that will help them to help their children not to be victimized by a bully. They believe that victim mentality is not an option. They look for the *why* in order to handle *what* the bully is doing to their child, and in the end use it as a process to empower their child to conquer the bully. They will do whatever it takes to put an end to bullying attacks in their children's lives.

The second group comprises parents who do not know what to do or how to support their children; they are in a catch-22—all their efforts to help end in frustration and pain. In some cases, these parents were bullied in the past or are still experiencing bullying behavior. Such parents are confused and do not know how to help their children because they are or have been victimized themselves. Because of their experience with personal bullying attacks, they are very hesitant in making a decision but end up making the wrong decision, thereby aggravating the situation.

The third group comprises parents who are not willing to fight, and they believe that changing location will help their children not to be a victim of bullying behavior; hence, they will transfer their children from one school to another. But this group fails to identify why their children are easily susceptible to the attacks of bullies and their followers and, in the process, fail to support their children.

The last group of parents are bullies themselves. They bully their own children with words and actions, either consciously or subconsciously. These parents do not realize that their actions are having devastating effects on their children.

Parents of the bystanders

The influence of the parents of bystanders is as crucial and important as the other parents because in most bullying environments, the bystanders are always the majority. The parents of bystanders active in educating their children to make the right choices in a bullying environment will help put an end to bullying in schools. When bullying is wiped out from the dictionary of teenagers, it will transform the world we are living in, even for future generations.

Parents of bystanders need to be more attentive to what their children tell them about their day in school and all that transpired. Most times parents will hear about the bullying of another child in the summary of their child's day in school. It will be of great help if parents don't overlook any piece of information their children tell them about bullying; in fact, it is an opportunity for parents to educate their children to stand up to support those being bullied. I believe when all bystanders speak against any form of bullying in their classes or schools, the strength of bullies and their followers will be broken, for bystanders are a majority force that no bully or follower wants to contend with. Remember, in unity lies power.

Positioning of Parents

Parents are the transmitters of wisdom in the lives of their children; they are the baseline where children learn what is right and wrong. Parents are

PARENTS ARE THE ANTIDOTE FOR BULLYING

to inculcate into children the wisdom that will enable them to do the right thing; this will be possible given the right positioning of the parents. The positioning of parents in the lives of their children will determine how far they will succeed in their responsibilities as a parent and the way their children will relate with them. Parents have authority over their children—to be a promoter of good conduct and not bad behavior such as bullying. When parents support or promote bad actions, such as bullying, they have only succeeded in denting and weakening their authority. When children detect weakness in their parents, they use this weakness to manipulate and control them; the danger is that in some cases, parents are not even aware that they are under the manipulating grip of their children.

When any authority figure has a lapse, there is bound to be confrontation, interference, and opposition from external forces. Parents are no exception, whether parents of a bully or parents of a victim. Either way there is opposition that is contending to undermine the authority of the parents. If the positioning of the parents is not well defined, the effects of these external opposition factors are reflected in the lives of their children.

Furthermore, some parents are not aware of how their positioning affects their authority in their children's lives. This is especially true at home where external influences such as TV, games, social media, and more are dominating the upbringing of a child instead of traditional home parenting. Where external influences are more active than the parent, it becomes an emergency situation because parents are not there to teach and enlighten their children on the practicality of life; in such situations, children are bound to misbehave and engage in mischievous acts, such as bullying, because where an authority is not ruling and prevailing, every evil will work.

The issue of parents being the antidote for bullying is two-sided. Just like a sword that has two edges, the parents of the bully and the parents of those being bullied have their responsibilities to carry out. The existence of a follower depends on the availability of a bully; thus, the existence of parents of a follower depends on how well the parents of the bully and victim carry out their responsibilities. How successful parents will be in their responsibilities depends on their positioning.

Parents are like a GPS

Parents are the Global Positioning System (GPS) in giving directions to their children at all levels and stages in life, moving from one point to another in order for their children to arrive at an enviable destination. The destination of a child's journey becomes colorful when the parents are there to give him or her direction and guidance, especially when there are distractions, situations, and external influences that want to derail or stunt the capability of a child, preventing him or her from reaching a destination.

It is the responsibility of all parents to come together and act as the GPS to help schools help children stop bullying in order to make a bully-free zone. Thus, parents make a difference in children's lives by becoming a GPS in the vanguard of eradicating bullying in our society and being the GPS that will rescue a child who is drowning in the sea of bullies. Parents, decide today to be a GPS to a child who is trapped in the web of bullies; show him or her the way out of the web. The directions and guardians that children need to stop bullying and to help those who are being bullied lie within all parents. So, parents should take it upon themselves to ensure no child is bullied, not even for a second. Such an initiative would have a tremendous impact in making our school environment a bully-free zone. Parents, could *you* be a GPS in the life of a child who is not yours by showing him or her how to smile again and leading that child on a road that will restore his or her faith? Parents, will you make a difference in the lives of your children by being their GPS and role model with positive attributes that will anchor them to an enviable destiny?

The Role of Parents of Bullies

Parents of bullies need to know that there are differences between a leader and an oppressor. They should not camouflage their children's behaviors as developing leadership skills. These parents should know that they are raising queen bees and tyrants in place of leaders. Sometimes parents of bullies do not cooperate with schools when teachers complain or share observations about their child's behavior; to them, the teacher is blowing the incident out of proportion. Parents, especially mothers, have a vital role to play by not being on the offensive when issues are brought to their attention about the behavior of their children.

In short, parents need to check their roles in promoting bullying in their children, whether directly or indirectly, whether consciously or subconsciously. There are some parental factors that might enhance bullying in a child. These factors might be seen in the foundations laid by parents, which are sometimes directly or partially responsible for bullying in children. This foundation can fall under some of the following:

- Behavior of parents
- Conversation style of parents (the way they communicate)
- Response of parents
- Cloud Parenting/Cloud homes (discussed in a later chapter)

Parents are also the beneficiaries of their legacy in their children's lives.

Behavior of parents

The way parents act and conduct themselves toward others influences the behavior of their children; it transmits a behavioral current that will eventually mold the behavior of their children. When children see their parents involved in actions that are not acceptable in society, children might think that it is acceptable, thereby practicing the behavior of the parents as normal.

To every parent out there, if you are really honest with yourself, you know or can identify or recognize that the effects of your behavior on your children are seen by you even before any other person notices it. But what you do with this discovery will determine the behavior of your children in the future. The environment of a child has a great impact on the child because it influences the attitude and the personality of the child. If a child grows up in an environment where lying, fear, dominating, and competing in a negative way is predominate, then the seed has been sown in the life of that child. Parents should realize that they are not only a parent but a tutor in their children's lives.

Naturally, when you hear about the reading of a will or an inheritance, your mind goes to properties and, in some cases, money after the death of the testator. But what most parents fail to realize is that their behaviors and actions are inheritances too, which are being read to their children on a daily basis while they are still alive. Parents must realize that their legacy is in operation in the lives of their children. The parents will also be the beneficiaries, whether the legacy is good or bad, because whatever you sow is what you will reap.

Conversation style of parents (the way they communicate)

Conversation is fundamental for communicating and exchanging ideas via the spoken word. The power of conversation cannot be undermined because it is the medium for expressing one's thoughts, opinions, and feelings, which is crucial.

The conversations parents are having in the presence of their children or with their children are not just mere words but seeds that grow in their mind. Once the seeds are sown, the parents and the environment (external influences) water the seeds until they grow, and they can have either a positive or negative influence on the child. When the outcome of a conversation is negative, it becomes an evil tree with roots that can destroy others under the tag or identity of a bully.

Parents should realize that their words during a conversation are part of the fundamental principles that shape their child's destiny. When we acknowledge the power of our words, we realize that they are not mere words but an instrument or weapon that can destroy, defend, or nurture someone in love. We all should learn how to choose our words in order to make the right conversation and use our words to positively impact others. Children are taught by their parents to speak, and they are corrected on how to use the right words and vocabulary. Most times these children pick up their parents' vocabularies, so it is important for parents to always remember that when they are having any form of conversation, their children are listening and will definitely put into practice what they learned from their parents.

For example, you could be a parent who always exaggerates by blowing things out of proportion, or you could specialize in spoiling, tainting, or defrauding other people's personalities with your words. Or, you could use your words as a well of refreshing water that quenches the thirst of the people around you. Nevertheless, your words are having effects on those around you, and the nearest beneficiaries are your children. That is why we need to be conscious in choosing the right words to covey our thoughts and opinions. When our words are spoken right, they are like apples of gold in settings of silver, and that is when we can really make a positive impact in the lives of our children and those around us.

Response of parents

When parents respond and treat other people in an aggressive manner, their children are always watching and seeing the response of their parents. They are copying this response because it is like a mirror, and whatever is placed in front of a mirror is what is reflected back. Parents applauding the queen bee or bullying attitude of their children will certainly send the wrong signal to the child that it is acceptable or normal, and eventually the urge to control or dominate others has been laid as a foundation for the child to build on.

That is why the response of parents to the attitudes of their children has a lot to do with bullying. Whenever a parent praises and compensates a child's bad behavior, they are not only telling the child that it is acceptable, but they are also empowering the child to take their negative action to the next level. This will continue and develop into bullying at the slightest opportunity to practice the bad behavior that the parents have applauded in the past. Most times the school is the breeding ground where bullies exercise the seed of bullying that was planted and nurtured from their homes, the company they keep, or their environment. The training and upbringing of a child should not be done outside the home, but rather inside the home, especially since people tend to believe that the schools are not doing enough to stop bullying.

When the correction of a child is ignored by parents, the tendency of being subjected to negative influences is high, and a child whose parents support his or her negative behavior tends to be more difficult to correct in school; hence, the hands of the teachers are tied due to the response of parents to their children's behaviors at school.

The Role of Parents of Victims

In the life of every child there is a treasure, and wherever there is treasure, there is always maximum security and protection. Therefore, it is very important for every parent to provide and enforce maximum security for the protection of their children from negative infiltration.

It is vital for the parents of children being bullied to take it as an attack not only against their child or children but against them, especially when their child is not able to stand up for himself or herself. It is not an issue that should be swept under the carpet, nor should it be wished away. The moment you realize your child has been targeted by a bully, do whatever you can to protect, support, and empower your child in order to stop the attack.

The children who are bullied most often are those who have a good home upbringing, children their parents taught to be respectful, humble, and not to be involved in any fight. Children who were not taught at home what it means to be respectful or to keep their hands to themselves or to keep out of fights will always target those children with a good home upbringing. These bullies believe that such children are the weak links in the group, which is why parents of victims need to encourage their children to come to them and talk about their experiences. This will help the parents to know what steps to take in order to support their children.

The first step is to ask the right questions, which will help you identify the reason behind the attack. When parents ask the right questions, the problem is half-solved because the parents' findings will enable them to know in which area they need to support their child. Indeed, each question will bring them closer to the solution that might work for their child.

These are some likely questions that need to be asked:

- Why is your child being bullied?
- Are other children in the class or school experiencing such bullying?
- If yes, how often are the other children being bullied?
- Who are the bullies?
- Is it the same person or a group of people bullying your child?
- What is the motive of the bullies?
- What are the observations and responses of the teachers in school?
- What is your child's reaction to bullying?
- How does your child express his or her emotions to bullying?
- What does your child need to know about boundaries?
- How do you set boundaries?
- What are your strategies to empower your child to stand up for himself or herself?

The ability of parents to ask the right questions and provide honest answers sets the stage for the role they need to play in order to help their children in the midst of a fierce bullying environment. In some cases, the questions parents need to ask might be different from one child to another, but one of the important keys for parents is asking the right questions, which will be a trigger for finding a solution to the bullying attack. Once the right questions have been asked and parents have received honest answers, then parents can devise a strategy.

This strategy should be tailored to fit the needs of that particular child. What works for one child being bullied might not work for another; hence, parents should endeavor to empower their children according to their children's needs. The capacity to empower children being bullied comes from parents identifying why their children are susceptible to bully attacks. Most of the time, instead of parents asking the right questions in order to arrive at a profitable solution, they take the easy route by moving the child to another school. Asking the right questions, however, will lead to solutions that will empower their children for life against any form of bullying.

It might be necessary for parents to relocate their children to another environment, especially when it is a case of life or death. But before reaching that point, ask the right questions, and leave no stone unturned before deciding to move the child to another school. Whatever made your child susceptible to bullies, if not addressed by identifying the problem, will make them susceptible again in a new location. Hence, changing schools is not necessarily the right solution; it should be a last resort.

Changing Schools is Not the Ultimate Solution

Most parents of children being bullied at school are quick in making the decision to move their children to another school in order to avert bullying attacks. But that is not the best option for solving the problem. History has shown that this option has not produced the results parents or children want to see. Changing schools is not the ultimate option and is always confirmed when the children are bullied again in their new school.

Most times parents are busy asking the wrong question of *what* are the bullies doing to their child, instead of asking *why* are they doing it. Until parents know the *why* behind the actions of the bully, there will be no solution to *what* the bully is doing. Parents' failure to deal with the root of the problem, which is trying to find out why their children are the target of bullies — there will be no solution. Until the right questions are asked and the right answers are found, taking your child to another school is like postponing the battle for another day.

The most disheartening part of bullying is that most of the victims are children who are well nurtured from home, but the parents failed to equip them for the battles existing in our world. They are taught by their parents to be humble and respectful but not taught that boundaries are necessary for the protection of lives and property or to maintain their territories; hence, these children are being sent to a battlefield of *warfare* but are being equipped with the mentality of *welfare*. It is important for parents to work on their children's weapons by building their self-confidence and self-esteem in preparation for the bully's assault. A bully's first point of attack is to disarm your children by attacking their confidence before the bully advances to dominate and control the victim into submitting to his or her bullying supremacy; hence, focus on the *why*.

The Answer is in the *Why*

Most parents of victims are always looking for the easiest way or a shortcut to resolve bullying problems. They fail to look beyond the quick fix, which is moving the child being bullied to a new school or environment. They fail to identify or deal with the *why* behind the bullying of their child, which will eventually result in history repeating itself in terms of their child being a victim of bullies again. Until the issue or the problem is identified and dealt with appropriately, there is a 100 percent chance of history repeating itself. You cannot guarantee that the new school does not have bullies, and neither have you as a parent equipped your child not to be an easy target for bullies to prey on.

Until parents try to discover the cause of their child being a target of bullies in school, there will be no room for the child's recovery. For example, if the reason why a child is continuously bullied is that the child has a low self-esteem and low self-confidence, then until the parents work on boosting the self-esteem and self-confidence of the child, the problem is not yet solved. Even when the child is moved to another school, the bullies there will easily fish him or her out in the new environment. Some children are taught to be respectful and love others but are not taught how to say no, or to speak against any form of abuse that someone might want to inflict. As a result, the child is easily victimized by his or her peers.

Keep in mind that continuously changing schools as a result of bullying will only destroy the stability in the child's life. When a child or even adult is not stable, it affects and reflects in every area of the person's life, including his or her actions and performance. Stability is vital in the growth and development of every child; it is the core for discovery and developing and maximizing children's potential. The pathway of empowerment for children is a lifetime booster and will be a propeller in the discovery and development of the hidden potentials in children's lives.

Empower Your Children

Parents are cultivators in their children's lives, while schools are the fertilizer that will help ensure what parents have already planted yields a good harvest. Parents are in their children's lives to empower them to shape their destiny, enabling them to rise against any storms in life, including the storms of bullying. Empowering children from home will not only build confidence that will help them shape their destiny, but it will also help them know their worth and value—and not seek validation from others who want to prevent them from achieving their life's endeavors.

When parents endeavor to bring out the best in the lives of their children, it boosts their self-confidence and self-esteem; and when parents help their children to cultivate self-confidence and self-esteem, they are empowering their children not to be someone's slave or victim. Building the self-confidence of a child is empowerment, while teaching a child at a tender age the importance of having boundaries in life is another form of empowerment. This will equip them to know when to say *yes* and *no*, when to *speak* and be *silent*, and when to be *humble* and be *tough*. All these forms of empowerment will help children to differentiate when they are being lured to aid and abet in an atrocious activity or coaxed into a victim box. It helps them to bounce back when they are being thrown against the wall by bullies and their followers.

Empowerment of any child can be more effective when parents keep watch over the company their children keep. Parents can be building the self-confidence of their child, but when the child is keeping company with the wrong crowd or mingling with those who have a victim mentality, the efficacy of parental empowerment becomes void. Thus, the empowerment of a child can be more effective when parents keep watch over the company their child is keeping, especially when the child is a victim of bullies already. Such children should avoid the company of those who will magnify the victim mentality in them, which will eventually lead to a pity party. Having boundaries enables a child to evaluate his or her associates in order to know which company he or she needs to exit or to abide. Setting boundaries will be a lifesaving empowerment in the midst of life's storms, including the bullying storm.

The area of empowerment might differ from one child to another, but there are certain areas where we all need empowerment, which is common to all humans. Below are some of these areas:

- Empowerment of love
- Empowerment of self-description
- Empowerment of setting boundaries
- Empowerment of being humble and tough

Empowerment of love

When someone tells you he or she loves you more than you love yourself, it is a huge problem, and something is seriously wrong. It can become an opening to abuse or maltreatment. It could also victimize the person because he or she has been programmed to believe another person's love is more crucial than loving himself or herself. The reality is that some children do not love themselves. Such cases are alarming, especially when this red flag is not being noticed by their parents.

When this error is not addressed and handled, it becomes a challenge for children. Whenever any person tells them they are not lovable or worth loving, they automatically believe the lies that are being sold to them. When this mentality is not corrected and children do not know how to love themselves, it affects them their entire life.

During Christmas one year, I met a forty-year-old man. As I wished him season's greetings, I asked him if he would be celebrating with his family. His reply to my question was shocking. According to him, in his words, he said, "I am nothing, I have nothing, and nobody is interested in nothing like me." It was disheartening for me to hear these words from the mouth of a grown man, and these words got me thinking. Where did things go wrong in his life? Although I tried to encourage him and gave him some uplifting words, it seemed like it was falling on a brick wall. At that moment, the question that came to mind was, how many adults and children out there in this world have been programmed by life's storms to believe they are worthless, and nobody cares enough to even notice them? Until children learn to love themselves, they cannot accept the love of others or appreciate their uniqueness or potential.

I came to the realization that parents loving their children, telling them how God loves them, are empowering and setting a precedent for children to love themselves. This becomes a lifetime jackpot that never runs dry but is always new every morning as they wake up. It is there every day as they walk through the streets of life. Teaching children to love themselves is an inoculation that gives children a self-description of *I am who I am and will not wait for bullies to define me or my worth in life*; hence, children loving themselves and acting on their love for themselves empowers them.

When a person is contented with himself or herself, it boosts his or her confidence and emits an aura of 'I love myself,' and no matter what people or life throws at the person, he or she glows in the midst of life's challenges and victories.

Empowerment of self-description

The truth is that most parents are doing their best to be the perfect parent who endeavors to empower his or her children to stand on their own two feet when they are outside the protection of their parental umbrella. That is why it is crucial for parents to give their children a self-description that will energize them even when they are confronting obstacles such as bullies.

In the storms of life, giving children wings is not enough without telling them how to flap their wings and fly in the midst of life's storms, just as the mother eagles do with their eaglets. Parents are not only giving children wings but also teaching them how to flap their wings and soar high above bullies by using the winds of challenge to discover their inner strength of resistance, thereby giving them a positive self-description. Thus, in the midst of bullies, the self-description of a child can either be a weapon of empowerment or defeat.

> *"A person standing at the edge of a ditch or cliff does not need much force or distraction to fall into the ditch or from the cliff, all he or she needs is a little distraction and the person falls into the ditch or from the cliff."*
> —*African proverb*

Children who are not equipped with a positive self-description or self-confidence are easily belittled, victimized, and attacked by their peers. It is crucial, then, for parents to give a self-description of upliftment in order for their children not to trudge through life being battered by the opinions of others. Instead they will walk through the streets of life with a self-assurance of "I am worthy to be whatever God has created me to be"; these children do not rely on the validation of others to define them.

The description children form of themselves will determine their path. When children are continuously reminded at home of their worth, and that they are valuable, a treasure to their family and society, such words of praise or encouragement will boost the child's self-confidence. It instills in the child a self-confidence that is unbreakable even in the face of life's challenges, such as bullying. Parents should endeavor to give their children a self-description that will empower them through life because an excellent description of who they are is a life booster.

Empowerment of setting boundaries

Human beings tend to abuse and misuse people and opportunities; it is only when you have boundaries that you can escape from being a casualty of such people. In as much as boundaries are used to protect goods and properties, they are also vital for the protection of human lives and peace of mind. Still, most people fail to realize how much their daily existence depends on setting boundaries in their lives. In order not to be wasted by selfish, self-centered people, such as bullies, parents need to teach their children how to set boundaries. Setting boundaries helps people know what is acceptable and unacceptable, depending on the standard people have laid for themselves. These boundaries transmit a clear message to those they come in contact with that there are limits.

It is predominant for parents of children who are being bullied to teach their children the importance of setting boundaries. Teaching a child how to set boundaries will help the child earn respect and privacy, which everyone deserves. However, deserving something does not mean you will get it; situations and people will want to resist you, even when it is your right to have the respect and privacy everyone deserves.

In every realm of life, boundaries are very important. That is why buildings have walls. The walls are boundaries erected to protect lives, properties, and privacy. Just as we use walls as boundaries in our homes, in life we build invisible walls of boundaries in order not to be trodden upon by bullies looking for prey. Parents should teach their children not to allow anybody to walk over them, and never keep silence when they need to respond in return, because to a bully, bullying is a fight for territory and domination.

Once you stop fighting for your rights and stop protecting your territory by enforcing your boundaries, bullies will automatically invade your territory and turn you into prey. That is why parents need to teach their children to form their own meaning and opinions, to speak out for themselves on issues, when necessary, and to avoid drifting between or concurring with the opinions of others. Any person in a group who has no meaning or say of his or her own is an easy target.

Parents should let their children know they are worthy and that they have a choice in any situation that confronts them; hence, they decide the game plan for their lives and not the bullies. Life's circumstances do not have to overwhelm them or incapacitate them because they can be both humble and tough. This will be possible when children have been taught to set boundaries and enforce them. Doing this is a choice that attracts responsibility.

Empowerment of being humble and tough

Learning how to set boundaries will help children to know that they can be humble, respectful, and tough. This will help children to know when to be humble and when to be tough. Parents should teach their children to be humble but not timid. Being humble yet tough or humble and not foolish is a signal children need to transmit in order not to be swallowed up by their peers. It is a characteristic found in bees; bees can produce honey and also sting when necessary. Help your child to be sweet like honey toward all men and women but rise as a bee, speak for himself or herself when necessary, and ask for help by the appropriate authorities.

Parents should tell their children to be humble but not to be humbled by bullies. When a child is being humbled by bullies, he or she has no choice in the process where someone else takes charge of his or her life and dreams. The child is brought to his or her knees by force or actions that are detrimental. Therefore, it is the responsibility of parents to bring up their children to be respectful and humble while refusing to be humbled. If children are not taught the difference between being humble and being humbled, they might be indirectly assisting others to trample over them. Thus, teach them to resist and not assist bullies in their atrocities against them.

This will be possible when parents teach their children the skill to identify or recognize what is acceptable and what is not acceptable. A child being humble and respectful does not mean the child should be the trampoline that everybody springs upon in order to have fun or make jokes.

In reality, people are ever ready to walk over you when you allow it; your child does not need to be a trampoline or a stepping-stone for others. Your children need to learn when to stand up for themselves and speak up or ask for help when necessary. Teach your children to be humble but not timid and humble yet tough by focusing on their watchword. That way, they won't be swallowed up in a bullying environment.

Below is a true-life story of a girl and two boys who were bullied but were equipped by their parents to conquer.

Chloe's story: Chloe is a beautiful young lady who was brought up with good manners to care for and help others; with this mentality, Chloe was equipped to go into the world, but the reality that Chloe encountered was that having good manners and caring for others was not good enough without having boundaries. Thus, Chloe later found out that the equipment she got from home for her life journey was not strong enough to confront and handle the battles in the world of bullying.

Chloe was bullied in primary school between the ages of six and eight for about three years by the same group of bullies. The bullying attack started when she was in her second year in primary school. She was in a class of about thirty students, where twenty-seven of those students were always picking on her. They bullied her inside and outside the classroom, sometimes in the presence of their teacher.

Chloe was continuously tormented and tortured by the bully and his followers with any opportunity they got; it all started with pushing, throwing things at her, and tearing books and turning her chair or table upside down. It was a hard, lonely three years for her because the bully and his followers, the majority of the students in the class, came to school every day to torment and isolate her from the group. Any time Chloe attempted to play or participate in any activities in the group, the bully plus his followers used it as an avenue to torment and ridicule her by ensuring that she always lost, which eventually empowered them to oppress her all the more. Throughout the three years of continuous attacks from the bullies, Chloe found comfort and courage from a girl in the class who refused to cooperate with the agenda of the bullies. According to Chloe, this girl (the voice) was a source of strength and the only reason she woke up in the morning to go to school, despite the attacks of the bullies.

For three years, Chloe was bullied from one class to another by the same group of students under the supervision of different teachers, but there was no change in behavior of the bullies despite having different teachers in each of the classes. According to Chloe, all the teachers in the different classes were aware of the bullying but did not have enough capability or knowledge on how to handle the situation. Thus, Chloe went through the torment and isolation until her parents took her to a new school. But her parents did not stop there; they sent her to a school that taught people defensive sports. This program empowered Chloe to build her self-confidence and taught her how to protect herself, especially in the midst of bullies.

In high school Chloe encountered another bully who was always picking on her and throwing away her stuff. Unfortunately for this bully, the Chloe in high school was different from the Chloe in primary school. Chloe had developed herself mentally and physically with the training she got from defensive sports, which enabled her to handle the bully in her high school class without any external help. Chloe taught the bully a lesson, and that was the end of bullying for Chloe in school.

Although Chloe conquered her bully, the scars of her past experiences still affect her today. She finds it difficult to trust people, and any kind of kindness from people always has to go through analysis and scrutiny. Chloe is a nice person with a heart full of love, but the scar left behind by the bullies still confronts her once in a while, and that is the battle Chloe is still fighting today.

Sean's story: Sean was a quiet, nice young boy with low self-esteem and zero self-confidence; this attribute of Sean was known by his parents and those with whom he came into contact. The bullies were aware of it too, so they capitalized on it; the bullies feasted on Sean's weakness to torture and isolate him in school.

Once his parents learned of the torture Sean experienced in school, they did not do or make the common mistake most parents make by sending their child to a new school. When they found out their child was being bullied in school, they chose to take the hard path in order to deal with the reason *why* their son was an easy target for bullies. They believed that when they handled the reason behind their son being susceptible to bullying, they could empower their son not to be the victim; hence, bullying would not be an issue but a workover. Sean's parents decided to let him stay in his current school and acted quickly to help their son by empowering him with necessary tools that would boost his self-confidence and self-esteem. They sent him to a combat or fighting sports school that helped him build his self-confidence, which helped Sean to develop his self-efficacy.

Sean successfully finished his old school and was able to put the bullies where they belonged. When the bullies saw the new Sean emerging from his low self-esteem and zero self-confidence, they witnessed a former victim become a conqueror, and all because his parents made the right choice and invested in empowering their son.

Bradley's story: Bradley is another young man who was well nurtured at home and who moved with his family from a different continent to another. Bradley was taught by his parents to be humble and respectful but was not told that boundaries are necessary in order to survive and maintain your personal territory. Bradley moved to a new society with a different culture with his old mentality from his previous country, but this mentality was used against him. In Bradley's new school, he was a target for the bullies, and a particular group of bullies was always picking on him.

Bradley told his parents about the bullying attack in school, and the parents told him to stand up for himself. Bradley adhered to the advice of his parents by handling one of the bullies while he tried to bully him. Unfortunately for Bradley, the only advice he received was to stand up for himself; his parents never empowered him to stand up against a group attack. So, the bully conspired to beat Bradley up after school on his way home, and a group of boys manhandled Bradley, which led to Bradley moving to a new school in a different city. Even in the new school, Bradley did four years' study in less than three years because of the experiences he'd had in his previous school.

For Bradley, school was not a place to study but a place of torture, and he did all he could to leave the school environment as fast as he could. Bradley did not enjoy his high-school days, but he endured them. While speaking with Bradley's mother, I could see and feel the pain that Bradley and his family went through during the dark hours of bullying. It was an emotion that no words could express. For Bradley's mother, when the bullies tortured her son, they were torturing the family, and the emotions I saw could attest to what they experienced.

Your words set a wheel in motion in the life of your children, and these words can either justify or condemn them.

Power of Your Words

Your words are the forerunner of your actions, and all actions are an indirect expression of words spoken in the past. Thus, words are the raw material that triggers actions. It can be direct or indirect words as a result of what we are exposed to. If we all understand the power of our words, we will learn to be more careful to choose our words before we speak. Words are the bedrock of our thoughts and actions; that is, what you hear can be an opening to a thought, which will eventually be seen in your actions. Whatever words pass through your ears or eyes can become a pattern to generate a thought wave, which is being executed in your behavior. Parents' words have the power to make or break their children, to encourage or discourage them, to heal or hurt them, to enthrone or dethrone them, to empower them to embark on the pathway of victory and success, or to throw them from the pathway of victory. Your words automatically affect and impact the future of your child.

Parents, your behavior and the words you speak around your children create your children's personalities. Just as children depend on their mothers for oxygen and nutrition in the womb, so do they depend on their parents' words to shape and develop their personalities. The words you speak to your children in the face of bullying, especially parents of victims or victors, will either motivate them to advance to conquer or demotivate them into surrendering to the ambush of bullies.

Parents should give a good orientation to their children at an early stage about which words and actions are and are not acceptable. The kind of words children are exposed to matters a lot because words can create a bully or victim mind-set in a child. Parents, never forget that your words set a wheel in motion in the life of your children, and these words can either justify or condemn them.

When the child's environment permits all negative words or actions of bullying, the tendency to create a bully is very high because bullies come from environments where there is bullying. No one is born a bully; bullies are created by their environment; hence, a fruit never falls far from the tree.

We must realize how important our words and actions are because words are the foundation for our thoughts and actions. There is a general saying, "Change your thoughts and change your life." I strongly believe that if we control the words that we allow to go into us and change the vocabulary that we are exposing ourselves to, we can change our life. Remember, our thoughts depend on a seed to grow. Also, that seed contains the words we absorb, and the wrong words and pictures produce wrong thoughts; in turn, wrong thoughts produce wrong actions. Word patterns motivate our thoughts, which later create our ideology, forming the bedrock of speech and our actions.

Your words are your identity.

Some people say, "You just need to open your mouth to speak for a few minutes, and I can tell who you are." *What does that mean?* It means that your words are your identity. Since our words are our identity, it becomes crucial to be selective of how we express ourselves. There is never a second chance to make a first impression. Hence, expression is the birthing of impression that people eventually use to label you. Parents, since we know now that the words we speak create our identities, my questions to you are the following:

- What words are you planting into your children?
- What wheels are you setting in motion by your words in the lives of your children?

External Influences

External influences can corrupt a child from a good home. When a child spends more time outside, or within the home with an external figure or device other than their natural parents, it is possible that the external influences might be competing with the values and teachings of the parents. This can lead to the child's personality or behavior being molded by the character of the authority figure in the child's life. When the authority figure is a bully, the chance of the child being influenced by the bully is higher. In some cases, a child becomes a bully as a result of associations and making the wrong choices due to an external influence unknown to his or her parents. Children from good homes have been cloned into being an accomplice of bad and questionable behavior because of external influences and continuous associations with bad company.

Parents have to go the extra mile in order to prevent such influences from totally corrupting their good work. They must sensitize their children to be able to discern when external influences want to derail or manipulate or coax them into doing the wrong things or exhibiting negative behavior that will be detrimental to their lives and family. Also, parents should not be in denial when a negative report of their children being influenced by external factors is brought to their attention. Denying it can lead to total corruption, which could be averted if the parents step in when the complaint is brought to their notice.

The place of taking responsibility for your action or behavior is the foundation of accountability, accountability to yourself and the authority figures in your life.

Foundation of Accountability

Accountability creates room to make the right choices and to correct the wrong choices. In the place of accountability, a person is put on the life barometer of checks and balances. It is a place where people are held liable for the consequences of their choices by becoming compliant with the instructions of certain authority figures; thus, in the lives of children, parents are there to lay the first brick of accountability. They are there to ensure the children have a foundation of being accountable to themselves, and that authority figures in the children's lives are well established and defined. Parents are in their children's lives to nurture, train, teach, guide, and prepare them for life's journey—a journey that needs preparation and guardianship. It is very important for all parents to teach their children the importance of accountability in order for them to know that they are responsible for their actions and the choices they make, and also to know that all actions and choices have consequences.

Every action attracts consequences, and the consequences will be determined by the gravity of the action. Choice carries rewarding virtues, and the rewards are in all levels, sizes, forms, and shapes. Accountability will give a child a sense of responsibility for their actions, which will eventually help him or her to make the right choice.

When parents teach a child at an early age the importance of being accountable for his or her actions or behavior, it stays with the child. When children come to the place of taking responsibility for their actions and themselves that is the birth of accountability to themselves and to the authority figures in their lives. Of course, there might be external forces or influences that might try to derail them. It might work for a while, but the foundation of accountability to authority will always prevail.

When a destiny is built on a solid foundation of accountability, the storms and winds of life might blow, but the foundation will remain strong. When the foundation of the child's accountability is shallow, the winds and storms of external influences will blow, and the possibility of the child being carried by the winds is greater because the foundation of accountability is not there or is too shallow; hence, there is nothing to keep the child standing. The strength of the foundation of accountability influences the ability to choose, especially when the choice is between good and bad.

Parents, especially mothers, have the power to influence their children and bring a permanent change to any situation, and that is the reason their role in eliminating bullying in schools is pivotal. They cannot be secluded from the change process because they are the catalyst of change, and change is achievable when parents are 100 percent on board in the antibullying campaign.

Parents should help schools preserve education systems for our posterity by being the wind of change that will blow wide and free to bring tranquility to our schools.

7

Bullying in School

SCHOOL IS LIKE a highway where different cars drive to get to their destination. The highway doesn't determine the capacity and the capability of the cars that drive on it, but there are rules that guide and control the movement of cars on the road. These rules might be different from one highway to another, but the destination of the cars is determined by the driver behind the wheel just as the cars are different from one another on the highway, so too are their destinations.

School is like a highway.

The destination of each driver on the highway is mostly predetermined; that is, the destination is known even before the journey begins. The journey is not always determined while the driver is in motion, but there are some who might be distracted on the way and some who might exit the highway before they reach their preplanned destination. But that has nothing to do with the highway. Also, not all drivers on the highway have a specific destination; there are drivers on the highway for joyrides, while others are there to get to a specific destination. Just as the highway is a route for a journey to a destination, so is school, because not all students have a vision of what they really want to get out of it; some are there just for a joyride. These students have no destination other than driving through school and going nowhere, and they will do everything possible to distract or frustrate others who have a destination. They do this by being a tyrant in order to break their focus. It is very important for us to know that the highway is their access route to their destination and not their destination, just like school.

In every student's life, the school is the highway he or she drives on to get to his or her destination. Students' destinations cannot be decided by the school alone but also by the students themselves, the company they keep, and their parents. Just as we have different cars on the highway with different manufacturers who decide the capabilities and functionalities of the car, we also have different students in school from different backgrounds and mentalities. The mentality of the student is programmed by the student's environment.

The behavior of a bully is not and cannot be controlled by the school alone because the tendency to bully begins from somewhere. Most times it is from the environment the bully is coming from and the people they are mingling with. People say that the schools have the sole responsibility to eradicate bullying; however, a school's influence is limited. A faulty foundation cannot be easily repaired once the construction process has been completed.

The foundation of a child will determine what the school has to build on, but if the foundation is faulty, the school can do only so much to correct it. This is not easy because the person who laid the foundation knows what went into the construction process. That is the way we all are. Our parents know what raw material went into each of us directly or indirectly.

Bullying is a Raging Fire in Schools

School is a place where students interact socially, and it is a perfect place to settle scores. As a result, schools have become a breeding ground where bullying activities and recruitments are being carried out. Many students are actively involved in one form of bullying or another setting the school's environment on bullying fire, and this bullying fire is raging. The result is a toxic atmosphere in schools where some students have been burned by the raging fire of bullies. Some of these students recovered from their burns because of the support system that was available to them; some students have scars that they use as reminders of what they conquered; still others have been disfigured by the scars. Some students did not survive the burns because they were unable to recover. Due to all these atrocities going on in schools, school authorities have become firefighters trying to put out the bullying fire that is raging in schools. We all have a role to play, especially parents, in helping schools stop bullying. It is up to us to make our school environments conducive for learning.

Until parents take it as their responsibility to put an end to bullying in schools, bullying activities will continue. Parents should not ignore it just because their children are not yet the victims. They should remember that any fire that is not contained will result in devastation in the future. The onus is on us to avert the pain and heartache associated with bullying because no parent wants to lose his or her child to a bully, and neither will any parent want to switch positions with those parents who lost their children in the cross fire of bullies. Therefore, whether you are the parent of the bully or victim, making our schools a bully-free zone begins with parents. If you want a change, make the change, as changes occur when responsibility is accepted. Change, then, begins with you and not your neighbor.

Bullying in Elementary or Primary Schools

Bullying behavior is rampant in elementary or primary schools. To see children actively involved in this illicit behavior is disheartening. It is evident that schools are having trouble putting an end to bullying activities within their four walls. For the sake of posterity, it is crucial for parents to step up in helping schools to eliminate bullying tendencies in children because it is easier to groom a child than to correct an adult.

All children deserve a bully-free environment to study in and the ability to explore their world and discover their potential. But schools are not always safe for children because of bullying activities that are dominating and controlling the atmosphere. Even in primary schools, innocent children are put under pressure by bullies. It is a nightmare to see children in elementary schools engaging in bullying behavior, and most young bullies come to school to practice what they saw at home or on television or with their peers. At this age, they are more pliable and susceptible to influences in their environment. This dilemma requires urgent attention in order to weed out this evil behavior in children.

The atrocity and havoc of this behavior has made school a living hell for these innocent students who have lost confidence in themselves and their self-worth at such a tender age; these students are silenced even before they can discover their voice. In some cases, these students are forced to change schools as a result of bullying attacks; hence, they lose their stability in the process of moving from one school to another, and stability is vital for the growth and development of every child.

When a child is moved from school to school because of being bullied at a previous school, a vacuum is created in the child's life. If appropriate help is not given to the child who is being bullied in school, the student will develop a victim mentality that will eventually seep into adulthood, where he or she will develop poor self-esteem and lack self-confidence. When bullying behavior is not contained in primary schools, the bullies continue their behavior, making others miserable. In the process, they are developing their personalities and shaping their lives with a bullying mentality; hence, they take it to the next level of the educational journey, which is high or secondary school.

At this stage it becomes more difficult to groom children, once they are in secondary or high school, because of other factors that come into play, such as emotional and hormonal issues, as they are undergoing major changes in their bodies and trying to discover themselves. When they are in this phase of life, where these major changes are taking place, containing their bullying behavior is more difficult. It is vital to contain bullying behavior in elementary school to avert, the danger of it spilling into secondary or high school, but this will be possible only when parents of both the bully and victim cooperate together with the schools.

Parents Need to Know

I have heard parents say, "It is the duty of schools to stop bullying." Based on this statement, I believe parents are shifting their responsibility to schools to do their parenting for them. But there is no way schools can ever take over the parenting responsibilities because school was not designed to be a parenting institution.

Parenting and schools impact children's knowledge, but there is a clear distinction between the knowledge gained from schools and that received from home. Schools will not teach people how to love or have empathy for others; the best a school can offer is to teach students to have respect for each other. Neither is there any course in the school curriculum that will teach you not to gossip or how to handle the storms of life. It is the responsibility of parents to teach their children to love and have empathy for others because love for people will contribute to a stress-free learning environment at school.

Curricula have limits and duration; parenting, on the other hand, has no limit or duration—it is a twenty-four-hour curriculum that covers all facets of life. There is no specializing in parenting, but in schools teachers have their strength in a particular subject. There is no way schools can take over the tasks of parents because parenting is not in the school syllabus and will never be. That is why parents should not shift their responsibility to schools or expect teachers to be the primary player in eliminating bullying in schools or society. There is an urgent need for synergy between schools and parents to put an end to bullying.

Reasons for Bullying in Schools

There are different reasons why bullying occurs in schools, and it all depends on the bully. Below are some of those reasons:

- To dominate their victim
- To maintain territory in a group setting
- To make others pay for the crisis they are experiencing
- To take attention away from themselves because of something they are afraid of, or a weakness they are hiding
- To make someone lose his or her self-esteem and confidence
- To make someone's life miserable and unbearable

- To make someone an object of gossip and ridicule
- To create a segregation within a group of friends
- To ensure that someone is being ignored in a group
- To make someone an outcast in a group
- To silence a voice in a group
- To create a battle for territory in a group
- To create prejudices in a group

Discipline in Schools

As stated above, the school is a highway where different cars drive to get to their destination. Despite the different cars, the highways have rules that determine and control speed and behavior.

In some countries, there are disciplinary measures that ensure the speed limit for each road is obeyed and respected, such as camera control, highway patrol, police control, and so on. Such measures are in place for the safety of the drivers. Where there are no well-stated road-safety rules, or the rules are not enforced as a result of lacking disciplinary measures, anarchy and chaos will ensue.

Highway rules are enforced for the safety of lives and properties; likewise, discipline in schools is for the protection of lives and to inculcate values into the next generation. In most schools, discipline no longer corrects bad behavior because homes have not taught children what it means to obey authority or to respect rules and laws governing schools; hence, discipline in schools has no weight. Some students have gone wild to enforce their own form of discipline by bullying others, and it is quite disheartening that some teachers have become victims of such actions.

Schools have become like a highway with little to no disciplinary measures to bring in checks and balances. There is no discipline in schools, or the discipline mechanisms are porous; hence, students easily get away with any form of permissive behaviors such as bullying.

Discipline in schools can be more effective when the discipline of children begins in the home. Schools can then build on the disciplinary measures imparted to children by their parents. Parents are the cultivators in their children's lives, while schools are the fertilizer that enhances what was already planted by the parents. Thus, discipline at home and from home enhances discipline in schools.

Teachers are limited

There are different issues that limit the ability of teachers to perform their duties to the fullest, such as harassment from parents, bureaucracy in schools, fear of losing their jobs, digital empowerment of students, and the like. Put together, these issues have crippled some teachers' abilities to carry out their duties. School environments have been made a lie where the truth has been prohibited—an environment where teachers are afraid to speak the truth because of the consequences, such as the fear of losing their job as a result of continuous complaints and attacks from parents. What is the benefit of sending a child to school when parents and society have handicapped the teachers?

Although there are teachers who act against the norms and ethics of their profession but that should not be a reason to label all teachers as unprofessional. It is time for both parents and teachers to build a good communication channel, especially the parents of bullies. Whenever a complaint comes from school about their child's bullying behavior, parents should not be on the offensive or defensive, but rather take time to find out the full details of the complaint and investigate the process in order to make the right decision that will benefit all parties involved.

Some teachers are confronted by issues for which they do not have the training to handle. Take, for example, the student who is already high on drugs before coming to school. In such real-life scenarios, the teacher is not prepared or trained to handle such a situation; the teacher is handicapped, and any move from the teacher or other students in class will result in bullying. These scenarios bring about permissiveness in schools, where students cuss out their teachers and go free because discipline has been replaced by chaos. In order to get the full benefit of the teaching profession, there is a need for proper disciplinary measures in schools. The right actions will provoke the right behavior from teachers and students.

Teachers can be victims

The atmosphere in a class can be determined by the teacher or the bully and his or her followers. If a bully controls the dos and don'ts in a class, and the teacher does not have the capacity to put the bully in his or her place, then the bully has taken ownership of the class, and this will set the pace.

Some teachers are being continuously bullied in one form or another, and the digitalized world we are living in has compounded the problem. Teachers are being policed and monitored by students who are using their digital gadgets as a weapon in recording activities within and outside the classroom to intimidate their teacher; in fact, teachers are being confronted on a daily basis, and it is taking a toil on their ability to teach effectively.

Other teachers are losing their ability to execute their tasks because the voice of bullies is louder than the voice of teachers. This eventually makes the classroom a confrontation zone where the teacher is busy putting out the fires the bullies are constantly setting. This has a huge impact on the atmosphere in the classroom as well as the performance of the teacher because the energy of the teacher is being geared toward bringing order and structure instead of teaching. In such situations, the teacher is always on his or her toes—under pressure—which can result in the teacher being stressed out.

For example, when an unpopular student tries to ask questions in the class, and a bully makes a derogatory comment about the student, and the teacher refuses to step in immediately, the situation will escalate. Such an atmosphere is not conducive for learning. The bullies are now in charge and in control of the classroom atmosphere.

There are cases where teachers are even the victims of bullying actions from their own students, especially when the students detect a weakness in their teachers. They use this weakness against the teacher by not listening to them, ignoring their instructions, and calling them names, even when lessons are going on. An example is a student making animal sounds in class while the teacher is facing the board to write. The aim of the bully is to intimidate the teacher in order to take control of the class, and that is the reason why some teachers cannot stay long in a particular school. They have lost ownership of their class.

Role of the School

The role of schools working with other institutions in putting an end to bullying cannot be underestimated, but it should not be tasked to the school alone. Putting an end to bullying requires the combined effort of schools, parents, medical professionals, and other law enforcement agencies.

The role of schools is vital because the teacher can easily identify the behavior of the student and know if the child is a bully or not. However, the teachers should not use the power of their office to pursue their personal ideology but to carry out their duty in total compliance with the ethics of their profession. Any student who needs help should be supported accordingly, and judgment should not be passed quickly on the child, especially when he or she is willing to change and be a better person.

Bureaucracy in schools

Due to bureaucracy in the school systems, there is little to no room for change. Schools are sometimes not open to new ideas in terms of how to handle present-day challenges. Old weapons are being used to fight a new war in schools today, such as cyberbullying, where students use social media as a platform to vent their anger or dissatisfaction with each other.

In the course of writing this book, I met teachers who were open to new ideas and were willing to make changes, but the school directors or principals were stuck within bureaucracy. They believe that the system they used in the past, which is failing them, is the system they will continue to use. They are not ready for a change, even when the teachers see the possibilities and potential to make a bully-free atmosphere in their class, and the refusal of the principal to cooperate with teachers has crippled these opportunities. But what the directors or principals fail to realize is that in using bureaucracy and politics in schools they are losing the next generation.

In order to prevent this from happening, school directors and principals need to be open to new ways of operating and to not underestimate the capabilities of anyone. After all, you can learn from anyone if you are open-minded and not biased. It is high time for schools to go through an innovation process for the benefit of the students and the education system because their system of bureaucracy is failing when it comes to handling the chaos of bullying in schools.

Parents are the transmitters of wisdom in the lives of their children; they are the baseline where children learn what is right and wrong by inculcating into their children the wisdom that will enable them to do the right thing. Thus, stopping bullying to some extent is doable when parents and schools work together as a team.

Schools cannot do it alone

To be a parent is a privilege and honor that comes with huge responsibilities, which when faithfully carried out yields benefits and a special satisfaction that cannot be compared to or experienced in any other area of life. Parents have been entrusted with a human life to nurture into greatness. That is why shifting their responsibilities to others, especially to schools for the upbringing of their children, is an error that has led to havoc in schools. Children are not being nurtured because they were lost in transit when parents decided to give their responsibility to the school.

Parents shifting their responsibility to schools are like farmers deciding to plant their seeds in the air instead of in the ground. This is the mistake most parents are making when they decide to leave the upbringing of their children to schools. Parents are subconsciously planting in the air instead of in the ground. Seeds must be planted in the ground where it bears roots downward into the ground to absorb nutrients; the benefit of the nutrients from the soil will begin to grow upward where the plant grows blades, leaves, flowers, and fruit. The home is the soil where the destiny of a child is being sown, except in rare cases where some blessed teachers take it on themselves as a responsibility to go the extra mile beyond their professional mandate to be a succor to a child in need. But that is not an excuse for parents to transfer their responsibility to schools.

"Anything left to chance has no chance."
—*Pastor (Dr.) Paul Enenche*

Parents who want their children to have an impact on the world must invest their time, love, and resources in order for their children to succeed in life. Leaving the upbringing of your child to schools alone is a gamble.

Parents leaving the training of their children to schools are like leaving the upbringing and development of the child to chance and, as we all know, anything left to chance has no chance or any guarantee of producing the good or right result. The practicality of life is not based on probability but on reality. As stated before, what you put into life is what you get out of life. There is no way a house can be built without the foundation, and neither can the school do the job of the parents.

Parents always say schools should do more with regard to stopping bullying in schools. But in reality, if parents do their homework on their children before they start their educational journey, there will not be room to transfer their responsibility to schools because the hours children spend in school are limited compared to the time they spend at home. Below is an example of time spent in class

Hrs p/d	MPD	# of Student	# of Subject	ABPD	Hrs spent	MPSPD	MPSPS
6.30	390	20	5	75	315	15.8	3.15
6.30	390	25	5	75	315	12.6	2.52
6.30	390	30	5	75	315	10.5	2.10
6.30	390	40	5	75	315	7.9	1.58

MPD   : Minutes per day
ABPD   : Average break per day
MPSPD : Minutes per student per day
MPSPS : Minutes per student per subject

Figure 2. Example of time spent in class

When you divide the total number of hours spent in school by the number of students in a class assigned to one teacher, there is little a teacher can do to bring effective change; hence, no long-lasting impact will occur in correcting bullying behavior. In the table above, assuming there are twenty-five students in a class with 390 minutes (6 hours 30 minutes) daily to spend in school, if you remove the break and other times, the teacher will have only 315 minutes for the whole group. As a result, each student will directly or indirectly have 12.6 minutes per day, and that is 2.52 minutes per student per subject, assuming they have five subjects per day. The million-dollar question is this:

Is this time enough for the teacher to impact change permanently without the support of parents?

As they always say, charity begins at home and not in schools. The school can only build on the foundation that was already laid by the parents or the environment the child grew up in. The best the school can do is either build or amend the existing foundation. As we all know, repairing the existing foundation is not that easy, and it needs all the expertise in that field, especially when dealing with human lives in order not to cause more harm and damage.

Parents should help schools preserve education systems for our posterity by being the wind of change that will blow wide and free to bring tranquility to our schools.

Reasons Why Parents Should Not Leave it to Teachers

Assuming the teacher's time is equally divided between the students, there cannot be an impactful change because of the following:

- There are cases where teachers do not have one-on-one student time on a daily basis.
- Often attention is not directed to the issue due to time constraints.
- The number of students assigned to each teacher is sometime too much for them to handle.
- The areas to cover during the school year are increasing.
- Most children get lost in the crowd.

Note: Bullying behavior is rampant in schools, and it is disheartening to see children actively involved in this illicit behavior. Help from the parents is needed to make our schools safe learning environments

Parents are order-keeping disciplinarians (OKD) because it takes discipline to establish order, and it takes order to birth structure in any area of life.

Parents are OKD (Order-Keeping Disciplinarians)

Discipline is the birthplace for order, while order is the catalyst for structure. There cannot be structure in any area of life without order, and order cannot be kept without discipline or disciplinary measures. Parents are the disciplinarians in their children, and when parents omit this key principle in their parental responsibilities, there is bound to be deficiency in successfully bringing order and structure in a child's life.

Carrying out parental obligations by applying discipline, when necessary, births the possibility of bringing and maintaining order and structure in children's lives, even when there are external influences that aim to undermine parental investment in their children's lives.

In any area, it takes discipline to make a difference; if there is no discipline at home, order and structure cannot be implemented; and there cannot be an establishment of parenting principles without order. Thus, where there is no order, there will be no structure; and where there is no structure in life, there is a rupture in behavior. Order enhances structure, which becomes the springboard to perpetuate the principles of parenting and the foundation upon which schools are built. For schools to succeed in establishing order and structure, the discipline of a child must begin at home. Children must be taught that there are consequences for every action, whether good or bad; good actions will bring rewards, while negative actions will bring discipline.

Parents are in their children's lives as a cultivator, while schools are fertilizers that enhance what parents have already cultivated

A child who has not been disciplined from home in the area of respect and honor for others will certainly not deploy it in school or society; hence, a child who has not been taught to respect and obey authority from home will eventually not obey or respect authority in schools. Similarly, a child who insults his or her parents at home will see nothing wrong with insulting his or her teacher or fellow students. A child who plays the boss at home will certainly want to play the boss of his or her teacher and fellow students. Parents are in their children's lives as a cultivator, while schools are fertilizers that enhance what parents have already cultivated. Parents are also in their children's lives as an anchor and order-keeping disciplinarian. They bring out the best in them and root out weeds that might attract disorder, through parenting with discipline and love.

Bullying is a nightmare, but cyberbullying is a living nightmare.

8

Cyberbullying and Cloud Homes

BULLYING IS A nightmare, but cyberbullying is a living nightmare. Bullying has now graduated from the traditional bullying settings, which involve physical contact, to cyberbullying behind the net and social media. This type of bullying is dangerous, and the effect on the bully's target spreads faster than a wildfire, which becomes more difficult to put out in schools and in our society in general.

Cyberbullying begins as a drop of water that trickles from a crack in a dam. When the crack is not closed, the water gushes out in full force, capable of destroying valuables that block its path. Whenever you are involved in cyberbullying, you have intruded into the life of another person; it is not a game. Rather, you are an intruder, and the activities of an intruder are not lawful. It is illegal and there are consequences. Therefore, when you want to flow with the crowd in cyberbullying, remember you are involving yourself in an illegal activity.

Cyberbullying is the most dangerous form of bullying; it is a sheer evil because there is no form of safety from it. This form of bullying is without boundary; it penetrates the safety of homes without the parents knowing what is going on under their roof, undermining the identity and privacy of those who are being bullied. The danger of cyberbullying is that it takes place via the computer and mobile phones. Sometimes the identity of those behind it is not easily known—they will go to any length to hurt others as they derive satisfaction from doing it.

The use of the Internet and social media is growing, and people are being drawn to it, looking for love and relationships. In our society today, people tend to identify with large groups via social media and avoid investing in personal relationships. People are no longer investing time in building a real relationship, which is a core value for our existence. People are being victimized because of no solid base for most of these social media relationships, especially when the person has become so addicted to social media that they become a prey for the cyberbullies. The bully will do anything to isolate his or her prey, and if the prey involved does not cry out in time for help, it becomes very destructive. Cyberbullying is dangerous. When victims are bullied on social media, whenever they go online they are being confronted because whatever is on social media does not go away easily.

The difference between cyberbullying and physical bullying is that the physical bullying might fade out when there is no more physical contact between the parties involved. But in the case of cyberbullying, whatever has been put online does not disappear easily. Cyberbullying covers a large portion of our society, and that is why it is very dangerous to those who cannot protect themselves. Cyberbullying occurs on different fronts, from intimidating to terrorizing prey by posting messages online. They lure innocent children into sexual activities online, taking their rights from them by manipulating them into illicit activities, which later results in harassment. Due to the danger associated with cyberbullying, schools and parents need to be educated on what is happening online. There should be accountability at all levels, including with the Internet providers.

Cyberbullying in Schools

Cyberbullying occurs through the Internet and social media. Mobile phones have become weapons for cyberbullying in schools, instead of devices for positive communication. Unfortunately, our youth today think it is acceptable to engage in cyberbullying as the norm. The aim of using social media as a tool for bullying is to isolate the victim and to spread damaging posts about the victim in order to make the victim vulnerable and an outcast in the school.

There are two major ways in which cyberbullying is being carried out in schools:

- Through group chatting and texting
- Through sending and forwarding information via social media

Cyberbullying through group chatting and texting

Cyberbullying through group chatting and texting begins when someone sets up an account on a chat site or app, and the person decides who will be in the group. The danger in this is that a person's permission is not needed before he or she is added to the group—all a bully needs is the telephone number of the selected people who will be in the group, and the person added to the group has no power to control what goes on in that group chat except the founder. A bully can befriend someone in order to get his or her telephone number so he or she can use it for cyberbullying.

When a bully is the owner or the founder of a group chat, the bully with his or her followers now uses it as a platform to carry out cyberbullying activities. In this platform most teens are involved in libelous activities through their group chatting and texting, where the reputation of another person is assassinated in order to make the life of the targeted prey miserable, which eventually isolates the victim from his or her peers. They sometimes add the phone number of their victim to the group chat without permission, and one of them starts an inappropriate topic on the victim. Everyone in the group will be commenting and responding to the comments of others in the group, and these bullying comments are being seen and read by the victim. Their aim is to torment, frustrate, and ridicule their victim in order to make the victim an outcast in school. Such actions make the world of the victim seem small and suffocating, and he or she has no place to turn.

Cyberbullying through sending and forwarding information via social media

Another way that cyberbullying occurs in schools is when information, incidents, pictures, and more are being spread quickly through social media. One person might have negative information about someone, and it is then spread throughout the school by sending it to another person who will later forward it to another, and the process will continue until the circle is completed. Eventually the story becomes the topic of gossip and scandal in school. The victim has no place to turn or hide from the scandal because the atmosphere in school is unbearable and tormenting.

Cyberbullying can lead to physical bullying, or physical bullying can lead to cyberbullying. It can occur both ways, depending on the parties involved. Most physical bullying occurs outside school hours, while cyberbullying has no restriction to it; it can happen during and after school hours. The tragedy of cyberbullying is that the victim is always confronted whenever they go online, and there is no way to change it, unlike physical bullying where you can always change schools or environment.

A War Within

A war within occurs when friends decide to use social media as a scandal media to air their differences and anger. Cyberbullying among friends is always ugly and dirty because the parties involved are people who have intimate and private information that they place on social media to hurt the victim. Such actions or activities in social media pierce deeper than any other form of bullying. Cyberbullying among friends is like when a person's worst enemy is a member of his household; the war becomes difficult to fight because the battle is at home, which makes the fight more delicate and dangerous compared to an outside battle. A battle from outside is more easily won than a battle from within because the victim's strength and capability or his or her weakness is not known to his or her enemy.

Cyberbullying among friends is tragic because whoever launches the attack knows the weapon to use in bringing down his or her victim. It becomes an emergency situation where things fall apart, and the center cannot hold the friends together. The effect or pain of such actions run deep, and there are cases where such actions or activities have led to the death of one of the parties involved in a scandalous battle among friends.

Students (teenagers) are another group that uses social media as a scandal or segregation media. They use this platform to hurt and torment their classmates who they do not like because of one thing or another. This group is not necessarily friends but acquaintances of the victim, and they conspire to hurt or disgrace the victim because of hatred or a quest for revenge. They set traps and keep a close watch on the victim, hoping the person will slip or make some mistake they can use as a weapon to defame the victim on social media. The scandal will eventually segregate or isolate the victim in class or school.

Effects of Cyberbullying in School

Cyberbullying is a living nightmare that the victim is living every day. He or she cannot hide or escape the agony because it is now a part of his or her life. The effects of cyberbullying on the victim cannot be described; it includes living in shame, fear of being the subject of gossip and ridicule, loss of freedom to walk around freely in school, and constant confrontation whenever they go online. As a result, the person's freedom is stolen, even within the four walls of his or her home.

The psychological effects might not be seen, but the victims are stuck with them for life. It is a nightmare that never ends for the victims and their families. Cyberbullying takes away the dreams of the parents whose children lost their lives to cyberbullying. Cyberbullies should always remember that any time they decide to bully another person, their actions are taking away the dreams and aspirations of the victim's parents.

Cyberbullying Content

The content of a person determines what the person can deliver, and when the content of a person is hate, intimidation, and abuse, that is all the person has to offer and deliver. Content is proportional to delivery; therefore, the content of a bully is directly proportional to his or her actions or behavior toward others.

The mind is the archive of the eyes and ears because the mind is the storage facility of the eyes and ears; thus, your content depends on what you allow to go inside you. Whatever gains access to your mind is what you will assimilate. Hence, what the mind stores creates the mentality of the person. Exposure is equal to expression, so whatever children are exposed to is what they will eventually express.

Bullies and victims are only expressing or exhibiting what they are made of, because whatever a child is exposed to goes into the child, and this determines what comes out. When a child is exposed to the noise of technology, then the reality of life's actions and dealings with such a person will be automated, whether the person is the bully or victim. The reason is that his or her content plays a major role in determining on what side of the fence he or she is standing.

When parents do not monitor what enters the mind of their child, they will not know what is influencing the makeup of their child's personality. We are living in the technology age, which can also be a disruptive age. There is too much noise outside, and the inside is empty; there is no space for quiet meditation or development of the mind.

The thinking, or meditation, and the human's instinct is no longer fully utilized; that is why a person is asked to send a naked picture of himself or herself through mobile phone or other online devices. The victim will not even think or process the reason behind the request or the consequences of complying with such an action. Foolishly, he or she will comply by sending the picture, which can be detrimental to him or her. The reason for this is that little attention is being paid to the development of the mind; hence, the content that will be expressed or exhibited is damaging. Technology is eroding and undermining the authority of parents and infiltrating the children with toxic content.

Technology is only making the world a global village while disconnecting people from investing in true and honest relationships, creating a macro relationship that has no depth, which can be easily shaken or destroyed by any slightest wind.

There is an emotional part of human beings—a very important part of our existence—which is missing in our advancement in technology. The technology age is what is real to most youth, and they are being programmed all the time to respond to this plastic lifestyle, which is eroding the empathy inside them. This lifestyle is the content that is being developed in most youth today. It is not surprising to see their attitude or response to other people's hurt and pain because the content is enrooted in them. Reality is disappearing because society is supporting and gearing more toward the disruptive side of technology, which is the basis for all turbulent behavior among people and their relationships, especially young people.

Sexting

Sexting, the sending of nude or sexually explicit photos or messages via mobile phones, has become the norm among teens. Since little or no value has been placed on sex in our society today, teens and youth see it as normal to engage in sexting online. When adults place little value on sex, why should teens respect it? The danger of sexting and other sexual activities online is that most, if not all, teens and youth involved in these activities do not know or realize the gravity of posting naked pictures of themselves on the Internet. It is very important for parents to be educated on the new terms and language being used on social media.

Only when parents and authority figures are aware of these terms can they help their loved ones by educating them on the implications of posting inappropriate pictures on social media. As for those forwarding these degrading pictures, they should be lectured on the implications of just clicking on the send or forward button on their phone. Their victims are stuck with the scars for life, even when the wound eventually heals. Then there is a chance of implementing a change in their mentality because most of them do not know or realize the implications of their collaboration in sexting or cyberbullying.

In some countries (like Canada), cyberbullying is a crime if someone is involved in libelous behavior or the sharing of naked pictures of any individual online. So, parents who do not want to be entangled in a legal battle should educate their children to deviate from such behavior. It would be a source of protection for children when other countries emulate those that have already implemented such laws.

Cloud Parenting and Cloud Homes

The home is the breeding ground for a child's character development; it is the place where the fundamentals of life are taught to a child. Most parents believe they are the ones in charge of their homes and family, but unknown to them there are external unseen influences controlling the affairs of their children through the channels of social media, the Internet, and online games.

Today, the latest gadgets and devices are now competing with parents in the area of upbringing and educating their children. There is a danger when the duty of a parent is being taken over by social media, or the parents' quality time with their child is being taken over by all the apps that are available out there. When the welfare and upbringing of a child are being compromised, and the influence of the devices is more predominant than that of the parents, then it is no longer parenting but cloud parenting. When this occurs, the home is no longer a home of refuge, but a cloud home, where external, unseen forces operate through the instrumentality of the Internet-connected devices that invade the home. In such situations, the control of the parents is threatened, and the irony of it is that most parents are not aware of it; thus, disaster is looming without the parents' knowledge.

A cloud home is where technology and social media have so invaded the home that the role of the parents has been relegated or nonexisting as a result of this; automatically, technology and social media dictate what the child does, and this influences the behavior of the child, hence cloud parenting.

CYBERBULLYING AND CLOUD HOMES

When a home is a cloud home, any external forces can access the home through social media, and activities on the Internet can corrupt the children in their home without the knowledge of their parents, thereby sowing weeds instead of wheat. The children become like a city without walls that can be easily accessed by any wind of segregation or scandal media that blows.

The tendency to create a bully or a follower becomes high, and so is the risk of a child becoming prey to cyberbullying in such an environment. The parents are not aware of what is going on under their roof; therefore, they cannot control what seeps into their homes. This lack of awareness has opened the door of many homes to be invaded by influences from the cloud technology, where traditional home settings have been changed into cloud homes. Homes are being run remotely from the unseen cloud world.

Parents ought to have a more prominent place in the lives of their children—not social media or games. But the reality today with teens and young people is that social media, apps, and gadgets are more prominent and active than the authority of parents. That is why most homes are targets of the disruptive side of technology, and modern gadgets are now contending with parents. Most parents are ignorant of these gadgets and not even aware of what they are contending or fighting with. To avert this unknown contender, they should endeavor to know the trends in the world of their young children. That way, they won't fall into oblivion or obscurity to what is happening in their world. This will help parents in their parenting duties not to be left behind on the sidelines with regard to what is going on in the lives of their children.

Most of the time parents think they have all the loose ends tied up, only to find out too late that there were loose ends that were unknown to them, which could be detrimental to the lives of their children. This is the danger of cloud parenting, where external forces infiltrate homes and have access to children without the knowledge of the parents, creating openings and loose ends that parents have no knowledge about. Many parents are diligent but only few are vigilant so parents must continuously be vigilant because the infiltration of external influences through modern devices is beyond what parents can grasp. Parents, be careful, especially when you think you stand, lest you fall. So that you don't fall, try not to participate from the sidelines in the lives of your children and the issues confronting them, including bullying.

Who is in Charge?

Whatever you commit yourself to will eventually dominate you because what controls your focus, mind, and emotions will enslave you, especially when your endeavor and pursuit are wrong. In the past, a servant had a physical and known boss/master, but now there is another form of servanthood, where individuals, especially young people, willingly register to be a servant to the gadget they bought with their own money.

Instead of owning these gadgets and social media pages, now the gadgets and social media pages own them; this is the truth. Yet most people are not aware or they refuse to accept that they are now servants to what they bought with their own money. These devices are now their taskmaster who decides how they live and what they do.

Ask any young person today who is in charge of his or her life, and he or she will tell you their parents or their guardians, or himself or herself. The truth is, young people are not in charge; rather, their devices and social media are in charge. Most young people are programmed and controlled by social media and their devices on what to do, reacting to every wind that blows through a social network; hence, they are being enslaved without even knowing it. They believe that they own their devices and social media apps, but in reality, these devices own them, because their lives and actions are being programmed and controlled by social media; they are being pressured and oppressed without even knowing it. Some are now addicted to their devices.

A Need for a Manual

Parents are investing a lot in providing their children with all the latest devices, which is quite good, but parents need to also have instruction manuals for their children, just like the way manufacturers have a user's manual on the dos and don'ts of a product. Also, parents need to have such manuals tailored to suit their family settings, especially when their children are still young, and when they have a great influence in their child's decision-making process.

However, parents using parenting manuals will work only when the foundation of honesty and transparency has been laid in the lives of their children. This will help the children to be open to discuss issues with their parents in all their dealings, including on the Internet. There have been cases where children were living double lives on the net, even when parents thought all their parental restraining and security codes on their computers or Internet accesses were in place to protect their children. But unknown to them, their children decided to live a life of double standards by using the computer or smart phone of their friends—hence, a double life. One is known to their parents and the other unknown. They have been caught in the cross fire of cyberbullies where they become casualties.

There is an urgent need for parents to have mission statements and parenting manuals that suggest checks and balances to prevent their children from using their devices or gadgets as weapons to hurt others or from supplying ammunition for others to use against them. This will discourage the children from using their devices as a weapon for bullying and also protect them from being a victim of cyberbullying or being enslaved by the devices.

A Need for Revolution

Revolution can only take place when we all participate and work together to put to an end to the epidemic of cyberbullying, when we don't support it and do not applaud any derogating postings online. There is the need for a continuous campaign in our schools that any form of cyberbullying is not acceptable and is not normal. No one should allow such a practice that might lead to the hurt or death of another person.

There is an urgent need or cry for our young people to be educated in order to avert addiction to this shallow lifestyle that has nothing to offer in times of life's storms. When people are aware that a mere device is the one in charge of their lives and is controlling their actions, they develop the tendency to make a change because no one will be happy to be tagged as a servant to a gadget or any form of device they are using for cyberbullying. This awareness is the beginning of a learning process that will help children to distance themselves from being enslaved by gadgets or social networks.

When our young people are educated on this front of the disadvantages of being owned by their gadgets and social media, they will become enlightened, which will help them not to fall victim to the bait of using such platforms for bullying, since it is useless to set a trap in front of a bird. It will help them to know the reality of life because life is not lived in their devices or on social media pages, where you have thousands of people as friends that are not known to you and not impacting your life or you having no life-changing impact on theirs. You are just living a life in a bubble, making no effort to know those around you.

It is high time we all learn how to invest in real friendships and relationships. People should not use social media to replace the fundamental principles of building a true relationship. If we do not start educating ourselves to invest in building true friendships and relationships, we might lose the next generation. There is the urgency to attend to this issue on all levels because we are now living in the iWorld. Of course social media has its benefit to the development of our society, but it can never and should not replace the principles of human existence.

Eliminating Cyberbullying in Schools

Eliminating cyberbullying begins with working on our mentality or mindset, especially the young people. There is a question we all have to answer: Who is in charge of our life? There are limits others go to in stopping cyberbullying, but there is no limit on you as a person if you decide not to be a party to bullying on the Internet or decide not to be a victim. So, stop supplying bullies with ammunition to fight you. When the two important parties do their part—and with the cooperation of parents, schools, telephone companies, social media companies, members of the chatting groups, and each of us—there is hope for a change.

It is time for us to use our dictionary more frequently in order for us to know the meaning of words. For example, a lot of people have lost the full meaning of *social*. It seems the word "social" before "media" has been replaced with *segregation* and *scandal*; hence, most teenagers use *social media* as a *segregation media* and a *scandal media*. Also, *digital world* has been replaced in the vocabularies of teens as *digital war*, where they express their anger and dissatisfaction with their peers. Once we all have a clear meaning of words, then we all will know how to use the words and what they stand for. I believe the intention of the social media founders was not to use social media as a platform for scandal and segregation, neither for the destruction of others.

My questions to you are the following:

- Are you living in a digital world or a digital war?
- What are you doing with your social media page?
- Do you have a social media page or a segregation or scandal media page?

Respect is a vehicle to motivate and influence others positively in any sphere of life, including the workplace.

9

Workplace or War Floor

MOST TIMES THE seed of bullying is sown in a person from a tender age. The seed grows within the person as he or she develops in every stage of his or her life. This seed of bullying will develop roots that are deeply embedded in the person, producing fruit in his or her actions and behaviors when dealing with others, even when he or she is a full-grown adult. Failure in containing bullying in children is the major sponsor of bullying in the workplace. This has led to atrocities and chaos in the workplace, which can eventually make the workplace unbearable for the victim; the work floor has become a war floor.

It is very sad to see adults engaging in bullying activities, which occur in all spheres of our society. There is the misconception that bullying behavior is more common in people from a low-education background and with blue-collar jobs, but the reality of bullying is that it cuts across all demographics; thus, bullying at work occurs in all working environments, whether in politics, medicine, education, or management. It is an operation that runs from the top to the bottom of most establishments. Bullying on the work floor is being carried out by different groups, but in this book, emphasis will be given to these three major groups:

- Gossip bully
- Oppressive bully
- Physically aggressive bully

There is no excuse for bullying adults in the workplace. Their parents or environment might have made them a bully, but as an adult they should realize that the mistakes from their past do not have to mold their future actions and behaviors, especially when they can differentiate between what is bad and good. They are conscious of the urge to hurt someone or make an environment unsafe for another person. It is time for them to unlearn and, if necessary, seek help from an expert.

Most times nobody wants to be identified as the bully; therefore, some of the bullies are very subtle in operation. This is very common among women in the workplace. They carry out their bullying agenda through gossip, manipulation, and propaganda. They are the *gossip bully*, and when their manager has weak leadership skills, the bully within the group capitalizes on the weakness of their manager and decides what happens on the work floor.

In some extreme cases, there are even physical assaults. However, in these cases, the victim can identify his or her enemy and will know that there is a battle. But in the cases of subtle bullying on the work floor, the victim might be dining and drinking with an enemy without realizing it. This is dangerous because the victim is always caught unaware that he or she is sitting next to a ticking bomb. Whether bullying in the workplace is physical or subtle, it all goes back to honoring yourself and others.

A gossip bully is like the flight deck of an aircraft carrier where fighter jets of rumor mongers land to gather wrong information and take off with negative propaganda as a weapon to hurt, harm, or tarnish the reputations of others.

Gossip bully

A gossip bully on a workplace is always involved in a parasitic relationship rather than a mutual one. The major aim of gossip bullies is to achieve their agenda at any cost, despite the detrimental effects their bullying will have on their colleagues or the smooth flow of operations on the work floor—a place that ought to develop mutual relationships. The major propagandist of gossip on a work floor is the gossip bully. Gossip bullies use their words as weapons to tumble others, especially on the workplace. They use words as a weapon at the office by spreading rumors about others to tarnish their image at work; they sow negative words about their colleagues to assassinate their character. Gossip bullies are conniving in their operations; they are propagandists of lies who are volatile and heartless in promoting their agenda by scraping and grinding the personality of their victims.

Gossip bullies use words as venom to attack the personality of their colleague in order to isolate the colleague from the team and make the work floor uncomfortable for the victim. Gossip bullies carry out their operations for different reasons, but most times they use it to gain favor and promotion at work. In some cases, these bullies are the ones who will befriend the victim in order to get intimate information about the person, which they will use in office gossip.

These bullies are very subtle and manipulative. They will use any form of manipulation or anyone to climb the corporate ladder; their success is always at the expense of others. Most times gossipers have personal agendas to fulfill, and they will go to any length to ensure that their plans are executed, while they are willing to use anyone as a weapon or ladder who foolishly complies with their operation, consciously or subconsciously. The irony of this is that managers, team leaders, or supervisors on most work floors have aided and abetted gossip bullies in achieving their goals. What a gossip bully fails to realize is that success and affluence can only be accredited to hard work, honesty, and fair play, and not by the promotion gotten at the detriment and expense of another person.

Most victims have lost their self-confidence because of a bully who has decided to use his or her mouth as a weapon of destruction instead of protection. Such actions have cost some victims their jobs. However, victims must realize that no matter how relentless a gossip bully might be in his or her actions, he or she will not succeed if the victims and the other colleagues on the work floor do not give ear to the gossip of the bully. The victim gives ear to the gossip of the bully by allowing the comments of the bully to incapacitate him or her, while the colleagues give ear to the gossip bully by joining him or her to spread the bully's propaganda. Either way, the victim and the colleagues are enforcing the agenda of the gossip bully.

"Advice is a stranger: if it is welcome, he stays for the night; but when he is not welcome, he leaves the same night."
—African proverb

If not entertained, gossip in the workplace will not continue, but whenever you give your ear to it, you are entertaining it and accommodating it. Comments and propaganda from gossip bullies should be abhorred in offices because the words of gossip bullies are always negative with the aim of personality assassination. Such behavior should not be applauded or entertained because negative words are cheap, whereas positive words are rare gems that are exclusive, expensive, and highly valued. A gossip bully cannot operate without accomplices. Either way, those who listen to office gossip are also promoting office gossip because without wood, a fire goes out; and without supporters, an office gossip fire goes out, which will eventually make the office a work zone and not a gossip zone.

Oppressive bully

Oppressive bullies on the work floor use the authority invested in them as a channel to oppress those under their watch. An oppressive bully can be the manager or an employer who has decided to make the office an empire, where what he or she says is final. In such situations, the staff members are only on the job because of their financial needs.

This group believes they deserve respect from their subordinates, but they fail to realize that respect is earned and not demanded. They are harsh and autocratic in their dealings with those around them, and the feelings of their staff do not matter to them as long as they get what they want, when they want it. The means to an end does not matter to them as long as they get their expected results, while the opinion of those working for them is not needed in the decision-making process. Whenever things are not working well on the work floor, those working for them are blamed. Oppressive bullies are found in all realms of workplace, but they are more brutal within low-income jobs because they believe if you do not comply with their rules, even if they are inhumane, you can make use of the exit door.

There are those who use their position to get whatever they want from those reporting to them. There is another group of oppressive bullies who are not necessarily the authority figures in a workplace but still very active in intimidating, harassing, and oppressing their coworkers. They are so used to oppressing people that it's become a way of life for them. The difference between an oppressive bully and aggressive bully is that, in most cases, the oppressive bully doesn't get into physical fights like the aggressive bully. He or she usually uses his or her position, authority, or privileges as a weapon in oppressing others, and some workers have remained victims of an oppressive bully because of the fear of losing their job.
Note: I am not promoting laziness or complacency on a work floor but only asking for balance.

Physically aggressive bully

Physically aggressive bullies use physical attacks on their victims to inflict harm and pain in order to express their anger and dissatisfaction on the targeted victim. Such bullying occurs in most workplaces, but it is common within the civil service/public sectors, such as health care and education, where workers are being bullied and attacked by those they were rendering their services to. It is usually as a result of these bullies not being satisfied by the services they received or being frustrated by being ignored or pushed around.

There are other groups of aggressive bullies. Take, for example, coworkers who throw fists in order to communicate a message to their coworker because they are irritated by the coworker's personality. Whatever the case, aggressive bullies go into physical combat in order to communicate their displeasure or anger to the victim.

Workplace or Political Party

When you hear the word *politics*, the words that come to mind are government, party politics, political parties, election campaign, campaign manifestos, democracy, and so on. But today, the reality of the word politics is deeply rooted in our lives and our dealings more than we truly realized. Politics has become synonymous with our daily lives even when we claim that we are not politicians. It affects and impedes our decision-making process and conflicts with our power of choice, especially in our dealings with other people. It is transmitted throughout all spheres of life, including the workplace.

Work floors have become a political arena where political parties are formed with political campaigns and rallies being exercised daily, depending on the political party. Thus, most workplace constitutes different political parties, where those who are not on the ruling party are easily victimized or expelled by managers and supervisors. These managers or supervisors have turned some companies into their personal domain where a political free-fight club is legitimate. The candidates of the ruling party decide the rules of the political free-fight club, where people's welfare is being tossed like dice, while the livelihood of a person and his or her whole family is being tossed away in the wind because of selfish interests of bullying supervisors, managers, or coworkers.

When an employee decides to turn the work floor to a political party, where a political caucus rally occurs, new "political members" are being recruited, while those employees who do not form an alliance with the existing ruling party become outcasts within the company. Such actions within a workplace make the atmosphere tense and not conducive for those who are not within the political caucus; hence, the pressure is on them to always prove themselves in order not to lose their jobs.

The irony is that even if they are doing a great job and their performance is highly profitable to the growth of the company, they are always discriminated against; these are the casualties in any reorganization within companies. But life is not a casino where you play games; it is a reality in which we are all living every day. So, stop playing games with people's lives because life is too fragile to be used to satisfy your quest for power. For a peaceful and cordial relationship on the work floor, there has to be room for understanding each other by seeing in your colleagues the basic necessities of life that you also need to accomplish for your own family to meet its basic needs. It's also worth remembering that the first thing that brought you to the work floor was to meet your basic needs prior to developing yourself by climbing the corporate ladder.

Negative Tolerance Sponsors Bullying on the Workplace

Tolerance is good; it creates room for understanding. It is the place of seeing things from another's perspective and putting oneself in another's shoes before drawing conclusion or passing judgment. When negative behavior such as bullying is being tolerated, it becomes negative tolerance, which can have harmful and disastrous effects on society.

Negative tolerance is the major sponsor of bullying on the workplace because office policy has indirectly accepted bullying. Even when it is not stated in the mission statement of companies, it has been written by the staff by their behavior/attitude on the work floor, especially by managers who tolerate bullying under their watch as a result of them being a bully themselves or having a soft spot for the bully on their team. This leads to a lack of commitment on the part of the manager to the mission statement of the company.

It is important to know that bullying in the workplace will not exist without the direct or indirect consent of the managers, because no matter how concentrated alcohol might be, it is not able to intoxicate a person without the person drinking it. The smell of alcohol does not intoxicate;

intoxication occurs only when you decide to drink the alcohol. Likewise, bullies cannot operate when the environment doesn't accept it. Bullying on the work floor is a result of the workplace ethic, which allows or makes the environment susceptible for bullies to operate. Either way, all those who gave their ears to gossip bullies or who turned away when an aggressive bully was physically attacking their fellow colleague are the main sponsors of bullying on the work floor. The mentality is that someone else will speak for the victim, and this none-of-my-business mind-set has promoted the physical/aggressive sort of bullying on the workplace.

There is no neutral stand when it comes to bullying, whether on a work floor or otherwise. You are promoting and enforcing bullying in the environment because saying or doing nothing in a bullying environment is empowering bullies to operate easily without opposition or confrontation, which only makes them more brutal in their quest.

Some Managers are Enforcing Bullying

Managers are in charge on a work floor; they ought to decide how their office is run on their watch, whether it will be a work floor or a war floor. Their behavior is either enforcing or abating bullying in their office; a bully cannot operate when the environment does not tolerate or accept it. Bullying on a work floor is the result of negative ethics, which has become the norm in some workplaces, allowing or making the work floor susceptible for bullies to operate.

When a manager in an office becomes involved in office politics and favoritism, having a soft spot for a colleague within his or her team, it weakens and influences the manager's ability to make the right judgment because he or she has been blinded by the interests of the bully. The end result is *bullying*. In an office where a gossip bully is actively in operation, the managers become puppets in the bully's hands, and the bully controls and decides the dos or don'ts on the work floor. In such cases, the manager exists as a figurehead, but the person running the work floor is the gossip bully. The gossip bully draws the plan, while the manager executes the plan, and it becomes the tail wagging the dog.

A Free World

Today we live in a free world, a world of freedom of speech where everyone has the right to speak and air their views. But this freedom of speech does not permit us to use our mouths as a weapon for the destruction of another. Neither is the world so free for us to use our words and actions to push another person into an early grave.

The world is free but not free for you to hurt or harm others by your bullying behavior and schemes. Bullies use their words as weapons in different facets of life to torment, intimidate, and isolate their victims in order to make life unbearable and miserable for them. The world has become a free world where people are not sensitive to the feelings of others. It has become a world of selfishness and self-centeredness, where people use others to get to the top or achieve their selfish desires.

It's a free world, but bullies make the world not free for their victims.

In spite of all the freedoms we have, there is a part of our existence as human beings in the free world that we are not permitted to exhibit, and that is tampering with another person's life. Life is sacred, and it exceeds a person's capacity to replace or return a lost life. That is why it is important for people to always remember that the world might be free, but there is no life that is free.

There is no substitute to a life that has been destroyed, and neither is any life free for destruction by your bullying actions. There is nothing to give in exchange for a life that has been destroyed due to bullying, and neither is there any comfort for parents or families who lost their children to a bully. We are living in a free world, but the truth is that no world is free for you to bully others to depression or death, and neither is emancipation a legal ground for depravity.

A Workplace, Not a Permanent Residence

A workplace is like a marketplace where buying and selling takes place, where you pack up/close for the day and go home. No one stays in an office forever. At the end of the day, you will eventually leave the company. Either you are fired, or you get a better offer elsewhere, or you are asked to go for early retirement, or you retired at the appropriate time, or you passed on, or the company went into liquidation, or you are sent home due to restructuring within the company. Even when you are the owner of the company, you can't stay there forever. One way or another you will exit the company you built, and another person will take over the office that was yours.

Bullies should realize that their offices are not their permanent address or personal property to be used to torment or bully the lives of those working with or for them in a company. Neither is it their legal right to oppress others irrespective of their position within the company hierarchy because no position you occupy authorizes you to make the lives of those working with you miserable. Bullies should always remember that their employment in any company is like a product with an expiration date. Wherever there is an entry sign, there is always an exit sign. The day you were employed was the day the exit sign was switched on, and your exit from the company only depends on how long it takes for you to get to the exit door. For you it might be longer, while for others it might be shorter; either way, your exit from the company is guaranteed. Therefore, for the benefit of the company, your colleagues, and yourself, be useful by making your office a work floor and not a war floor, by providing your reasonable service to the company that gave you employment.

A child who was not taught respect, esteem, and value for others will certainly lack the ability to respect or value other people, because where respect is not designated, honor is mostly absent.

A Need for Respect

Bullies on workplace are mostly on a mission in their relationships. Their relationships are not mutual; their major aim is for their personal interest and achieving their agenda at all cost despite the detrimental effects it can have on their colleagues on the workplace. There cannot be a true corporation without respect and value for those you work with. People are willing to help and work with you when you place value on them and the services they are bringing to the workplace. Thus, bullies on the work floor should realize that a company cannot be run by one person; every employee has his or her own unique service to contribute to the progress of the company.

Courtesy is the building block for respect, while respect is the birthplace for honor. You cannot truly honor those you do not respect, and neither can you celebrate those you do not honor. The disheartening reality today is that the word *respect* has become a rare gem that is hard to find. When you go to a public place, a place that is popular with young people and adults, take a seat and observe the way the majority of them behave or respond to elderly people. You will be shocked by what you see because the majority of them do not know or understand what it means to be cordial and respectful.

Respect is a vehicle to motivate and influence others positively in any sphere of life, including the workplace.

Even among children, the word *respect* has been deleted from their dictionary; this is likely because parents are no longer there to infuse in them how important it is to respect others and themselves. A child who was not taught to have respect, esteem, and value for others will certainly lack the ability to respect or value other people because where respect is not designated, honor is mostly absent. Having respect for others needs to be taught because respect is the birthplace for honor, and wherever there is honor there is adoration, appreciation, and celebration; hence, there is no room for hatred or bullying.

There is a great need for the word *respect* to be restored to the vocabulary of our youth, especially teenagers, in order for them to know the full meaning of honor and to learn how to value and celebrate those around them. When children are not taught the full meaning and benefit of respect for others' opinions from a tender age, the result is reflected at school and in the workplace, where backstabbing others to get to the top becomes a lifestyle in spite of the detrimental effects it has on others. It is more beneficial to be respectful and have regard for others because it is easier to motivate others when respect is on the ground. Thus, motivation flows from the direction of respect, and where there is a mutual respect, there is a vehicle to influence others to be more committed to their duty and bring their best to the workplace in order to meet the organization's goals. Respect is a vehicle to motivate and influence others positively in any sphere of life, including the workplace.

A Need for Honor

Honor is all about value and respect. To honor is to highly esteem and to have regard for another person. Honor begins from the value you place on yourself because the place where you honor another person is the place where you have honored yourself. Honoring yourself and other people adds value to your life and those you choose to honor. Whatever honor you place on yourself is what you give to others. If you do not like honoring others, you will certainly lack it in your life; thus, in a situation where you don't honor yourself, you have nothing to give to others. Honoring others starts with you having honor for yourself, and then you can transmit it to those around you.

Life is real—a reality; it is not a show. So, any dishonoring behavior being exercised on others has a tremendous effect. All work-floor bullies who specialize in using scandal to dishonor their fellow colleagues and to climb a professional ladder confirm that they have no value for themselves despite the place they might be occupying in life.

Bullying in adults on the work floor goes back to what values bullies placed on themselves. Bullies on the work floor must realize that their actions are not all about trampling on another person or using another person as a ladder to be popular in a group. Rather, the act of bullying or honoring others is all about content. It is important, then, for adult bullies to know that their content determines what they exhibit and what flows from them to others.

Food for thought

- The behavior, attitude, and mentality of a parent is like an aura that rubs off on their children to build their personality. Parent, beware of whatever you do or refuse to do, as almost everything is being transmitted into your children's lives.
- Bullying behavior is rampant in schools, and it is disheartening to see children actively involved in this illicit behavior. Parents, help are needed to make our schools a safe environment for learning because it is easier to groom a child than to correct an adult in order to avert bullying behavior in our society.
- Bullying activities are increasing in schools, and parents should not ignore it just because their children are not yet the victims. Remember that any fire that is not contained will result in devastating effects in the future. The onus is on us to avert the pain and heartache associated with bullying.
- Never use your strength as a yardstick to bully others because your weakness could be other people's strength. Hence, stop using your strength and ability to set the standard for others.
- The quest for power and recognition should be earned and not demanded...Thus, be careful in your journey to power. Ensure it is not at the detriment of others, and never take the position you are in today as your right; instead, see it as a privilege.

PART 3

Treasures are not found in perfect places, so do not under-estimate anybody, because there are treasures in each and every one of us. Therefore, be the propeller through which those treasures are being discovered and birthed in the lives of those around you.

10

Bullies (You) are Better than Bullying

There cannot be a fight where there is no dispute or quarrel, and there cannot be a bully where there is no anger, bitterness, hurt, hatred, and jealousy. Most bullies are people who were hurt, whether in the past or present, who have decided to use bullying as a channel to alleviate their hurt. Some bullies have been incubated with hatred for others, while others operate purely from jealousy or envy. In the process of their being bitter, hurt, jealous, or envious, they have misused and abused their free will by making the wrong choices. They became bitter instead of better.

This bitterness has led bullies to become like a pond that never flows, and because they are not flowing, they eventually end up stinking as a result of clogging their life with illicit behavior, such as bullying, which is detrimental to them and society. Bullying is a choice, and most times a bully chooses to yield to negative emotions, through harming and hurting others instead of dealing with the issues that are responsible for the negative feelings that have triggered his or her choices and actions. Until bullies decide to unclog their lives with love, they will always stink wherever they go because of those wicked and hateful ways they resort to, and there is no room for fresh things to flow into them. Hence, they will be decaying and wasting away without knowing because they believe they are harming others. But eventually they will partake in the fire they kindled.

BULLYING

Bullying is a learned behavior that sets the pattern of your life, which will end up framing your world and defining your life. Since bullying is a learned behavior, it is also possible to unlearn bullying; but you must decide to stop bullying other people. If you decide to continue to bully other people, then you are saying to yourself that you don't care about the souls of others because you do not know the value of your own soul.

Bullies should not view with complacency the destruction of anyone because whenever you are bullying others, either with your words or actions, you are saying to yourself that you care less about your own soul. You might gain a temporary satisfaction, but your soul is doomed because you are involved in an illicit activity. Always remember that bullying is trespassing, which involves invading the lives of the victims, and such action or behavior is a crime and should be treated as such. All forms of trespassing are handled as a crime, and trespassers are prosecuted accordingly, especially when they are being caught. In a nutshell, a bully is a trespasser.

Some bullies do not know that they are bullies or trespassers, and neither do they understand the gravity and the consequence of their actions. While some derive pleasure from bullying others, others do not realize or recognize their actions and activities as bullying. That is not an excuse to continue with such illicit behavior or activities because the normal human being should know when he or she is trespassing or invading the territory of others. For those who do not know or realize that their actions or behaviors toward others is bullying, here are some words that summarize bullying actions in ONE word:

- Persecute
- Oppress
- Torment
- Intimidate
- Harass
- Force
- Subjugate
- Subdue

BULLIES (YOU) ARE BETTER THAN BULLYING

- Dominate
- Tyrannize
- Trespass

The irony of bullying is that people who are bullies do not want to be called or tagged or identified as such because they know it is not an acceptable behavior; yet, they still indulge in it. Any bully who does not want to be tagged or identified with such names should make the right decision to stop engaging in bullying activities. Your decision to make a change makes you a better person and gives you an identity that will position you to express your good potential.

Why is it important for you to make a change?

You were not born a bully, but your environment made you a bully. Now that you have identified your actions as bullying, please decide today not to be controlled anymore by the environment that has made you a bully. Make the right choice to be a better person to yourself and to society in general because you have something good to offer to the world. What makes you a good person is when you have the consent of others to govern over them. But for bullies, the consent or permission of their prey is never requested before they launch their attack.

Whenever you subject people to a hostile situation by frightening them in order to make them do what you want or to comply with your wishes, or whenever you intimidate them into submission without their consent, you are not human. It is only in the animal kingdom that the consent of the other animal is not needed for control. You might be able to subdue and oppress the person for a while, but in the end the person involved in your agenda of bullying is better than you because using force to reign over others makes your world grow smaller and insignificant.

Look at it this way. There has never been an important or well-recognized individual who has received a standing ovation or a Nobel Prize because he or she was a bully. There is no future in bullying. As for any action that you cannot publicly defend, why do you want to give yourself to it? Nobody wants to associate with a bully. Any person who uses force to oppress others has no place in the hall of fame.

Bullies should realize that the more they push someone into a wall, the higher the tendency the person will bounce back. However, the way the person bounces back might be positive or negative. Whatever the outcome, you are responsible for his or her actions, which are sometimes bloody and tragic.

In reality, we were created with a heart and not a stone. There is the human part of us that has empathy that might have been ignored or buried by a bully in the journey of life. It is never too late to make up your mind to activate or make use of the empathy part of you that you have ignored. Stop bullying and start connecting with people.

Bullying will cost you more than loving; bullying will cost you more than you are willing to pay, and it will deprive you of life's opportunities. You will never lose by loving, but you will always lose by bullying. If you do not want to be a loser, stop your practice of bullying and dominating others around you. When you refuse to put aside your bullying activities, you are not only a loser but a fool because bullying dwells in the bosom of fools. Of course people make mistakes, but in the case of bullies, they maximize mistakes when they choose to bully others.

If you are willing to change, there are people out there who are willing to support and help you to become a good person, a person people will want to associate with; this is only possible if you stop your bullying practices. You can only be useful to yourself and those around you when you are happy and healthy. All this can happen when you decide not to bully again.

Bullies are Trespassers

Bullying is another form of trespassing where the bully encroaches and intrudes into someone's life, privacy, property, and rights. It is an act of infringing on the privacy of another, without the consent of the person, to cause harm and pain. Trespassing is a violation of human rights, which is illegal and it is a crime. Crime never yields good results because after committing any crime, including bullying, you must pay. Thus, any bully who indulges in bullying activities is indulging in a vicious activity, and such a person should realize that he or she is a trespasser.

People are bound to sometimes make poor choices, encroaching or trespassing on the privacy and territory of others. But the difference between a nonbully and a bully is his or her ability to discern when he or she makes a bad choice and to deviate from it. In the ability to differentiate between trespassing and respecting the privacy of others lies wisdom. Bullying is a compilation of bad choices to harm others and encroach on the privacy of others on a continuous basis—to everyone's detriment. Such behavior is a crime that has consequences.

Bullying might seem right to a bully, but in the end, it is a way of inflicting harm, pain, and even death. It is an encroachment, and it is trespassing that must be sabotaged in order to save lives and make school environments a place where positive knowledge can be transmitted to children.

We might be different in our ways of life, but we are all humans; hence, let us celebrate our uniqueness, respect our diversity, because in diversity lies beauty and power.

Human Beings are Limited

Bullies are trespassers who always invade the privacy of others without permission, based on reasons best known only to them. The reasons bullies give for attacking others are despicable and unbelievable. But what bullies fail to realize is that whatever they are harassing or tormenting their victim about is being transmitted into their lives in another form; thus, human beings are a limited species.

Human beings are limited in strength, capacity, capability, knowledge, wisdom, time, relationships, emotions, and resources. Hence, wherever you are today as bullies, stop looking down on others because of their limitations. There is this general saying, "take the limits off, or no more limits," but the reality is, you can gear your attention to take limits off in certain areas of your life, while other areas remain limited. In short, refuse to bully others because of the limitations in their lives that are obvious to you because what you see in others as a limitation might be represented in your life in another form.

No human being is unlimited. In one way or another, we all have our limitations, and there is no one on earth who can boast to being unlimited. That is why no one is a *one-stop shop* for all, which is why we have a division of labor. Thus, as human beings, we are a limited species with the ability to specialize in any field we choose in life. While in the midst of our specialties, we still have lapses we try to cover up from others. Bullies still have areas in their lives that are not totally endowed; hence, come down from your high horse of bullying and stop bullying others. What you see in others as limitations is being channeled/communicated in another form in your life as a limitation. Remember, you are a limited species and not an unlimited superhuman.

Whatever are your dealings with others today, you might be the best in your field or class, but remember you are not sovereign because you still have your weaknesses and things you do not know. Bear this in mind in order to avert unnecessary, arrogant bullying behavior. In all you do, especially with others, try to gain an understanding. Try to see things from the perspective of others. Put yourself in the shoes of those you choose to bully, and see if you would be happy to swap positions with them. Only when you understand that you are not perfect but have limitations can you easily live in harmony with others. Endeavor to treasure those in your life who you believe to be weird because treasures are always hidden in the vessels you least expect. Always remember that we might be different, but we are all human; hence, let us celebrate our uniqueness and respect our diversity because in diversity lies *beauty* and *power*.

> **Treasures are not found in perfect places, so do not underestimate anybody, because there are treasures in each and every one of us. Therefore, be the propeller through which those treasures are being discovered and birthed in the lives of those around you.**

Treasures are Always Hidden

Treasures are never found on the surface; they are embedded in the inner core of the carrier. Treasures are found in hidden places, especially where you least expect them. Many nations are blessed with natural resources that are mostly found in the deep depths of the earth. In human beings, greatness and potential (treasures) are not written or found on the foreheads of people, and neither are they written on the foreheads of those who are in the realm of power, influence, and authority. Be careful because the person you are bullying or choosing to bully might be the next president, prime minister, first lady, Bill Gates, Oprah Winfrey, attorney general, or the world's number one surgeon.

The destiny of a person can never be determined because of his or her background or his or her race; it is only through time unraveling that we can see the potential and greatness of a person. So, beware because greatness and potential could sit in that boy or girl you choose to bully; you can never tell if the person you are bullying today is going to be the next banker or entrepreneur who will decide your fate tomorrow. You might be biting the finger that might feed you tomorrow. It is crucial, then, for you to always remember that life is a seed, and whatever we sow, we reap.

Think about these questions the next time you choose to get involved in any bullying activities:

- How will you feel if the doctor who will decide your fate is someone you bullied in the past?
- What will you do if you are in crisis, and the only donor who will save your life is the person you bullied while in school?
- What if you were involved in an accident and the first person who came to the scene to rescue you was one of your victims from your previous or present bullying atrocities? What do you expect the person to do for you?
- What if you are desperately searching for a job in order to keep your head above water, and the person who has the key to your employment is one of your victims from your past illicit activities?

- What if the person closing a business deal that will bring your company into the limelight is one of your previous victims? Do you think the deal will go through or be aborted?

Of course human beings are expected to forgive and behave professionally, but never forget that the wound of bullying cuts deeper than any physical injury, and not everybody is capable or strong enough to forget the pain of yesterday. You might not know the content of tomorrow, and being ignorant of what tomorrow will bring will not stop tomorrow from coming, but the only guarantee that your tomorrow will be better depends on your actions today. Whatever you do today is a seed that has been sown into your future, and it will certainly yield fruit. But sometimes you might not be ready for the harvest you will reap.

Always remember, greatness is never written on the forehead, and treasures are hidden in places you least expect them to be; thus, the child you are bullying today is a carrier of greatness only waiting for time to unravel the greatness inside.

You might not know the content of tomorrow, and being ignorant of what tomorrow will bring will not stop tomorrow from coming, but the only guarantee that your tomorrow will be better depends on your actions today.

You are Accountable

Bullies should realize that whatever they do today does not just disappear with the day, but it goes ahead of them, waiting to either haunt or help them into a new phase of life. Always remember, your deeds do not evaporate but transcend into your future, waiting for your arrival.

Whatever the reactions and actions of those people who were bullied, it is the bullies who are responsible; hence, they should be held accountable for the outcome of their bullying activities. It is very important for bullies to know that their decision to terrorize another person through their bullying activities is killing or aborting the dreams of victims and their parents, especially in the cases where the victims lost their lives by committing suicide or being pushed into depression, where the victim becomes incapacitated through bullying attacks.

You may or may not be identified in the end, but either way, you are accountable for the death of another soul, and his or her blood is on your hands. There is no way you can escape paying the price for your actions because your conscience is there to torment you. Whether you believe it or not, it will certainly affect and set in motion the cause of your life because your actions are not for mere fun or to hurt another person, but they set the course of your life in motion. The outcome will be your dividend for life. Wherever you end up in life or how you proceed in life will be reflected in the sum total of your dividend—what you sow in your life and the lives of others around you. Life's journey is a combination of different junctions that are connected as you move through life, and the ink you choose to join the junctions in your life will reflect in your pathway. Remember, bullying is one of the negative inks so avoid using it.

"How far you go in life depends on your being tender with the young, compassionate with the aged, sympathetic with the striving, and tolerant of the weak and strong. Because someday in your life, you will have been all of these."
—George Washington Carver

Here is a true-life story to illustrate the quote above:

Bryant, who I previously wrote about in this book, told me that there was someone who was always mocking him because he used a wheelchair. He said the last time he saw the person, the person was incapacitated because of an accident and eventually used a wheelchair just like him.

It is vital to always remember when dealing with others that what we sow is what we will eventually reap. To all bullies who specialize in tormenting others, especially people with disabilities, be careful what you sow into the lives of those around you because you might eventually be in their position. It's time for all bullies to take an inventory of their bullying activities and actions by analyzing the pain, heartache, devastation, depression, low self-esteem, and even death that their actions have caused. They need to know the extent to which their actions have destroyed others and to take ownership for the havoc they have created in other people's lives. They need to do this to prevent future occurrences. The laws of sowing and reaping are real.

Count the Cost

Every second, minute, and action counts in life. A person's decision to bully others changes the direction of his or her life and of those he or she chooses to bully. Most times bullying is a deliberate act that is consciously carried out by bullies, which has a grievous effect on the victim with repercussions on the bullies. Even though they might not admit it or are not aware of it, their toxic behavior is affecting them directly or indirectly.

For their own benefit, it is vital for bullies to take an inventory of their bullying actions. It will blow their minds to realize that as much as they are hurting the victims, they are doing themselves even more harm. This is because they do not have the time or energy to discover or develop their own potential because their focus is occupied by their desire to intimidate or dominate others. As a result, the potential of the bully is being buried because the bully does not have the time or capacity to explore his or her potential; that is, the bully is subconsciously digging his or her own downfall without knowing it, all because his or her focus is dominated by and fueled with hatred for others. The bully should instead invest his or her time in using his or her potential positively, which would eventually make the bully useful to humanity. In addition, bullying limits a bully's ability to form healthy relationships with others. As a result, his or her world becomes smaller, and in the process he or she loses lifelong friendships and opportunities because of illicit behavior.

It takes a lot of adrenaline pumping through their bodies in order for bullies to plan and execute their evil actions. The effects of such actions are massively destructive to their health and mind, even though they have become hardened or heartless. When bullies take inventory of their actions, they will see how futile their lives have become as a result of their actions and the injustices they have personally brought on themselves, because bullying will only short circuit their potential and opportunities in life. In the end, bullies are creating havoc in their own lives as much as they are hurting their victims because the cost of their actions has tremendous negative effects on them as well as their relationships.

Take a moment to reflect on your relationships today and make amendments where necessary. Choose to build broken relationships in your life that were damaged as a result of your behavior. Decide to be your brother's keeper today, because every one of us needs a friend and not a bully.

Be Sensitive Again

Bullies, no matter how far you have gone or the magnitude of the havoc you have created in the lives of those caught in your web, it is never too late to turn over a new leaf. Take a moment to reflect on all your actions and the damage they have caused in the lives of your victims and their families. You will realize that your insensitivity to others has driven someone to physical and emotional death. Through your bullying actions, you might have killed someone emotionally, mentally and sent some of them to an early grave. Never forget, whatever actions or paths your victims end up on in life is at your expense, and they are being accumulated in your life as your résumé. Thus, you are compiling a curriculum vitae that you will not be proud to present publicly. Become sensitive again in order to avert having a dent in your life that will disqualify or affect you in the future.

You must realize that the license you have given yourself to hurt others does not only have a toll on the victims, but on their families and society as well; hence, wherever you are today, become sensitive to the pain and heartbreak of those you have chosen to prey upon in your quest for power.

It is time to put all hatred and bitterness aside because wherever the seed of bitterness is sown it produces problems, which will eventually defile many, including you. For your own good and the betterment of humanity, it is crucial to put all bitterness and prejudices aside to become better—even the best in life.

Be Better, Not Bitter-Be the Best, Not a Bully

Being better is more profitable to you than being bitter. The difference between better and bitter is just one letter, but it will have a tremendous impact on your life and on the lives of those who come into contact with you. The effects of letters *E* and *I* can be either life preserving or life destroying; that is how powerful these two letters can be, depending on which letter you choose to apply to complete the word B[ ]TTER. Placing the letter *E* to fill the missing gap in B[ ]TTER will have an immeasurable effect on your life and those around you. In the alphabetical order of letters, the letter *E* comes before the letter *I*, and when you choose to place one of these letters in B[ ]TTER, it can pull you up or pull you down life's ladder. Thus, placing *E* to fill the missing gap in B[ ]TTER to become better will only move you upward, while being bitter with the letter *I*, which comes after the letter *E*, will only move you backward. Being better brings out your best, which will catapult you into the realm of greatness; hence, be the best and not a bully.

Being better makes you the best, while being bitter always produces negative fruits, such as bullying. It is vital for you to be the best in life because every action and moment counts in life journey, and they all attract consequences, which can have positive or negative effects. What is good about being better instead of being bitter is that there is always a window of opportunity opened for each of us to make amendments to the areas of our lives where we have been bitter, in order to avert the negative consequences that bullying always births.

Every day is a new day, a new opportunity, a new possibility, and a new chance. Develop a good, positive attitude in order to create a peaceful, joyous atmosphere wherever you go each day. Your life is like an open book that you are writing, and it is open for people to read with or without your permission. People might not remember your face and your name, but they will never forget your good or evil deeds. Your deeds in the lives of those around you are always remembered; even when you are long gone, your deeds are your legacy. In life, being the best and not being a bully will be more beneficial to you because it will enable you to utilize your energy positively, and it will energize you to be focused on discovering your strengths while in the process helping others to be the best in their life's endeavors. Your decision to be better and not to be a bully is your doorway to a great destination; hence, wherever you are in life today can be traced back to the decisions you once made. The sum totals of your choices are reflected in all you are today. If you are not happy and are not the best where you are today, decide to make amendments in order to produce enviable results.

Give Compliments and Appreciation Instead of Bullying

Just as bullying touches the lives of those who are bullied in a negative way, a compliment touches the lives of those receiving it in a positive way. It is very important for parents to teach their children to give compliments to others by being the examples whom their children will learn from, especially the parents of children who bully others.

Compliments and appreciation are double-sided words; they are words given by one person, and the benefit or the satisfaction is received by the giver *and* the receiver. It helps you to eliminate selfishness and a self-centered mentality, and it takes your focus from yourself and helps you see the goodness in others. Compliments are a booster to the self-confidence and self-esteem of those who receive them, and it helps someone to know you care, and that is *why you* noticed what you are complimenting the person about. It communicates to the person receiving your compliment that someone is watching out for them in a positive way to support and lift them up. Bullying is the opposite, where a bully is looking for someone to torment and pull down.

A compliment is a power key that has a magical effect on the giver and the receiver. It puts a smile on the face of the receiver and gives a positive kick to the giver because of the transformative effects the compliment has on the receiver. Thus, the giver of the compliment goes with the magic smile of the receiver, which becomes an aura that follows both parties whenever they reflect on that moment and the responses that transpired. Compliments encourage a person who was discouraged, a person who perhaps felt overshadowed, and it helps a person who is isolated emerge from isolation by giving them a reason to carry on or go that extra mile.

A compliment is a message to a person, saying, iCare that much about you to notice something about you that I am complimenting you on. Instead of bullying others, give compliments so that your life will be complimented. Compliments boost the confidence of the person receiving them and make the person giving them feel accomplished, and as a result he or she has positively touched the life of another. In compliments lies the power of appreciation, which is the birthplace of connectivity. No one rejects true compliments; people connect easily with people who believe in them, and that is what you do whenever you compliment another person. You are telling them "you are able" and "I believe in you for your inherent strength that might not be seen by others."

Endeavor to Invest Time Positively

Life is a seed, and time is a seed. Our journey on earth is being measured in time; thus, anything you spend your time on, you are indirectly spending your life. When you invest your time in an illicit behavior, such as bullying, you are indirectly planting your life. Wherever you choose to plant your time/life seed, it will grow and yield fruit accordingly; hence, in any bullying attack it takes time and energy on the part of bullies to carry out their atrocities, which means bullies are investing their time and energy negatively toward their own downfall and that of their victims. In as much as bullying is a negative sowing of time and life seed on the part of the bullies, it is crucial for bullies, for their own benefit, to endeavor to invest their time positively in knowing their victims. It takes spending time with someone for you to actually know the person, and it might surprise you to discover that the person you think is weird in one area of life might be a container or well of wisdom, insight, and ideals in another area of life, which might just positively impact your life's journey. Endeavor to utilize your time by investing it to know those you choose to bully. You might discover that they are streams of wisdom to your problems. Remember, discovery is the birthplace of solution, and your solution might be in the hands of that person you choose to bully.

Have an Open Mind

We all see things from our own perspective, but that does not necessarily mean that we are always right and others are wrong. There are always two sides to a story, two sides to a coin, and that is why it is crucial to see things from different angles. Your view from one angle will certainly tell a different story from another angle.

Have an open mind to see things from different angles by putting yourself in the shoes of your victims whenever you have the desire or urge to embark on your bullying atrocities. If you are honest with yourself, you will not want to be in the position or condition you want to put your fellow human being in. So, have an open mind in your dealings with your fellow human beings, and you will be surprised that things are not really the way they seem to be from a different angle. Your viewpoint from a keyhole will certainly be different from an open window and from the rooftop.

First refuse and then deal with that urge in you to bully another person because of your narrow or keyhole perspective of that person. When your bullying damage or harm has been done, it will take the mercy of God to undo the impact in that person's life. Endeavor to avoid the pathway of destruction because when the damage is done, especially for those who have killed themselves because of your bullying atrocities, you might not find the opportunity to repair the damage or recall the wrong choices you have made, even when you truly, carefully sought to undo the wrong. Avoid this pathway of bullying because life is fragile and irreplaceable. One death as a result of a bullying escapade is one too many for the vacuum it creates in the family, which can never be filled. Bullying is a pathway to avoid; choose not to embark on it.

Live Simply

As human beings and for the peace of humanity, when each of us sees one another—whether bullies, victims, followers, bystanders, or the voice with a mind that is open and straightforward without any hidden agenda or selfishness—we will come to a place of knowing that we are not perfect. Then we can adjust and be more sensitive to the weaknesses of others by living simply.

SIMPLY

S	→	See
I	→	In
M	→	Me
P	→	Prospects and Potentials
L	→	Lurking In
Y	→	You

When we apply the word *simply* in our daily dealings with others, life will be peaceful, and the stress level will drop or be eliminated. Then there will be room for understanding, which eliminates finger-pointing or isolation of others within a group. Especially for bullies and their followers, it is crucial to apply the word *simply* in your dealings because whatever you see in others (your victims) also exists in you; thus, I appeal to you to see in your victims S I M P L Y.

Questions for bullies:

- As a bully, would you love to swap positions with the person you are bullying and experience what he or she is going through?

If your answer is *no*, please let your answer convince you to stop bullying.

To be victorious in any sphere of life, the first person you must defeat is yourself, because if you can conquer your limiting mentality, you can conquer anything.

11

Be the Victor and Not the Victim

Most victims are still living their experiences every day, even when the bullying happened years, months, weeks, days, or hours ago, and when help is not rendered early to victims, or the victims do not seek help for themselves today, it will eventually affect their tomorrow. Hence, they grow up with the victim mentality, thereby finding it difficult to separate themselves from the attack and the experiences they had as a child; this mentality will keep them imprisoned, affecting whatever they do. In such situations, they are not open to new opportunities or do not have confidence in themselves or others.

When you hear the word *marriage*, the first thing that comes to mind is a union between a man and a woman in a traditional marriage, but the word marriage is now synonymous with other words or phrases. Just as the car manufacturing company uses the word marriage as a process of joining the engine to the body of a car during manufacturing, so are people subconsciously marrying themselves to their past pain, hurt, and bullying experiences. As a result, they don't see beyond what they went through in the past; meanwhile, they are separating themselves from all the possibilities and opportunities in front of them; hence, they are subconsciously married to their past hurt, and they have automatically divorced themselves from their future.

BE THE VICTOR AND NOT THE VICTIM

"To be married to the past is to be divorced from the future."
—*Pastor (Dr.) Paul Enenche*

To be stuck in the past is to forgo tomorrow's opportunities and dreams. Until you let go of your past pain and experiences you had as a result of bullying, you cannot lay hold of your future. It is time to have a new dream and not allow your past torment or pain to mortgage your tomorrow because your future is bigger and brighter than the bullies. The bullying experiences might be painful and cut deeper than words can explain, but remember, you are far more worthy than where the bully or bullies mapped out for your life.

You are not responsible for the opinions, actions, or attitudes of others toward you, but you are solemnly responsible for your responses to their actions or attitudes toward you. Thus, you cannot conquer a bully with a victim mentality or response, and neither can you have a great tomorrow holding on to your past pain or victimization, because your mental picture of yourself determines what tomorrow will bring.

You have one life to live, so live it and enjoy it; under no circumstances should you allow a bully to sabotage your life because only you will determine how you anchor the ship of your destiny. Of course the support of others is necessary, but your ability to keep afloat in the sea of bullies lies in your buoyancy. Your life is not about the bullies, but it is all about *you*. Stop subconsciously enforcing or enhancing the programming of the bully in your life. Any time you allow bullies or your past experiences of being bullied to torment you or keep you bound, you have succeeded in wasting your time. Let it be known to you today that you have not only succeeded in wasting your time, but your life too, because time is life.

Time is Your Life

Our existence on earth is being measured in time; that is how vital our time is, and it is the one thing that the bully wants to steal from his or her victim. When a bully succeeds to control what the victim does with his or her time, the bully has succeeded in controlling the life of the victim. Common to all the different groups of victims is the *time* that the bully has stolen. The bully took too much time from them and, in some cases, the bully is still in charge of their time, even when the attack happened decades ago.

Whenever bullies come to torment you or segregate you from a group by putting you in box with the label *victim,* the bully has come to steal a part of your life from you. Once this happens, the bully will end up controlling what you invest your time in by gearing your focus on the picture of yourself as a failure or an outcast, which will eventually lead to self-pity and depression. Most victims are still held captive by the attack from a bully, even when the bully is long gone. They are stuck in the experiences of the past, and some of them keep on investing time to replaying the picture of the scene in their head. Instead of moving forward, toward opportunities that abound, they keep going on a retrogressive movement, which might eventually lead to stagnation and confusion.

Once this happens, the bully has succeeded in distracting you from your focus. Whatever comes to distract you will eventually give you direction, and whoever gives you direction controls your time. When a bully succeeds in controlling your time, the bully has automatically succeeded in controlling your life, because the life span on earth is measured in a frame or window of time. That is why birthdays are celebrated within the window or frame of time. Always remember this when you celebrate your birthday; you are indirectly celebrating time, which is your life. Therefore, do not allow a bully to control what you do with your time (your life), because when a bully controls your time, he or she is indirectly controlling your life.

Bullying is beyond tormenting or isolating someone within a group; bullying is about stealing a part of someone's life. Most times victims are not even aware that the operation of a bully goes beyond the actual scene of attack, and that it cuts deep into their tomorrow, especially if they don't have the proper help to boost their confidence in themselves.

It is high time for any victims of bullying who are still under attack, or still replaying the scene after a decade or months or weeks or days, to understand that bullying is chopping away at their lives. They should rise up to take their lives back by moving forward to reach out for their tomorrow themselves, by not allowing any bully or their followers to control what they do with their time, because time is life.

Time is so crucial to our existence to the extent that people spend money in getting teachings/training on time management. But what most people are investing in is learning about life management. That is how vital and crucial our time is. It is simple arithmetic—how you manage your time is how you manage your life, while the value you place on your time is proportional to the value of your life; how you define your time is how you define your life, and where you invest your time is where your life investment is. Living the experience a bully gave to you will control your focus and eventually your time, which is your life.

> *"A man who dares to waste one hour of time*
> *has not discovered the value of life."*
> *—Charles Darwin*

As the clock ticks, so too is your life clock. Any passing years, months, weeks, days, minutes, or seconds cannot be retrieved. Your life is all about time. That is why when you are sixty years old you cannot turn the time back to become thirty or forty years old again. Your life clock has passed that time of your life, just as the annual calendar cannot be set back to the fifteenth or eighteenth centuries, or the seventies or eighties. Your time (life) is too precious for you to waste on bullies and their agenda, because no matter how rich or poor you are, nobody can afford to buy back yesterday, and neither can you preorder the next second or minute. That is why you should not waste any minutes or seconds. Time is a commodity that cannot be bought; it is too valuable and essential for your existence but too expensive for the wealthy, the rich, and eventually the poor to buy. No one can buy back yesterday, last month, or last year, and neither can you place an order for the next seconds or prepay for time; that is how powerful your time (life) is. Do not waste your time, and do not allow anyone to waste it for you or steal it from you.

In as much as what the bully is doing is painful and really hurts, the pain happened maybe a few minutes or hours or days ago. You have to let it go just as yesterday is gone, so that your tomorrow can be more productive. Any time a bully or situation steals time from you, it cannot be retrieved or bought back; therefore, be wise in order not to waste life because a wasted time is a wasted life. No matter what the bully is doing, your life is too powerful and valuable to be wasted on bullies; thus, in order to avert lamenting tomorrow, you must manage your today wisely. Your today will always be your yesterday once tomorrow comes, and tomorrow will always come. Your yesterday, however, can never return when it is gone.

Enjoy life and appreciate the mercies of the Giver of Life, and do not take the breath on your nostril for granted. The reason you are still alive is that you are breathing. It is vital for you to place more value on your time because the sum total of your life is measured in time, and how you spend your time will determine how your life is being spent. For this reason, it is in your own interest to be resolute with your time—I mean, your *life*.

Be Resolute

You must be strong willed not to allow any bully to have control and final word over your life or future, especially when the bullies are gone. Don't allow them to have rule over you, whether they are present or not. You shouldn't give them any power over you because the power you allocate to them is what they have to control and dominate you.

Your price tag determines the offer you get in life, and the value you place on yourself will determine the response you get from others. That is why you need to stand up for yourself; it is for your own best interest, and no one will have your best interest in heart more than yourself. The interests of others are secondary. To be a victor, not a victim, is in your best interest.

Decide whether you will be someone's victim or not; nobody can make that decision for you

BE THE VICTOR AND NOT THE VICTIM

To be a victor, you must have the desire, zeal, and persistence to block bullies, their words, and their actions by always having the mind-set that there is a limit they can't go beyond. There should be a place in you that they cannot touch or reach, and that place is your spirit because anything that cannot conquer your spirit will not dominate you. With your spirit, you are like a country with a military defense.

Be Focused

Your focus enables you to progress, advance, and conquer, or it limits, distracts, stagnates, and pulls you into despair. Your focus being on the positive or the negative will eventually affect your choices, actions, and dealings with others.

In the midst of a bullying battle, it is not the time to focus on the pain or your weakness; rather, it is the time to focus on your strengths, which will trigger your victory. When you focus on the wrong things, defeat is inevitable, but when your focus is geared toward victory, it transmits a message to the bullies that you are a force they cannot oppress or suppress into surrendering. Your focus on victory will keep you standing in the midst of battle because your focus is either on winning or losing to the bullies; hence, whatever your focus is in the midst of a bullying attack either forges you into victory or defeat.

The reality of life is wherever there is a tussle, what controls your focus will determine the end result. Therefore, in any bullying battle, when your focus is on winning, victory is the outcome, but when it is on fear or your weaknesses, defeat is inevitable because you are now double-minded. Being double-minded in the midst of challenges incapacitates your ability to focus because a double-minded person is always unstable; hence, defeat is obtainable. But when victory is your goal, focus becomes a propeller and fuel to advance and conquer. So, be focused and do not waver because victory is obtainable.

Advance and Conquer

Only the prepared person is confident and a conqueror. You need to prepare ahead of time so that no matter what comes your way today, you choose to conquer it in order to be a victor and not a victim. No one has your interest at heart more than you, and neither is there anyone who can guarantee your victory over bullies without your willingness, preparation, and determination to conquer. Hence, conquering in life is at the mercy of your preparation for the battle; therefore, be prepared and equipped to conquer.

> *"Give me six hours to chop down a tree, and I will spend the first four sharpening the axe."*
> —*Abraham Lincoln*

Be Prepared

There is no victory without preparation, and there is no victory without a battle. For any child or adult to be victorious in the midst of bullying, he or she must prepare from home because no athlete wins without a rigorous preparation prior to the competition, and neither will any student pass an examination without preparing or studying for the exams. Any child who does not want to be a victim of bullies must have some element of preparation and equipment in order to be victorious.

Bullies want to make you their victim, but the choice isn't theirs; that is where you are stronger than they are. You will never be too old to be victimized; it is only when you decide in advance not to be a victim that you will not fall to be one. Your mental picture ahead of an attack will be the basis for you to conquer any battle. If you can picture it, you can have it. Let the picture of a victor be permanently etched in your mind as your identity, and parents of young children should help their children by engraving the picture of a victor/conqueror in the minds of their children by speaking uplifting, not downgrading, words to their children, irrespective of their weakness.

In each of us is a conqueror; hence, you must fan the fire of a conqueror in yourself by preparing and choosing not to be a victim to any bully. Nobody is going to do it for you; it is a decision you have to make by yourself, especially in a society where there is no well-defined support system. Note that it is your duty to take the bull by the horns for your own benefit. The aim of a bully is to shut you down; nevertheless, your decision and vision as a conqueror will make you rise from the pit where the bully wants to bury you, in order to climb to the top as the conqueror that you are. Bullying is temporary, but your victory is permanent when you decide to rise above the agenda of bullies.

Bullies are problems and obstacles to be used as an asset to develop a strong will, just like the dust, to rise above whatever is trying to beat you down. Keep on saying and reminding yourself that you are a conqueror and will never give up, just like the dust, because no matter how hard you beat the dust, the higher it rises. No matter how hard the bully might terrorize you, say to the bully that you are rising above him or her, just like the dust.

Be a Winning Warrior

No one is a conqueror without a battle, or a warrior without a war, or a victor without a fight. The reality is that there is a bullying war or fight going on around you or even in your life and it is only the warriors who have equipped themselves who win the war. To be a winning warrior, you have to get yourself equipped by working on your mentality and not allowing anyone to brainwash or belittle you into losing your self-confidence. Be equipped for winning, and never forget that the time of bullying is not the time to be basking in self-pity or your shortcomings.

In a bullying contest, you are the greater one because of your inherent potential, and this potential will be enforced when geared toward your strength and not your weakness. All a bully wants is to program your focus on your weakness, and your refusal to believe the lies of bullies concerning who you are makes you a winning warrior. The battles of bullies are the battles of the mind; hence, when bullies are not able to conquer your mind, they cannot win the war. This is only possible if you decide to protect your focus, which is at the mercy of your mind, in order not to be distracted. Whatever comes to distract you only comes to give you direction, and no warrior asks for direction from an enemy.

For your own interest, take all the steps that will help you be the winner and the victor so that you can enjoy, not endure, life. Your future is bright, and your potential is enormous, so don't be stuck in your past because your past is over; you cannot change it. However, you can make changes in your future, which is beckoning you.

Parents are the Builders of Victors

In the life of any precious child, the parents are not only there to nourish, nurture, teach, guide, or guard, but they are there to build. They are there to build any broken walls in their children's lives; they are there to build areas in their lives where there are weaknesses as a result of external encroachment and trespasser invasion.

It is crucial for parents to protect or build the self-confidence of their children, as the case may be because human beings always act according to the way they see themselves. They behave in light of what they see. Therefore, if a child will ever conquer a bully, he or she must have the self-confidence to see himself or herself as a conqueror, winner, and victor, even before he or she ever encounters the bully; thus, the child should be endowed with a self-confidence that is unmovable. The greatest help and support a parent can give to a child who is bullied is the gift of love, which will engulf the child to be secure in his or her parents' love, boosting his or her self-confidence and self-esteem in the process of empowerment and recovery.

Parents, empower your children with love and let them know that they are your beloved because your love for your children will empower them to climb over any mountain, including the mountains of bullies. Empowerment with words of love from parents builds an unmovable foundation in children, which eventually deepens the root of their self-confidence. Parents should never forget that a bully will never succeed in his or her operations without destroying the self-confidence of his or her victims; hence, in any bullying battle, the first thing parents need to safeguard is the self-confidence and self-esteem of their children. When the self-confidence of a child is intact, he or she will soar above any storm like an eagle and rise above whatever a bully throws at him or her.

Knowledge is Critical for Victory

Knowledge is an empowerment that enables you to handle or terminate any confrontation. The more knowledgeable you are of who you are and your self-worth, the easier it becomes to handle the pranks of bullies. Parents should enlighten their children; it is empowerments that will help children terminate the captivity of bullies because victory will begin from what children know about themselves, especially from those who love them. This knowledge they have about their strength, self-worth, and capacity will eventually become a weapon they will use to terminate attacks. Knowledge will always give you an edge in any sphere of life, especially when you choose to appropriate the knowledge you have in the midst of life's challenges, such as bullying. When a person who is being bullied sees himself or herself as conqueror, then victory is inevitable.

Victory begins when a person deals with bullies from the perspective of a conqueror and victory because it is not possible to think like a victim and not end up as one. Your knowledge of your hidden strengths is the catalyst for your victory; thus, victory begins in discovering who you are and your inner strengths.

Therefore, knowledge is critical for victory. What you know will keep you afloat in the midst of a bullying sea, where the bullying battle is raging. Your knowledge of your strength, ability, and capacity will make you conquer and not quit or surrender in the midst of battle; thus, knowledge is a key for survival in any life battle.

To be victorious in any sphere of life, the first person you must defeat is yourself, because if you can conquer your limiting mentality, you can conquer anything.

IM and OR are the Difference between Victim and Victor

It is crucial for victims to remember that the difference between victim and victor is just two letters—*IM* and *OR*. These two letters will make a world of difference in your life, whether you are tormented as a victim or celebrated as a victor. The impact of these two letters is determined by your decision, which is the reflection of the choice you made and who you choose to believe as an adult or child. Either you believe in yourself or you believe the lies that the bullies are selling to you. Never forget that bullies are like sales reps who want to sell their products to you, but the ball is in your court to either buy into their lies or reject their offers.

For the children who do not understand the gravity of these two letters and their tremendous impact in their lives, it is the duty of their parents to nurture their children to believe in themselves and have self-confidence that does not need praise from another person to blossom. In the process, teach them as they get older to know the difference these letters will make in their lives, and how these letters will reflect in the choices they make. This will eventually help them from being victimized by their peers.

It will be more beneficial to you to make the choice of using the attacks from bullies as an incubator to discover your strength; use it as a furnace to enhance your potential as a refined gold by reaching out to your future while cutting connections with past pain. Never forget that your future is beckoning you with brightness; you decide whether to go to that glorious future or to hold on to your past pain and limiting experiences. It is your choice to go for *IM* (*In Me*), which is the victim in me, or *OR* (*Over Reproach*) victor over reproach.

> "*The flame of French resistance must not and shall not die.*"
> —*Charles de Gaulle*

You are the one who will fan the flame of a victim mentality or victor mentality (winning warrior spirit) burning in your life. But never forget, either way you are fanning a flame—the victim's flame or the victor's flame. Whatever flame you choose to fan will determine who you become in life.

Always remember you were not born a victim but a victor, despite what the bully is saying and doing. Below is an example of what victors say and think of themselves. I am:

V	Valuable
I	Intelligent
C	Courageous
T	Tenacious
O	Optimistic
R	Radiant

Valuable	I know my self-worth; I don't need validation from a bully to define who I am. I am too valuable to myself and society to allow a bully to make me insignificant to my world. I choose to be valuable to myself and my world by not being a victim or relinquishing to obscurity and irrelevance. I carry a well of treasure in me. I am a walking treasure to myself and my world.
Intelligent	I am too smart and intelligent to believe the lies and the pictures the bully is painting about me. I refuse to be what a bully says. I am too smart for a bully to distort my focus; I am bigger than the bubble the bully wants to put me in. I am not ignorant of my capability and capacity.
Courageous	I cannot be deterred by a bully or his or her attacks; I am too brave and audacious to be alienated or isolated by any bully.
Tenacious	I cannot be wearied by a bully to surrender to his or her attacks and pranks. I am too persistent to give in or give way or give up to a bully to drown me in a bullying battle or to dictate my future.
Optimistic	I am confident in myself and hopeful, too. I have a future that cannot be tampered with by a bully. I am too needed

	to allow a bully to drown me in a bullying sea. My focus is geared toward success and not defeat.
Radiant	I am like the morning sun, a rainbow too colorful and radiant to be ignored. I glow and illuminate wherever I go; therefore, I am too significant to my world to be covered or overshadowed by a bully.

You are too needed to be swallowed up by bullies and their rants and too equipped to be wasted or stranded in life, even in the midst of bullying conspiracies. You have all it takes to be a victor and not a victim. You are too equipped for life's journey to be the victim; thus, make use of your equipment because it is in you, waiting for you to activate it to be the victor that you have always been. You have all you need to be victorious in life's endeavors, even in the midst of a bullying battle. You have what it takes to advance, conquer, and come out as a victor. You have been well equipped for life's journey just like any other conquerors who became victorious in life. Emulate other victors because you have the same equipment that gave them victory.

Remember, Nobody Remembers Failure

Wherever you are today, whether you are being victimized or about to step into the battle ring of bullies, never forget that it is for your own good to stand up and fight for your rights. No one has your interest at heart more than you do. Thus, standing up to fight in a bullying battle in order to conquer and not be conquered, to be a victor and not be the victim, is for your own good because nobody remembers failures in the hall of fame.

In the sands of time, it is only victors and those who have conquered that are remembered. The truth about life is that no one introduces or wants to associate with a failure; that is why it is crucial for you to stand up for your rights as an adult and for parents to help their little ones to believe in themselves by countering the lies of bullies.

Is bullying an easy battle? *No*, but in your determination not to give up in a combat lies the victory—that is what Nelson Mandela did in South

Africa. There were many Mandelas in South Africa, but there was only *one* Nelson Mandela. He is gone now, but his legacy still speaks in South Africa, even now, because he refused to be the victim of circumstance. That is the reason why people still remember him today.

For your own good, refuse to be a failure or a victim because nobody will remember you. Choose to be remembered, and not forgotten in a crowd because of bullies. Whatever might be confronting you today, you have what it takes to conquer it.

You Have What it Takes

In any bullying battle, never see yourself as the victim because you have what it takes to conquer anything bullies throw at you—and to be whatever you choose to be in whatever battle you choose to fight. This is only possible when you believe in yourself and know that you have what it takes to win.

Until you choose to believe in yourself that you are well able to conquer any obstacle and be whatever you choose to be, other people will decide your future for you with or without your consent. Thus, it is crucial to believe in yourself and not the lies or pictures bullies are propagating about you. Any time you believe or accept bullies' propaganda, you have given them the power to decide your future for you.

It is in your own interest not to believe or give a listening ear to the lies of bullies because who you choose to believe decides your future. You are too equipped for life's journey, just as others who have conquered bullies before you, to allow bullies to decide your future for you. So, choose to believe in yourself and not the bullies because bullying is not the end of who you are but a bend that can be used to create a new channel to explore and discover your potential—that is why you should not see bullying as the *end* but rather a *bend*.

> *When you give bullies your attention, they will give you directions that will derail you.*

Bullying is Not the *End* but a *Bend*

Although bullying hurts, pushing you into a corner or isolating you from a group, it is not enough for you to indirectly aid the bullies in their agenda by thinking the end has come for you. When you think like that, you have only succeeded in doing yourself more harm because the bully only tried to hurt you. Your reaction to his or her attempt to hurt you will determine if you have chosen to harm yourself or not. In a painful situation, there is still hope, but in a situation of harm, all hope might be lost. Do not come to a place where bullies make you believe that all hope is lost and that there is no way out for you.

When bullies tell you that your end has come, tell them it is not the end for you but a *bend*. It is a bend that will reinforce your inner strength and create an opportunity for you to mend what is crooked in your life. A bullying attack is not your end but a bend that will help you discover your hidden potential and strength that will empower you to conquer bullies.

It is crucial for you to know that the difference between *end* and *bend* is the letter *B*. This letter *B* can make a world of difference in what side you end up on in a bullying battle, either as the victor or the victim, the conqueror or the conquered. It is in your hands never to see challenges and conflicts as the end. See them instead as a bend that needs to be mended in order for you to fend for yourself in the midst of a bullying battle, to conquer and come out as the victor, and to live your life and fulfill your dreams and visions.

Please do not allow bullies to frustrate you to a point that you are thinking of harming yourself because you believe your end has come—it is not over yet! You are too precious to your family, the society, and to me, the writer of this book, and you are the reason this book was written. Think about it because you are too precious and needed by the world to be wasted. Never forget that those who are for you are more than the bullies who are against you. You are too radiant to be overshadowed by bullies, you are too needed to be isolated and ignored, you are too equipped to be stranded, and you are too valuable to be wasted.

BE THE VICTOR AND NOT THE VICTIM

You are in charge of your key, and whatever happens to your key is your responsibility; hence, endeavor to use your key positively to enter your future.

You Have the Key

Every one of us has the key to our future; you are no exception. Because you have the key to your future, you decide what to do with the key. Either you use the key yourself to open the door to your future or you give it to another person to use to lock you out of your enviable, bright future.

Always remember the key to your destiny is solemnly in your hands, and you decide what happens to the key and who gains access to the key. Whether you believe it or not, you are being discovered by others as a result of or due to the door of exploit you choose to open with your key. Or, you are being covered or overshadowed by others due to your refusal or fear to effectively make use of your key. Maybe you are putting your key into the wrong hands.

To be victorious in any sphere of life, the first person you must defeat is yourself because if you can conquer your limiting mentality, you can conquer anything in the process, eliminating any obstacle that might be a hindrance to your ability to make effective use of your key. Whatever you choose to do with your key is a decision you have to make, and whatever door you choose to open with your master key will reflect in your future. But remember, your master key is highly active and not dormant, so either you are using it to open doors that will be profitable to you, or others are using it to lock you out of your future. You are in charge of your key, and whatever happens to your key is your responsibility; hence, endeavor to use your key positively to enter your future.

You Decide

When the ocean of life issues rises and thunder roars, what will you do? Will you soar above the storms and the seas of life's challenges or be distracted and drown? Taking action is the wing and bridge that will make you soar above the storms and cross the oceans of life's challenges. Nobody will decide for you, so you have to decide while others are there to support you.

In every life situation, including bullying, your decision makes a tremendous difference. Since bullying is an attempt to break the will of the victim, the decision of the victims will determine the experiences the victim and bully take out of it. Since the victim has a say in the whole process, it is the victim who determines the game plan and not the bully.

Whatever you decide will determine in the end who eventually wins. When you decide to win and not whine in the midst of a bullying attack, you are taking action, which will eventually propel you to win. Your decision to rise above the attack of bullies makes you a victor, and in the process that decision is writing history for others to learn from and emulate. Conquering and winning in a bullying battle is not only about you alone; it influences others' decisions to believe in themselves, which sets up the battle ring for them to dare to fight for themselves.

Questions:

- What flame are you fanning in your life?
- What are you doing to furnish your will to win in the midst of a bullying battle?
- Parents, what are you doing to furnish your child's will to win in the midst of a bullying battle?
- Parents, how are you equipping your children for their life journey?
- Parents, what are you doing to activate and enhance the equipment of your children?
- Who are *you*? A victor *or* victim?
- What do you want? To be *forgotten* or *remembered*?
- Who have you chosen to believe?

No one can answer these questions for you. Only you will know the answers.

We carry out maintenance and repairs in most areas of life, but the most vital area is sometimes ignored, and that is the area of relationships. The greatest poverty in life is not having someone you can lean or count on.

12

Love Versus Hate

Hate is the birthplace of violence and persecution. It is the beginning of living a life of self-existing, where a person forgets that life cannot be lived as an island. But at some point, your existence and survival will depend on the help of another person, who might be the one you bullied in the past. Thus, there is no one that is self-existing, and we all need and depend on each other at some point, so there is no need to hate or indulge in bullying behavior. The truth about human beings is that no person on earth is self-existing or self-sufficient; we were created to depend on each other. Even when you are alone on a forgotten island, you still depend on nature for your existence; hence, it is paramount for us to drop the bullying mentality and start caring for one another, because your existence and survival on earth depends on your relationships and associations.

> *"Hateful and condemnatory thoughts crystallize into habits of accusation and violence, which solidify into circumstances of injury and persecution."*
> —*James Allen*

We all love ourselves consciously or subconsciously, whether we express it or not, but when you refuse to acknowledge and nurture the seed of love in you as a human being, life becomes empty. Then there is room to learn and nurture the seed of hatred that might have been sown by your association or the environment you came from; however, the harm of being hateful takes its toll on the hater and those they hate. A bully's hatred and desire to hurt another person does not only affect the mind, emotion, and will of the victim, but it also affects the bullies themselves, whether they are willing to accept that their atrocities are having a toll on them or not. Hence, it is profitable for the bully to unlearn his or her hate-filled lifestyle because he or she is also a beneficiary of his or her evil deeds in the lives of others.

> *"No one is born hating another person because of the color of his skin, or his background, or his religion. People must learn to hate, and if they learn to hate, they can be taught to love, for love comes naturally to the human heart than its opposite."*
> *—Nelson Mandela*

If only we can learn to extend a bit of love to another person, then we will have no room for bullying and prejudice. We are created equal, whether as a bully or a nonbully. We might have different skin colors, body sizes, and face shapes, but we all have the same red blood flowing through our veins. There might be a difference in our blood type, but there is no special blood for a bully or a nonbully. There are no differences between the oxygen that a bully and a nonbully breathes in; neither do we have control or quantify the volume each of us should breathe in.

> *Why, then, should we create this atmosphere of negative energy known as bullying?*

There is no special sun that shines on the bully or victim, and neither is there a special rain that falls on us individually as human beings. If we are honest with ourselves, we know that we have no control over vital things that ensure our existence. These necessities are available to the rich, poor, big, small, bully, or victim and include the rain, the sun, and the oxygen we breathe; therefore, it is time we realize that we are not in the position to bully or tyrannize another person, whether in our words or actions. Since bullying is a learned behavior, it is also possible to unlearn it if you are willing, because you were not born a bully, but your environment made you one.

> *"I don't like that man. I must get to know him better."*
> —Abraham Lincoln

You might not like a person or what he or she stands for, but that does not make you more superior. For the good of all, we must learn to be more tolerant of others because in variety lies beauty. Your decision to know a person better might be the key to a lifetime friendship since treasures are always hidden in places and in persons you least expected. A person you think is weird today might be your life support tomorrow.

We all are unique, so let us celebrate our uniqueness and not use our strength to destroy another. Never follow the crowd of bullies to destroy another person, but let love distinguish you from the crowd, and let love make you behave kindly and gently to those around you. Love will make you share and not take from others; love will make you respect others; love will make you care for others; and love will make you have an iCare (I care) and not an iBully (I bully) attitude by living a life of fellowship filled with love for those you come into contact with every day.

What is Life?

To different people life means different things, but whatever is your definition of life, it should be a definition where you come to the realization that life is interdependent, meaning we all depend on each other for our survival and existence. My perspective of life is the following:

L → **Living**
I → **In**
F → **Fellowship**
E → **Every Day**

Life is all about living in fellowship every day, but the beauty of it is that we are all responsible for the way we choose to live, and whatever pathway we choose will be reflected in our dealings with others.

There are people who have chosen not to live life in fellowship but have decided to live by bullying others, which is the opposite of living in fellowship every day. Even though they choose not to live in fellowship every day with people who come their way, it is never too late to make a new choice because the power to choose is inherent in us. When a bully makes a wrong choice by bullying others, it is still possible to make a new choice today by going through an excretion and detoxification process in his or her relationship with others, in order to build up the broken walls of his or her life. Therefore, make it a priority to live in fellowship with those around you in order to connect with them. In connectivity lies the power of fellowship.

Your willingness to go through the process of excretion and detoxification will certainly ventilate and rejuvenate your relationships with others, and then you can truly have a life—Living In Fellowship Every Day.

A Need for Detoxification

The power of filtration and separation, breathing in and breathing out, is very important for us humans. Our lives depend on it for survival, and that is why our bodies always flush out the harmful, toxic materials from our system in order for us to live healthy lives. This is vital because our existence depends on it, but most times in our relationships and associations, we fail to have a mechanism to remove toxic, wasteful influences and associates from our lives. Now is the time for you to look at yourself any time you breathe in and out or you use the restroom as your body removes toxic and wasteful substances from your body. Use that time to evaluate your actions, attitude, associations, and the company you keep. This will help you identify areas in your life that need reassessment, helping you to have a clear and broader view in order to make the right choices.

Detoxification is an opportunity for you not only to analyze the actions and behaviors of others but also to evaluate your actions or behaviors to people around you, in order for you to identify any of your negative actions, behaviors, attitudes, and mannerisms toward those people who came in contact with you at some point. This process helps you to be more conscious not to step on others in your crave for greatness and popularity at the expense of others. It will help you as parents, teachers, bullies, followers, bystanders, victims, or victors. The process of detoxification is necessary in order for you to be more accommodative and adaptive to the shortcomings in others by not using their uniqueness as a weapon to bully them.

When you continuously undergo a detoxification process in your mentality, you will identify the areas of your life and relationships that need rejuvenation. The purpose of detoxification is to remove toxic wastes that might kill you or keep you in bondage because of your negative mentality, which is the result of past experiences and exposures. After you have undergone detoxification, you will need to go through the nourishing or feeding process to sustain your relationships and identify areas that need an urgent nutritional, balanced diet of good conduct in order to maintain, sustain, and rejuvenate your relationships—and to restore and give vitality to keep them aglow.

A Need for Ventilation and Rejuvenation in Relationships

We carry out maintenance and repairs in most areas of life, but the most vital area is sometimes ignored: relationships. It is extremely important to invest in your relationships with others because the greatest poverty is not having someone you can lean or count on. We must take a step forward to ventilate and rejuvenate our relationships that are under strain as a result of our past toxic actions, behaviors, and associations as a bully or a follower. Rejuvenation in your relationships will bring increased vitality, restoration, and healing, while ventilation will remove the noxious, stale air of hatred from your life, allowing a wave of freshness, which is a major characteristic of ventilation.

Ventilating yourself and relationships will expose anything that is a threat, which can weaken your relationships, even yourself, from moving forward. When a heavy wind blows, things hidden are being brought to the surface where they can be identified and recognized as issues that need to be addressed, thereby helping you to know the areas in your relationship that need rejuvenation.

This will bring fresh air and vitality into all you do, therefore improving your contacts, increasing your productivity, and enhancing your value. It will eventually bring new opportunities, broadening your horizon and making you useful to yourself and others. To maintain a continuous freshness in your relationships, it is crucial to go through a bathing process in your mind and attitude to wash away any accumulated dirt that has been acquired consciously or subconsciously. The bathing process will remove any harmful wastes that might affect or interfere with your relationships.

We carry out maintenance and repairs in most areas of life, but the most vital area is sometimes ignored, and that is the area of relationships. Decide today to stop bullying and invest in your relationships with others, because the greatest poverty in life is not having someone you can lean or count on.

Restoration of Relationships

Relationships begin with initial contact, and they are the doorway to other people; thus, a relationship is the conception place for fellowship, which will eventually lead to the birthing of intimacy. At the place of intimacy parents can see beyond the periphery; it is a place where parents can see into their children according to the word *intimacy* (i.e., "into me you see").

In order to see into their children, parents have to have a relationship with their children, which when developed into closeness and fellowship will enable the parents to operate at a frequency that will aid them to diagnose whatever their children might be going through in different phases in their lives. Parents who have a relationship with their children will gain access to their children, and this access will help parents see beyond the actual pictures their children are painting for them, thereby positioning parents as a present help in the day of trouble.

But the reality today is different; most parents have replaced having a relationship with their children with providing for their physical needs. They are succeeding in providing their material needs and also interested in their performance in school but are failing to make provisions for their emotional needs, which is the core department of their lives that guarantees success elsewhere. Most of these children are starved for attention and admiration from their parents.

Sometimes there is no verbal communication and expression of how much parents love their children. Their love is being expressed through supply and the provision of their children's material, social, and educational needs by showing great concern for educational performance in school, which is quite good, but all these provisions should not replace the emotional stability of children or being physically present and active in their children's lives. Most times this area is ignored, and most of these children do not know what it means to love others and be loved. A child who is well loved and nurtured in love cannot be hidden because love radiates wherever it is found, and a person who is loved knows how to show and reciprocate love to others.

No parents want their children to get emotional support and attention from another person, especially if the attention is coming from a wrong person with hidden motives. That is why parents need to have a relationship with their children and fertilize the relationship with an expression of their love for them, by investing time and attention. A parent should be the first person children call when they need help and rescue. Parents need to position themselves as the first rescue number their children will dial in times of trouble. Parents, instead of strangers, should be the 112 or 911 numbers in their children's lives during crises.

Any time spent with children to influence them positively is an investment for their future and the betterment of the society.

Investing in Relationships

Relationships are investments that need nourishment and nurturing; relationships are progressive, and they grow and blossom depending on the nutrition you provide. Giving life and having life in your relationships enable them to grow, because the more time you invest in any relationship, the more you develop confidence in the relationship. Whatever you put into a relationship is what you will eventually get out of it; therefore, your relational capital determines your relational dividend. Any relationship you refuse to invest in will eventually yield minimum or no dividend in the end; hence, your relational capital is proportional to your relational dividend.

Success in any relationship is equal to the nutritional attention that the relationship is being fed and the rules guiding it. It is vital to have rules in every relationship, and abiding to these rules that govern any relationship is what makes it grow. Behind every relationship is a mission statement that is directly or indirectly stated, and this is the rule that governs every relationship. Your ability to have a well-defined mission statement and abide within the mission statement will be the fertilizer that will enhance the relationship because input plus positioning will determine the output or what you will get out of your relationship investment.

That is why it is never too late to go back and work on any relationship that has gone stale as a result of your toxic or harmful actions and attitude toward those around you. You need to invest in people by investing your time and resources into knowing people and making contact. Everything in life needs specific things to grow, such as water, light, time, and so on. Since every relationship needs time to blossom and flourish, parents should invest time to plant their children in order for them to flourish. Without planting there cannot be flourishing. The place of planting is the place of investing time with children; parents should not be absent-minded when investing time in their children, or else they will miss vital signals being transmitted by children, especially when they are facing bullying attacks.

The same is true in relationships, whether you are the parents, the children, the teachers, or the coworkers; time is vital in developing a relationship and friendship in order to get life out of it. Time is the fertilizer that you need to grow your relationship with your children, just as time plays a vital role in a planting process. If you can touch the life of your child by dedicating your time and resources, then you can gain access to his or her thoughts and experiences. Thus, any time spent with children to influence them positively is an investment for their future and the betterment of society.

For a relationship to be prolific there has to be time for a fertilization process that will help the relationship grow, and time for a respiratory process that will help to ventilate. This will bring in freshness and remove any toxic issues, rejuvenating and restoring the relationship, which will develop into confidence and trust. Time invested in a relationship will give it buoyancy and strength, which will eventually lead to companionship.

Relationships are built and not a free gift.

Companionship is a Result of Investment

Companionship is the key to surviving the wind of bullying. It provides a sense of not being alone and knowledge that someone cares and is there to hold your hand through the storm that might be brewing above your head in the form of a bully. Moreover, it is an assurance that goes a long way to empower a person who almost gave up or was on the verge of quitting.

In the course of writing this book, there were students I met who were bullied in school who decided to stop or refuse to go to school because of their experiences with bullies and their followers. In one particular case, when someone stood up as a voice and a shield to silence the noise of the bully in the life of a student, there were instantaneous changes in the student's academic performance, and he became vibrant because he had found a person, a companion, who believed in him at the height of his troubles, a person who gave him a great boost and reassured him that he was not alone.

This assurance can only be achieved through the seed of solidarity, and whereas solidarity is the birthplace for friendship and companionship, companionship gives security to relationships.

Parents are the first teacher in their children's lives, especially mothers; thus, mothers are the first teacher a child will ever encounter.

13

The Gift of Life

A CHILD'S WELFARE AND development from conception is the responsibility of the parents. The fertilization of the ovary by the sperm from the father marks the beginning of this great journey into parenthood, which entails a huge responsibility. Mothers have a major influence in the lives of their children during the pregnancy stage, but this does not underestimate the role of the father in the process.

There are other factors that come into play for the survival of the baby in the womb, but the mother's influence is pivotal. Just like the umbilical cord is the only lifeline for the survival of the fetus and a source of oxygen and nutrition from the mother, so are parents the lifeline from which a child learns and develops his or her personality. Parents are the first teacher in their children's lives, especially mothers.

> *"All that I am, or hope to be, I owe to my angel mother."*
> —*Abraham Lincoln*

Whatever a child becomes will be determined by the positioning of the parents in that child's life because the first angel or bully a child will know will be seen in his or her parents or guardians. When a parent is a loving parent, the child will inherit that characteristic, but when a parent is a bully, the child will sometimes automatically inherit the same bullying behavior.

THE GIFT OF LIFE

The Power of a Mother

God has placed a capacity in mothers that cannot be overlooked in the upbringing of their children. Mothers have the capacity to nurture and nourish their children, and that is why the key to ending bullying in a child starts with mothers. Mothers are the building blocks of the home, and the home is the backbone of the society. Whatever product a home has to offer is what it will eventually manifest in our streets. When there is no love, no moral values, or no respect in homes, it will certainly reflect in society, and it will be the society that bears the consequence by paying the price for the neglect in homes.

Mothers are the only angels their children might know when they are young, and if mothers are aware that they are angels in the lives of these precious gifts, they should learn how to speak and behave in the presence of their children. Since their words and actions are seeds sown into the lives of their children, these seeds are either words of life that will help children discover their potential or words of destruction that will eventually destroy them.

The truth about life is, you can only give what you have.

It is very important for mothers to overwhelm their children with words and actions of love rather than words of hatred and derogation. In the end, whatever words you sow into the life of your child will be what will eventually come out, whether good or bad. The truth is, you can only give what you have.

Mothers are the first teacher a child will ever encounter.

The emphasis on the role of mothers in stopping bullying does not exempt the fathers. Parents decide whatever method they might want to use for the training and upbringing of their children to be a blessing to their generation. However, the role of the mothers is much more significant because mothers are the first teacher a child will ever encounter; they are most times responsible for the implementation of the rules that govern their home. Since fathers often refer their children to their mothers, the role of mothers in the lives of their children is too crucial to ignore. Mothers should return and report to their duty post to be more active because their connection with their children through the umbilical cord remains even after delivery.

Mothers are a Gateway and Access Code

Since mothers are the gateway that brings children into the world, they are also the gateway and the access code to end bullying in our world. In reality, access can only be gained when the access code is active. Whether you want to gain access to your computer, bank account, home, or office building, your access code needs to be active, even if the computer or bank account is yours. If you do not have the right code, access is bound to be denied. If there is any chance of stopping a bully, the cooperation and involvement of the access code, which is the parents and especially the mothers, cannot be overlooked.

A loving woman is the backbone of a joyful family.

There is no family or home that can be successful in the upbringing of children without the help and support of a loving mother. Therefore, mothers need to rise up to their duty by being active in teaching their children to love and live in harmony with other people, irrespective of who they are or where they come from. You are in your children's lives to be a light to them by guiding and anchoring them to make the right choices, especially when they are young.

Teach Your Children to Love

As the first teacher a child will encounter, mothers must teach their children the language of love; wherever there is love, there is kindness, compassion, devotion, respect, and regard for others. Love is about sacrifice, where someone consciously decides to learn to see things from the perspective of others, especially those who are bullied. It is all about teaching children to put themselves in the position of the person they want or choose to hurt and segregate within a group. The teaching of love to children should be a joint venture between mothers and fathers because love (charity) begins at home and not in school. When there is love in a person's heart, there is no room for bullying. A heart filled with love sees what is invisible to the eyes and overlooks what is not perfect in others.

Love sees beyond what the eyes cannot see in a person; whenever love is present, there is affection in attendance.

Love sees beyond what the eyes cannot see in a person; whenever love is present, there is affection in attendance. Where there is love, there is warmth, and where there is warmth, it radiates. When radiation is present, there is an attraction, and where there is an attraction, there is the magnetic force that will bind people together, which is the basis for a solid friendship.

The best foundation parents can ever lay for their children is the foundation that will stand the test of time and the storms of life. Teaching your children to love themselves and to love others will create security and help them build self-confidence. There will be no room for them to look for confidence elsewhere or wait for another person to compliment them before they can believe in themselves. Teaching your children to love is much more beneficial to them because true prosperity and riches in life can be enjoyed when a heart is filled with love for oneself and others.

"Loving and unselfish thoughts crystallize into habits of self-forgetfulness for others, which solidify into circumstances of sure and abiding prosperity and true riches."
—*James Allen*

Love is a Universal Language

Love is a universal language that is easily received and celebrated wherever it is present; it will lighten any darkness—a sunshine that shines all over the world. Love distinguishes you from the crowd, and love makes you behave kindly to those around you. You might be in a place where you do not speak the language, but when there is love in your heart, you can communicate easily and be accepted. This is possible because love is a language that transcends or goes beyond words. Love speaks even when you are not talking; it is our badge for access, acceptance, and conquering any obstacles.

> *"Love knows no distance; it hath no continent; its eyes are for the stars."*
> *—Gilbert Parke*

When children are taught to love other people, they will see the stars in them, and there will be no room for bullying or dominating others. Life is worth living and appreciated when we do all in the spirit of love, because love is always giving and not enforcing its desires on others. When parents teach their children to love, they are teaching them the pathway to greatness.

Bullying will always fail, but love will never fail. Love will always open doors of opportunity for you, while bullying will only close doors of opportunity and even close an existing door. The greatest language any parent can ever teach his or her children is the language of love, which is engraved or tattooed in their heart. Where there is love, peace flows, which creates an atmosphere of tranquility and respect for others.

Love glows wherever it is present; it attracts joy and not sadness. Love is vibrant and not doomed. It brings satisfaction and not dissatisfaction; it gathers and not scatters; it offers unity and not disunity; and it pacifies and not aggravates. Love complies and does not contend; love exalts and does not halt; love cares and does not hurt others; love is kind and not wicked; love is generous and not selfish; love gives pleasure and not pressure; love is good and not grievous; and love is protecting and not bullying.

The best tattoo you can ever have is the tattoo of love engraved in your heart for God, yourself, and humanity, because where there is love, there is peace and not war. Love equips you for the journey of life; it is the only language that will still be spoken when you are gone in the lives of those you have touched and communicated with. Love is equipment that always stands the test of time.

Parents bringing up their children in love and to love are equipping them for life's journey. Therefore, investing in good and quality attributes in your children is the most rewarding investment of lasting value. This value will prove the test of time while you are alive and when you are gone.

> *"In the end, it's not the years in your life that count. It's the life in your years."*
> —Abraham Lincoln

Teaching Your Children to Love is for Your Own Benefit

There is an urgent need for parents to differentiate between financial love and emotional love. Financial love is parents providing material needs for their children, which is necessary, and most parents are succeeding in this area but failing in providing emotional love, which is the transmitter of life and energy from which all other necessities are built to create emotional stability.

But what most parents fail to realize is that teaching their children love and compassion from birth is an investment that will be of great value to them when the parents get older. When parents cannot care for themselves 100 percent, they sometimes depend on their children for help.

Most times the children are not there for them emotionally; however, some might provide material goods. But the core need of parents at that stage of life is sometimes lacking. This is the result of what some parents planted in their children, and the fruit of that tree is now reaped by the parents, because remember: whatever you sow you reap. For your own benefit, it is extremely important that parents nurture and nourish their children in love. Parents should always remember that when they invest time to nurture their children, at the end of the day, their children will nourish them. On the flip side, when parents fail to nurture their children, they are only tampering with their own nourishment.

Love is a Key

The key of love can open any door; even the doors of peace, unity, and greatness are answerable to the key of love. Most parents would want their children to be greater than they are, and for their children to be the best in their life's endeavors and not to be a queen bee or tyrant; hence, parents need to teach their children at a tender age to love people. Love and compassion for people is the pathway to greatness. No leader can lead without loving the people he or she is leading. Any successful leader who is making an impact in his or her field today is a leader who looks out for the welfare of others and pays attention to the interests of those working for him or her.

Love for people is a choice, and parents are in their children's lives to give them direction by guiding them to make the right choice to love and care for others. Love for people will distinguish your child from the crowd. Teaching children to love people will not only make them great leaders but will also help them to gain the knowledge they need to lead others, and this will position your children in the pathway of distinction.

Wisdom is the beginning of knowledge, and to love is wisdom.

Wisdom is the beginning of knowledge, and to love is wisdom; hence, once there is love, knowledge is bound to be productive, which will enable a leader to lead in greatness and tranquility. Love doesn't reduce you but makes you succeed in your endeavor. Love will always conquer the storms of opposition, and no one succeeds in a place of authority without a heart for the people. Love for people will always influence others to support your dreams and goals; thus, a loving heart is a heart for people, and that is the key that will ensure your success in the realm of authority and leadership.

Wherever you are today or whatever hierarchy you might be part of in society, always remember that love is the pathway through which a human soul passes from selfishness to kindness. At the end of your day or duty, what you have to take with you that will be of a lasting value is the experiences and the satisfaction of the positive impact you made in people's lives.

Love the Gift of Life

Love is a seed gift that a sower sows into his or her own life and the lives of others. The seed is sown only once but has a double reaping. The seed of love permeates and irrigates the life of the person who chooses to sow this seed into his or her life and the lives of those he or she comes into contact with. The benefit of this seed is felt by those who have chosen to live a life of the seed of love.

Love is a choice that is made every day in order to give meaning to life. The true beauty of life is seen and felt when life is lived on the grounds of love. When we all truly come to the place of sowing love in our dealings, there will be no room for rejection, segregation, or bullying.

Living in fellowship every day is possible when life is lived on the grounds of love. Love gives meaning to life and makes it authentic when you see in others yourself and your imperfections. Therefore, love is a gift of life that makes it possible to see the stars in others despite their weaknesses or imperfections. Let us come to a place of choosing love every day in order to have *LIFE* (*Living In Fellowship Every Day*).

> ***After the storm, it is love that will stand to say I conquer the storms of life.***

Questions to parents:

- Is there someone who can replace or take your place in your child's life?
- If no, then why transfer your responsibilities to others?
- What kind of equipment are you giving to your children for their life's journey?

No parent is perfect in his or her parenting styles, but that is not an excuse not to aim at perfection in your assignment as a parent. The willingness to be open to learn and inquire about information in areas that you need support will make you become perfect, because inquiring is the key to acquiring in life.

14

Appeal to Parents and Society

To all parents, wherever you might be today in your journey of parenting, it is very important to know that you are in the most rewarding assignment possible. This book is not about judging your parenting styles but making you humble enough to identify areas you need to address. It also lets parents know that there is an urgent need for them, especially mothers, not to applaud or tolerate any form of bullying behavior in a child. It is crucial because no parent or mother wants to lose his or her children to a bully or bullying, and neither will any of the parents of the bully want to swap positions with the parents whose children committed suicide because of being bullied.

Parents need to be fully active in the upbringing of their children by being there to counsel and guide them. In the multitude of positive counsels, there is safety and respect for others because your input in your children's lives determines their output or impact in life. Thus, it takes educating, training, and disciplining to arrive at excellence.

No parent is perfect in his or her parenting skills, but that is not an excuse not to aim at perfection in your assignment as a parent. The willingness to be open to learn and inquire about information in areas that you need support will make you become perfect, because inquiring is the key to acquiring in life.

Stopping bullying is possible and doable when all parents come together as a team, looking through the same lens to see the danger bullying is posing to our children, hence taking their responsibility more seriously by training and educating their children, instilling in them respect for others. When parents become more conscious and faithful to their responsibility, eradicating bullying will be possible. Bullying has surpassed the stage of who is right, or who is wrong, or whether your child deserved it or not. It is now time for parents to come together as a united force to put an end to bullying. In unity parents will stand to win, while in disunity or division they will fall.

Parents' decisions and actions send signals to children. When parents decide to be a rainbow that appears in the lives of those around them, their children learn from them, and their children automatically become a rainbow to a person who is in the midst of a heavy storm of bullying. Parents should teach their children to be that rainbow that breaks out against the odds, against the cloud of hurt associated with bullying, by being a source of strength, which gives hope and beauty to the victim despite the cloud. Parents, please carry out your parenting by example. Be that rainbow in your environment where bullying is dominating and becoming a way of life. Be that rainbow that will bring color against the cloud of bullying in your environment by standing against any form of bullying in our world.

The Voice of Parents

The voice of parents is essential in the upbringing of children and stopping bullying in our schools by teaching them not to take the simplicity of others for granted. Parents, let the voice your children hear be the voice of love because hatred will cost you more than love. Fill the heart of your children with love, and teach those who hate to love again; let them know that we might be different, but we all are the same, and there is greatness in every one of us. Therefore, we should not judge people by their looks or the color of their skin because the seed of an oak tree might be small, but it has the capacity to produce a great tree.

APPEAL TO PARENTS AND SOCIETY

Spend more time with your children, and be more sensitive to their emotions and needs. Do not allow signs or events to escape your attention, and watch the baselines for those little switches in their behavior. The little things that you let slip add up to becoming big issues that can be life threatening or lifesaving. Be a succor to your children, especially those who are being bullied. Parents of bullies should not allow bullying behavior to be exhibited in their homes but should educate their children on the importance of having regard for others and placing value on relationships. It will make our schools safer for learning and strengthen their relationships with others.

The palm tree is not a tree that can be ignored or overshadowed by other trees because of its usefulness and the depth of resources embedded in it. Just like the palm tree, the role of parents in eliminating bullying and finding a permanent solution to bullying cannot be overemphasized. Parents' support and collaboration in stopping bullying create a well of resources with unbeatable, unstoppable influences and effects of change that cannot be gotten from any organization or professional. This is true because at the end of the professional help, the children, whether victims or bullies, will go back home to their parents who are the sculptors that mold their children's lives.

Parents need to grasp the privilege of every moment to make positive deposits into their children's lives. Take advantage of every moment because life transformation occurs in a moment—a life journey is a compilation of these moments as every moment counts. Be an anchor that holds your children's lives together because whatever is not anchored can be easily shifted and influenced by external factors. Be the farmer that cultivates his or her children's lives to birth the potential and treasures within them, and in the process uproots the weeds of bad attitudes, bullying, or the victim or inferiority mentality. Parents are the umbrella that covers or protects children from the rain and the scorch of the sun, including bullies. But do not forget that when the umbrella is not open, the umbrella loses its usefulness. You need to be an open umbrella that covers your children by becoming more active in their lives, whether you are the parents of the bully, the victim, the bystanders, or the followers, in order to make an impact in their lives that will transcend your lifetime.

Parents are the Source While Children are Channels

Children are the representatives of their homes in society; hence, parents should endeavor to build their homes out of love, truth, and integrity so that their children can emulate the standard laid by their parents. In any home, parents are the source while their children become the channels that transmit to society what they got from their environment.

Parents are the source from which the personality and character of children are nurtured and developed, while children are the channel through which these attributes are disseminated into society to either build or corrupt it.

Parents' behaviors can be contagious; how they treat others is transparent for their children to copy and emulate. Parents, being the source, are in the position to influence their children to be a channel that represents their home in society. When love, care, truth, understanding, compassion, and integrity are what is issuing out of parents or guardians as the source in homes, their children will emulate those same characteristics, while in the process demonstrating and exhibiting these characteristics wherever they go.

When parents are too busy to be the source in their children's lives, external sources will influence and contaminate the child because of loopholes left open by the source, which are the parents. Hence, parents need to avoid this error, which can be detrimental to their homes and society. Parents need to remain the major source of influence over their children, especially when the parents are of an exemplary character.

Parents are the source of power that propels their children into progress and greatness. When children are successful in their chosen life endeavor, they become a source, a channel of positive influence to their generation. Whatever a child learned at home is being disseminated to the public. Thus, when parents supply excellence to their children, the children as the channel will produce prominent results in their endeavors and become eminent, which other children will emulate while they remain ambassadors of their homes, being deployed into society to carry the flag of their source—their parents.

APPEAL TO PARENTS AND SOCIETY

Children are the Ambassadors of their Homes

The greatest compliment a parent can ever have is to be told that his or her child looks like him or her or acts just like his or her daddy or mama, and they have the characteristics of their parents, especially when the child is doing great and excelling in his or her life. But it becomes a challenge to the parent when the character of the child is questionable, or a bully and the child are being referred to as a carbon copy of his or her parents. It is crucial for parents to always remember that their children are a reflection of the homes they came from, and they are ambassadors of their homes. Thus, parents need to teach their children to be good ambassadors, representing their homes wherever they are being deployed.

Since children are ambassadors of their homes and are deployed into society, the discipline of the children is mostly the responsibility of their parents. In any society, the discipline of an ambassador is the responsibility of the home country of the ambassador and not the responsibility of the host country; however, the code of conduct of any ambassador is given by his or her home country in compliance with the laws that govern the host country. So is the role of parents in the lives of their children since children are ambassadors of the homes they came from, and they are authorized by their homes to be their representatives in society.

They are ambassadors of their homes deployed into society to stand for the constitution of their homes and to raise the flag of their homes. Most children reflect the home they came from, and whatever flag a child is raising as an ambassador of their home corresponds to that home.

If a child who has been deployed from his or her home is being influenced by external factors to be an ambassador of bullying, it is the primary responsibility of the parents to recall the child for disciplinary measures because he or she went out of line. Children should be deployed from their homes as an ambassador of good will and hope and not of bullying.

No More Excuses

Sometimes giving excuses might be the best option to cover our shortcomings or mistakes, but in the end, such excuses will eventually cost us more than we are willing to pay. Excuses might seem like the right thing to do to cover up a bullying behavior in a child, but in the end its products are always disastrous. Therefore, to maintain peace, it is crucial for parents to put an end to excuses; it becomes vital, especially when the life of an innocent child is at stake.

In order to lessen the blame or to transfer the blame to others, parents make excuses for their children, even when they are in the pathway of harming others. When parents make excuses to justify a bullying behavior in a child, it sends a negative signal. The children, parents are trying to protect see it as an approval from their parents to indulge in bullying activities.

Whatever the reason behind parents' excuses for the bad behavior of their children, the results are detrimental. Making excuses for a child who is a bully transmits a message from parents, telling the child that there is pleasure in wrongdoing. Any parents entertaining bullying behavior in a child by giving excuses for such an illicit behavior are only lowering the standard for their children, which might influence the mentality of the child, resulting in a lifestyle of unnecessary compromise that might be detrimental or self-destructive.

Parents must always remember that their children are not just their children alone but also ambassadors of their homes, and whatever havoc or good they exhibit in society will be transmitted back into their homes. Certainly the home will benefit from the harvest of using an excuse as a cover-up for errors that could have been averted or corrected. The place of excuse is the place of compromise, which is the beginning of lowering the standard. Thus, whatever the reason behind making excuses in order to pervert the truth is an error that must be avoided because in the end, the truth will always prevail.

Revisit Our Culture

Things are changing and will continue to change, but some things should not change, such as caring for those around you, living as a community, bearing the burden of one another, being your brother's keeper, and standing for the truth. But the reality today is that almost everything is changing, including what is vital for our existence as human beings; those things that

APPEAL TO PARENTS AND SOCIETY

made us a community are eroding rapidly. We always say that we are living in a multicultural society, but in reality the society is now an individualist culture, where I alone is the prevailing culture instead of living as a community.

A culture of living as an island and not as a community has been the source of selfishness and disconnecting from people. This culture of isolation, of individuality, of believing the other person will take care of the issue, shifts responsibility to others and judges each other instead of loving and helping one another. The "I" mentality of "I am not my brother's keeper, but me, me, me" makes a person go to any length to get whatever he or she wants, no matter who he or she crushes on the way to achieving that desire. It has a lot to do with bullying in our schools and in the workplace.

There are some cultures where there is social control, where bystanders stand up for others and ensure that there is immediate intervention to put an end to bullying the moment it happens. In other cultures, children are taught not to stand up for other people. They are taught to look away when a person is being oppressed, while others are taught to amplify and aggravate the oppression of others. Today, some people are living the life of "it is none of my business" or "I don't care what happens to my neighbor," and this attitude or culture has led to seclusion and isolation where people are being bullied to death.

When you decide not to stand up for a change, there will be no change because it only takes one person to bring about change. But when everybody continues to think the same way with the individualism mentality, there will be no change. It takes a conscious decision to bring change, and this will impact and change the culture of isolation for good. We all have a role to play in changing the bullying culture in our schools and workplaces; no one is exempted because the trace of our footsteps in the sand of culture will determine the questions the next generation will be asking. Do not allow the next generation to accuse you for not doing enough to bring change that would have stopped bullying in our society.

The mentality that is prevalent today—of me and me alone—has created a vacuum of loneliness, where people are isolated as a result of not being there for one another due to busy schedules or pure selfishness.

People have disconnected from each other despite the crave or hunger for love and care. People have to go online to try to connect with people, and a lot of them have gone online to their own detriment.

We all might have different cultures, but what makes us human beings is not different; that is, our emotion, pain, joy, and need for love and acceptance are the same, irrespective of our cultural background. Thus, everybody has a role to play. A solution is found in a culture shift and everyone taking responsibility for their actions, irrespective of their race, sex, affluence, education, position, or status in society.

Society has a Role to Play

The torch of possibilities and greatness has been passed from generation to generation, and it has been handed over to this generation with the hope that this generation will faithfully pass it to the next generation with the light shining brighter than before. That is why investing wisely in the next generation is vital in every society; in fact, the best investment for any society is in their children (the next generation), who will eventually keep the light of the country burning or put out the light of their country, as the case may be, depending on what was the priority of the previous leaders.

Any society that does not place any value on children or make children a priority has no future. When a country neglects the welfare of children and youth, the country will have no future because children are the next generation who will eventually determine the survival and peace of their country. Whatever happens in the future is anchored on what the predecessor handed down.

> *"Freedom is never more than one generation away from extinction. We didn't pass it to our children in the bloodstream. It must be fought for, protected, and handed on for them to do the same."*
> *—Ronald Reagan*

The greatness of any society can be predicted based on its investment and the priority placed on the welfare and development of the youth because the lifestyle of the youth is a preview of the next generation. They are the picture of the next generation, foretelling what the next generation will be, and that is why the youth should be a priority of any government leaders who say they love their country, or that they are patriotic citizens of their country.

They must make the welfare of the youth a number one priority in their manifesto and ensure that there is a full implementation. Whatever peace or prosperity the present generation is enjoying today is the result of the price the past generation paid, while the next generation will be living on the legacy of the present generation. If you are a true patriotic citizen of your country as a president, prime minister, or citizen, your response or attitude toward the next generation will confirm how patriotic you are because the present generation reflects the hard work and patriotism of the past generation, and we are reaping the seeds sown by the previous generation. Therefore, the performance of any government or society in general is known by the impact they have on the youth and the legacy they left behind while they were in office.

It is great to talk about innovation, development, and success, but the mind of those you are governing must be at peace in order to flow in the same frequency before success can be actualized in government and in homes. An investment in the mind of the youth is an investment in the future; the wealth and destiny of any nation lies in the hands of the youth. Any society that refuses to invest in inculcating the right mind-set in the youth has no future, and its decision to leave the youth behind on the sidelines will have a grievous consequence on society. The price will be too high to pay.

> *"The empires of the future are the empires of the mind."*
> *—Winston Churchill*

When government and homes invest positively in developing the mentality of youth, it will make the homes or country a force others will want to reckon with. Ignoring the youth, conversely, will only lead to segregation, destruction, stagnation, and degeneration of the next generation. It is vital, then, for government to focus on developing the mind-set of the youth by guiding them in the right direction and by educating them on issues that are prevalent, such as bullying in schools and on the work floor. Addressing these issues and implementing a worldwide campaign against bullying will change people's perspective about bullying by sending signals that it is not acceptable, thereby changing the notion that bullying is an acceptable norm among youth. Changing this mind-set will be a great bequest to the next generation.

Just as society has a role to play in eliminating bullying, homes are the base where a child is being groomed. The position of the home and society in the life of a child is like the connection between a tree and its root. There can be no tree without the root; the strength of the root is reflected in the product of the tree, while the synergy between the root and the tree is seen in the fruit. The homes are the root, the tree is the society, and the fruit is the youth. That is why it is vital for homes and society to work together to leave an enviable and excellent legacy for the next generation. Remember that society reflects the sum total of all homes.

Our children's upbringing is the responsibility of the parents and should be run as a marathon, not a sprint. Each stage of a child's life is a bat being passed from the parent to the child. Parents need to watch the type of bat they are passing to their children to carry on in their life's journey.

Children are the Future

Bullying activities in schools are a prelude of what the future holds for a society where bullying atrocities have become the norm; hence, parents and authorities should come together to make our schools a nonbullying zone. Since children look up to their parents and authority figures for guidance, your stand concerning bullying today will reflect in the next generation. Children are either being groomed to impact their world positively in any endeavor they are guided to achieve, or they are being influenced or derailed by external influences.

Children look to their parents and authority figures to guide them and help them make the right choices. Whatever they are told they believe, and whatever words you speak over and over to them are being sown and cultivated in their lives, which determines their pathway. That is why parents and teachers should be careful not to sow negative words into the life of any child; the wealth of any nation depends on the children. It is crucial for parents and teachers not to see any child as a nonentity but rather as a reformer and a shaper of nations. Whether you believe it or not, the destiny of nations is in the hands of that little boy or girl you call your children or students or neighbor's children. The description a child has of himself or herself will determine the path he or she eventually ends up on. When a child is continuously told at home of his or her worth, such words of encouragement or praise will boost his or her confidence, while in the process instilling a self-confidence that is unbreakable, even in the face of life's challenges. Therefore, parents should endeavor to give their children a self-description that will empower them because an excellent description of who they are is a life booster.

Children are too valuable, precious, and dear to the continuity of any society; they are worth fighting for as they are the building blocks of any nation. Their peace is critical for the sustainers of our future because the future of every nation depends on them, for they are the wealth of their nations. When parents and authorities keep this in mind, it will be a fuel that will fire parents' passion to make a difference. Addressing bullying in our schools is addressing the needs of the future.

Food for thought

- Everyone has a story to tell, but be careful how you tell your story. It should give hope to others because in every mess there is a message. Always remember that there is someone waiting to hear your story of what you conquered to give him or her courage.
- You are not responsible for the opinions, actions, or attitudes of others toward you, but you are solely responsible for yours; thus, your mentality determines what you conquer because you cannot conquer a bully with a victim mentality.
- Life's journey is a combination of different junctions that are connected as you journey through life. Whatever ink you choose to join the junctions in your life will reflect your pathway. Bullying is one of the negative inks, so avoid it.
- Life might not be a bed of roses for someone today, but it's not your responsibility to make it a bed of thorns by your bullying attacks. Stop bullying and don't be a source of misery. Be a fountain of joy for someone in your environment.
- Validation can be profitable to you when it comes from your mentors or those who truly love you—not from those who torment you. Thus, do not believe the lies of any bully because his or her validation of you is to destroy your self-confidence. You are not a victim until you believe the validation of bullies. It is an error that must be avoided.
- Live life to its fullest because once a day has passed in someone's life, it cannot be retrieved. It is crucial for your own good to learn how to forgive and forget your past pain, hurt, or shame. When you are able to forget your past pain, healing can begin, and then the weight of bitterness and regret disappears.

Part 4

It is the responsibility of parents to ensure that the dwindling flame of their children's dreams and vision is rekindled so that children do not lose out in their life's endeavors.

15

Dreams and Purpose

Everyone has the capacity to dream and have a vision. For some, that part of their life is very active and intense, while for others, their ability to have a dream or vision has been distorted or made inactive because of painful life experiences such as bullying. Some have done something valuable with their dreams, which have become a reality, while others have nothing but the nightmare of the pain they went through at the hands of bullies, even if the bullying attack happened years, months, or days ago. Hence, their ability to dream or have a vision for their future is impeded by their nightmare—they do not have a dream or a clear vision that will bring them out of obscurity.

Dreams are meant to be chased, because what you chase in life is what you will fulfill. Fulfilling your dreams is the place of achieving your dreams.

Have a Dream

There is a niche with your name tag on it, waiting for you to discover and unravel it, a question waiting for your answer, a problem waiting for your solution—and all these are tied or connected to your dreams. While dreams are meant to be chased in order to fulfill them, a dream cannot be chased if it is not kept alive or the fire fueling the dream is not kept burning.

Until the fire fueling a dream is kept burning, the light of the dream will go out. Many dreams have been shattered and broken at the place of bullying, where the dreams of victims and parents have been cut short, especially for those parents who lost their child as a result of bullying. In order to avert shattered and broken dreams, parents need to help children keep their dreams alive by becoming the fuel that fires their dreams through a focused lens.

One of the major departments of parenting is to help children discover and develop their potential. It is the duty of the parents of victims to be a succor that will help their children not only discover and develop their potential but also keep their visions and dreams alive. Parents should help their children keep the flames of their vision burning because there is opposition wanting to quench the flame or derail and frustrate the birthing of your children's dreams.

It is your duty as a parent to be proactive in keeping the dreams of your children alive. Many children who were constantly bullied in the past, lost their dreams in the process of being constantly traumatized by bullies. Their dreams were aborted and replaced by the pain of the experiences they went through at the hands of the bullies. Their self-esteem and confidence were destroyed in the process, and all they have is the horror, the pain the bully inflicted on them physically, emotionally, and mentally. It is your duty as parents or guardians to avert such situation from being the story of your children's lives by helping them to build a resistance in order for the vision/dream not to be aborted. Many adults today who were once bullied have lost their dreams and vision for life to a bully.

Many people's dreams were destroyed as a result of bully attacks, while others have developed a victim mentality as a result of the assaults from bullies and their accomplices (followers). In the process they abandoned their dreams. While there is another group of victims who still have their dreams, but the dreams are not speaking because the bully stole these victims' voices to express their dreams and visions for life. But the reality of bullying is that some of the victims have no dreams of their own. They only have the dream the bully gave to them, and the most disastrous part of the dream for the victims is that the dream never ends. This has resulted in the victims losing their self-confidence and self-esteem, which has made them victims for life. They have developed the mentality that they are not good enough for anyone to believe in them or accept them for who they are. Hence, they are always trying to please others by becoming a bond servant in order for people to accept them. This low self-esteem mind-set has made some of them more susceptible to further victimization wherever they go; thus, they become a pawn for bullies because the door was opened in their past and has yet to be closed.

Some people in their thirties or forties, some even in their sixties, have lost direction and do not have dreams. Or, they have a dream but do not know how to keep the dream alive. They lost their dream to the attack and experience of the bullying they went through at the hands of the bullies; thus, they have forgotten how to dream and have expectations. Their dreams have been replaced by the nightmare of being bullied in the past, and they are still going through this torment, even though the bullying incident happened decades ago.

The memory of being bullied is bigger than their dreams and, as a result, most of them remain victims for life. The memory of what the bully said about them or did to them crippled their ability to dream or define themselves; hence, they always want validation by trying to satisfy others. Any time they try to do something nice it always backfires on them; either people find them too nice or hyper or irritating in their response, which always leaves them confused, and they spend more energy trying to satisfy others rather than discovering and living their dreams.

It is sad to see a person without a dream. Such an individual only exists but not living his or her life to its full potential—all because of the embargo laid on him or her by bullies in the past. The picture bullies draw for the person has more photographic effect on his or her mind than on his or her own dreams/vision. Such an individual is liable to fail and to be easily victimized by others; he or she goes through life without being satisfied because where there is no dream the person is bound to be frustrated. This is a disheartening situation where most victims of bullies find themselves as a result of their experiences at the hands of bullies, which has eventually crippled their dreams. They are living, but their dreams are dead.

The irony of this is, there are people who are dead, but their dreams are still speaking even decades after their departure from earth. There are dreams that have outlived their dreamers, and those dreams are still speaking long after the person is gone. Martin Luther King, Jr. had a dream, and Anne Frank had a dream, and their dreams are still speaking to us today even when they are long gone.

It is vital for both adult victims and parents of children who are being bullied to be vigilant by fanning the fire of their dreams and not allowing bullies or bullying situations in their lives to quench that fire. They must get rid of the little foxes that spoil the vine in order for their dream or that of their children to thrive. No matter how dark the night might be, it always gives way to the day, and no matter how terrible bullies are, they will always flee from those who resist them. Always remember that your victory over bullies is guaranteed when you do not succumb to their agenda, lose your ability to dream, or forget your vision for your future in the midst of a bullying battle. Never give up on your dreams; empower your children or yourself in order to resist bullies. Certainly, bullies will flee from you, because your dream is worth fighting for and is bigger than the bullies' agenda.

The dreams of Martin Luther King Jr. and Anne Frank are still speaking to us even though they are long gone, and what about you? *Do you have a dream?*

Questions:

- To children: Do you have a dream?
- To parents: Will you want the dreams of your child to be aborted by a bully or bullying attack?

DREAMS AND PURPOSE

Your future is wrapped in your vision; hence, the future of your children is wrapped in their vision.

Parents are Visionaries

In the midst of continuous bullying attacks, some children have lost their self-confidence and self-esteem, which has eventually affected their ability to dream and have a vision. The effect of their dreamlessness and lack of vision continues to limit them throughout their life journey. If help is not given to such children in time, they carry their low self-esteem into whatever they do. They accept whatever others throw at them as the best they deserve, even though they are worth so much more.

It is paramount for parents to become a visionary in the lives of their children to keep their dreams and visions alive. Parents should keep the flame of their children's dreams burning until their children are strong enough to fan their own flame, especially those children who have no vision as a result of it being impeded by circumstances and situations they have come against.

I believe parenting is not only providing for the needs of a child. It also entails parents being there for their children as a visionary, especially for those who have no dream and vision for their future as a result of being bullied in the past or presently. Therefore, parents need to be on alert in order to keep the dreams and vision of their children alive. What most bullies are using to ruin their victims is the corruption of their self-efficacy in their vision. Bullies do this using propaganda and lies, which are being repeated by their followers to tarnish the victim's reputation and self-confidence.

Parents are to be on the watchtower in order to keep their children's dreams alive; it is the responsibility of parents to help their children cultivate their dreams and vision in order for them to become a reality. It is the responsibility of parents to ensure that the dwindling flame of their children's dreams and vision is rekindled so that children do not lose out in their life's endeavors. When a dream or vision is corrupted, a child can be derailed.

Parents being visionaries in their children's lives is a crucial responsibility that must be taken to heart. When a child exists without his or her own dreams and vision, his or her life exists without relevance, which can leave a child susceptible to any negative wind blowing. For example, the winds of bullies can abort the dreams of your children, and when there is an abortion of dreams and vision, there is an abortion of destiny. Therefore, parents, keep the dreams and visions of your children alive because their future depends on it, and their future is being captured in the visions they have today.

When there is no vision, the future becomes blank, and when a person without vision enters the future, he or she is not aware because there is no known vision that will separate his or her yesterday from where he or she is today, or where he or she will be tomorrow. Hence, life becomes a drift that is being carried in at any direction by others, which eventually results in an aborted destiny. For those who have lost their ability to dream or have any vision for their future, their parents should take it as a responsibility to help their children by using their passion as a GPS or a compass to redirect them to the pathway that will lead them to their dreams and vision.

Give an Immunization Shot

At different stages of our lives, even from birth, we all received one form of immunization or another for prevention of different diseases. Also, in our daily activities, immunization is needed and crucial for prevention and survival in the midst of life's challenges.

As children receive different immunization shots to prevent certain diseases, the immunization shots are tailored to suit the needs of the child and the environment the child is living in. For example, a vaccine for polio will not prevent malaria. While the vaccine for polio is no longer needed in certain continents or countries, it is still in demand in another country or region. Therefore, the type of moral immunization shot parents give to their children in relation to bullying should be tailored to suit what is crucial and rampant in their region and what is personally needed for children to overcome their challenges.

Giving a child an immunization shot, in terms of praise, leads to self-confidence. It is like giving him or her wings and teaching him or her how to flap those wings to fly in the midst of the storms of life, like the mother eagles do with their eaglets. It takes skill in order to win, and for any child to be victorious in bullying battles, the child needs to be inoculated for victory. Parents should endeavor to equip their children with the necessary equipment, ensuring that this equipment or these skills are being utilized when necessary to guarantee their victory.

Parents should not allow bullies to encompass their children as a shield but teach and empower them with the skills necessary to break out of any shield the bullies want to use to confound them. Equip and empower your children with the victory vaccine that suits their needs. Giving children an immunization shot from home is a preventive measure that will prevent them from being infected by bullies' attacks. Of course, the immunization shot for one child might be different from another, but the effort is worth it because it will build in the child the resistance that will keep him or her from falling flat on his or her face in the midst of a bullying battle.

Since parents know their children more than anyone else, parents should give their children the immunization for their mind-set or mentality in order to prevent deficiency in self-confidence, self-esteem, and self-efficacy. Meanwhile, some shots will be necessary for enhancing and boosting their image, lifestyle, and boundaries—and for setting a standard against the agenda of bullies. Still, some children are not inoculated from home against bullying attacks, and they are bleeding profusely. It is never too late to help stop the bleeding by applying the medicine needed to bring about a permanent healing—so help in stopping the bleeding of those who were not immunized against the infestations of bullies.

Stop the Bleeding

No human being is perfect or completely self-sufficient. Also in parenting, there are no perfect parents who know it all or have it all covered.

We all have something to bring to the table, and we all learn one thing or another from each other. Some parents are aware that their children are being bullied in school but do not know what to do or how to support their children; hence, they are bleeding but do not know how to stop the bleeding.

When there is an accident, and there is an injury where blood is gushing out, it is the duty of those on the scene to help stop the bleeding in order to save the life of the victim, even before the medical teams arrive. A major concern of any medical team at any scene of an accident, especially when there is a sign of bleeding, is to stop the bleeding and ensure that there is no internal bleeding, which can be dangerous and life threatening.

Today, a lot of victims are bleeding from the injuries they incur from the bullying attack, and some of us are watching but making no attempt to stop the bleeding or to prevent any internal bleeding. It is the responsibility of the victim or the parents of the victim to seek help, and our responsibility to support them positively. That is why it is crucial for all parents to never turn away when they see a child being bullied. It is our responsibility to render first aid by stepping in to help the victim to ensure the bleeding stops, both external and internal bleeding, in order to save precious lives.

In the course of writing this book, I found out that there are some victims who are still bleeding internally from their bullying experiences, while some are busy reopening the wound; hence, the wound is not healing, and the bleeding is still gushing out in spite of many years having gone by since they were victimized. One particular victim I met is still bleeding profusely decades later, and this has affected her in so many ways. It has hinders her interactions with others and placed an embargo on her self-confidence and self-worth. In such cases, until the bleeding is stopped and the wound is cared for by applying appropriate support to initiate a complete healing, the victim is gradually losing out in life. To prevent further bleeding, the victim must learn to forgive for complete healing to take place.

Apply Forgiveness as a Medicine

Though the bullying attacks hurt, and some victims bleed profusely from the attacks, the hurt becomes more grievous if the victim refuses to let go of what transpired. Stopping the bleeding is not enough to bring about a complete healing process because stopping the bleeding is stopping the bullying attack. For the healing process to be complete, however, the application of medicine that will help heal the wound is another phase where the victim needs to be supported. This stage is more delicate if the required support is not provided for the victim right away; hence the hurting intensifies as the days go by, in spite of the bleeding having stopped.

This might eventually lead to another problem in the victim's life, as a result of the victim rehashing the entire scene over and over again. In the process, the incident that happened outside will now be transported internally, where it will eventually torment the victim who will not know the gravity of what he or she is doing to himself or herself. Such torturing sets a battle ring within the victim where he or she continues the bullying battle, without the knowledge of those around him or her. In such a situation, the victim is now the one inflicting the hurt on himself or herself as a result of reliving the painful experience. The irony of it is, since the victim is the one now inflicting the pain subconsciously, it becomes dangerous because most of the time those who love the victim are not aware that there is a battle raging within; thus, there is no sign of the victim's struggle, which would have enabled his or her family to help him or her appropriately.

In the course of writing this book, I met some victims who are going through the bullying experience again and again; they have unknowingly set the ring within themselves for the battle to continue. Some in this group experienced the bullying decades ago, but the battle is even more intensified and fueled by anger and resentment, which has kept the victim in bondage while the bully is long gone. They are constantly reopening the wound, and this has crippled their lives, especially in their relationships and their validation of their self-worth.

So, after stopping the bleeding, it is crucial to apply or administer the medicine of forgiveness, which will free the victim from any pain and all problems that the bullying experiences would have triggered in his or her life. Teaching the victims to forgive the bully and themselves will free the victims from self-condemnation, self-belittling, and any form of resentment that would have triggered the reopening of the wounds—in order for the healing process to take place and prevent any internal bleeding (internal battles) detrimental to the healing process.

You are Not Alone

Life is fragile and delicate. Life is lived every day; you have breath in your nostrils—that is the reason you should endeavor to live your life to the fullest in spite of the challenges you might face in your life's journey. The truth about life is that at some point, the storms do blow, but the timing and type of storm might differ from one person to another. The beauty of it all is that you do not have to face it alone, and that is why life is Living In Fellowship Every Day (LIFE). There is always someone known and unknown to you who cares and is willing to bear your burden with you.

To any child and adult being bullied who do not know what to do, or who are feeling alone in the midst of a bullying battle, you do not have to fight alone. You have to reach out because there is someone waiting at the edge of the bullying attack, stretching out his or her hand to support you and pull you out of the battle ring. All you have to do is reach out, and certainly there is a pair of caring hands willing to grasp you so that you will not slip. Always remember, there are people close to you who are waiting for you to give them the signal to come to your rescue. There is someone out there who wants to be a life jacket for you so that you will not drown in the bullying sea. There is someone out there saying to you iCare, and all you have to do is believe that he or she truly cares for you. You do not have to fight alone.

Wherever you are today, or whatever bullies are plotting against you, never forget that you are not alone. That is the beauty of us as human beings—we are all interdependent. Reach out to those who love you because someone cares for you, and so do I *(you can always reach me via my site at www.evelynekhator.com).*

Your Life Is for a Purpose

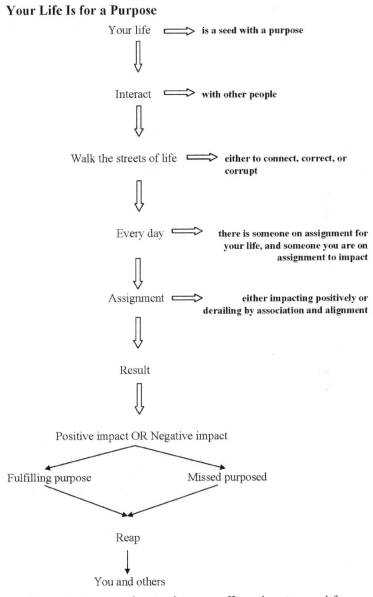

Figure 3. Diagram showing how you affect others in your life

Your Life is for a Purpose

Every day as we walk the streets of life, in our daily endeavor, we encounter people and leave an impression; in some cases it might be a brief or insignificant encounter, but at the end we leave an impression behind that might be detrimental or profitable to our and their future.

Our transactions on the streets of life by our actions, words, attitudes, and behaviors toward those with whom we come into contact leave a mark in their lives. It can be a mark of hurt, agony, bleeding, shame, defeat or joy, fulfillment, tranquility, direction, or upliftment that will redirect and impact the future of those you meet.

Consciously and subconsciously, your contact with each person you meet on your life's journey has an impact on them; thus, be careful of your transactions in the lives of those you meet. Your transactions are having tremendous impact in their lives, either positively or negatively, because your life is a seed with a purpose that blossoms to produce fruits that are reaped by you and those you encounter.

Parents are the bridge over troubled waters in the lives of their children. They are the shield that covers them from the storms of life, and the compass that redirects them on the right path whenever they miss their way in the journey of life.

16

You Have a Role to Play

Bullying starts with one person who usually pulls the bullying trigger where others are eventually initiated to assist in executing the agenda of the bully in the life of the victim. Likewise, putting bullying to an end starts with one person. It is possible to stop bullying when people are ready and willing to change. Change occurs when people decide that the time has come to make a difference. It is a choice, and this choice is easier to make when situations are weighted and the outcome is not palatable or acceptable. Then the desire for a change is triggered. The desire for change is a major factor that will eliminate bullying in our society. This starts when parents lay the right foundation while existing bullies decide to stop their bullying ways, and victims choose not to be victims. Then change becomes the vehicle to bring a lasting impact, which will bring about positive transformation.

All this is possible when all parties involved decide to make the right choices. This can be actualized when parents and society make the environment not conducive for any form of bullying. Since bullying is a combination of different factors, we all have a role to play to stop bullying in our environment by creating the awareness that any form of bullying will not be tolerated. When this message is communicated, the strength of bullies will be weakened, and their activities will be reduced. Now it is time for us to do what is right. We do not have to wait for a crisis or pressure to force us to do the right thing. Let every one of us be responsible by doing what is expected of us in order to stop bullying in our environment.

Bullies

All bullies and their followers should realize that their decision to bully a person does not only affect the person (the prey). It affects their family, friends, neighbors, and associates. Therefore, bullies should think first about how their attack harms not only the victim but the family and society in general. You know that when it rains, it does not fall on one person but on everyone where it is raining—so too is the rain of bullying. The rain of bullying actions is also falling on the bully, whether directly or indirectly.

A bully is also like a child who cries unnecessarily in order to get attention from his or her parents. Although the parents might feel the discomfort associated with the cry, the pain and headache from crying is the portion of the child. Thus, bullies, your actions and attacks on your prey might cause your victim some setbacks or might even lead to death, but the nightmare is all yours because peace is always far from the wicked. Bullies are always aggravated because their time is being invested in evil plots while in the process, they indirectly, mortgaging their peace. As a result, bullying affects every aspect of bullies' lives because bullies take their behavior into all they do, and this makes their world smaller. For their own benefit and for those around them, bullies must choose to stop feeding the urge or desire to hurt or bully others because anything you do not feed dies. Your decision as a bully today not to be a stumbling block that leads to the fall or death of another person, but to follow peace with all humankind, will make you a better person and empower you to utilize your potential for a positive course. You can make a difference in your society. For your own good, changing from being iBully to iCare will open more opportunities for you and broaden your horizon.

Followers

As we all know, a tree cannot make a forest, just as a drop of water cannot make a river without multiple drops accumulating in a single place. As well, a bully cannot operate alone without the help of followers (accomplices). It is high time for followers to decide today not to sell their birthright as a person to a bully by making use of their power of choice to do the right thing, realizing that in every action there are consequences. By so doing, the bully's strengths are weakened because the atmosphere will no longer support his or her action. Therefore, followers do not underestimate your power to make an impact in your generation in a good and positive way. It is vital for all followers to analyze and evaluate the associations they keep, because their behavior reflects who has been influencing them, and who they choose to believe.

When you are a follower of good deeds and actions, you will be at peace with others; that is the only way you can truly impact others, instead of using your potential negatively to defy or destroy others.

You need to ask yourself these questions in order to evaluate your associations and the path you choose to follow:

- What are the effects of this association (i.e., identify the advantages and disadvantages of the association)?
- Will you be proud to publicly talk about your activities and actions you engaged in with this associate?
- Is this the standard you want for your life?
- Is this the brand you want to build?
- Is this the legacy you want to leave behind when you depart this world?

Bystanders

Life is a journey where people help each other to reach their destination because life's journey is never taken alone. There comes a time in people's lives where the warm hand of support from another person is needed in order to fulfill life's journey. Bystanders need to decide if they will be that warm hand to help a person being bullied in the midst of the bullying storm. It is a choice bystanders have to make to assist someone being harassed by bullies. Also, it is vital for bystanders to remember that life is not static, but their actions today to help someone being bullied will make a world of difference, which will enable the victim to go through the turbulence of bullying without fear.

Bystanders are like spectators in a football match. They clap for the winning party. But they are not directly involved in the match, and at the end they go home without any price.

Bystanders will need to decide today if they will be a pacesetter by being a part of the antibullying campaign. This campaign is a journey for saving lives and rescuing victims from the clutches of bullies. When bystanders choose to ignore the cry of the victims today, they might be the target of bullies tomorrow, because a bully is like a pendulum that swings from side to side; thus, the pendulum of a bully might be on their side tomorrow.

Bystanders can only be a pacesetter when they choose not to concur, applaud, or ignore any form of bullying in their environment, especially not joining the bullying crowd or forwarding rumors about people on the Internet. Therefore, bystanders should deploy their strength to help someone who is drowning in the flood of bullying. Be that light bearer in order for your generation not to be swallowed up in the darkness of bullies. Be the pacesetter.

Victims or Victors

Whatever you become is only established by your mentality; when your vision to be a victor is higher than whatever a bully might throw at you, it will have no impact. The wind of a bully might be blowing now, and no matter how hard the wind of bullying is blowing against you, there is something in you the wind cannot touch or blow away; hence, weary out bullies and their followers by being tenacious.

BULLYING

This is only possible when you are determined to be the victor, when you draw the picture of a victor in your mind by continuously visualizing the victory and not the picture of a victim. Do not allow a bully to hold you down or put you in a box in order to silence your voice by making you an outcast in a group, hence rendering you useless, incompetent to yourself and to those around you.

Remember, all a bully wants is to kill your dream by taking your focus away and placing it on the dream the bully wants to create for you. This is only possible if you permit the bully to manipulate your focus. When the bully is in charge of your focus, then the bully can control your life and dreams, because what you focus on is what you will eventually attract.

It has been said that you feel in your body whatever you focus on. When you focus on the actions and agenda of the bully, you end up giving up your own dreams by replacing them with the agenda (dream) of the bully. When this happens you become the victim. This is only possible if you permit it; do not allow any bully to steal your dream because your dream is yours, and you will decide who wins. Either way, someone is winning, and whosoever is winning depends on who you choose to believe. Persist in not giving up or giving in to the plan of the bully, because the winning power lies in your hands.

Be persistent like the dust that covers up a car on an unpaved road; the harder the driver drives on the unpaved road, the higher the dust rises above the car and covers it up. Learn from nature, and be that dust that rises above the attacks and plots of bullies and their followers. Weary them out, swallow them up with the tenacity of the dust, and let them know that you decide the game plan.

The powers to win lies in your hands—not in the bully's—because whatever weapons bullies are using are the ones you gave to them.

Everything in life has a beginning and an end; life is always a journey of coming and going. Even the attack of a bully on you will come to pass, but how it will end depends on who you choose to believe and the pathway you choose to follow. It all depends on you because a bully is like a vapor that is here today and gone tomorrow without a trace (i.e., if you choose not to let them break you). If you do not have the strength to do it alone, ask for help from those people who love you and other appropriate authorities; you do not need to fight the battle alone. You asking for help do not mean that you are weak but strong.

Let the bully know that you know who you are. You might be different from him or her, but you know your potential. You have a dream and vision that no bully or accomplice can take from you. You are a volcano that cannot be ignored, silenced, or kept in darkness. You are bigger than the box that a bully wants to put you in. You should be proud of your uniqueness, capacity, and capability. You are special with great potential that the world is waiting to celebrate. There is greatness in you.

The Role of Parents

Some people believe the solution to bullying is complicated, that there has to be an advanced, delicate theory, but the reality of it is parents need to return to the foundation of training and teaching their children. A hungry, suckling child does not need anyone to tell him or her where to turn for food. The child turns automatically to the breast of the mother. Such actions come naturally to the child because he or she has been taught to suck his or her mother's breast right from birth.

Whether you are the parents of the bully or the victim, you have a role to play in the process of ending bullying. Parenting is an employment that does not have a retirement plan, and it is the most rewarding employment that you will ever gain. It all depends on your positioning in the life of your children. Parents are like a hand lens and a zoom lens that have different functionalities, which can either magnify by enforcing focus or minimize things. Your positioning in the lives of your children can magnify your children by bringing focus into their lives or minimize their abilities and potential.

You, as a parent, are the hand lens and a zoom lens in the life of your children. You are either magnifying or minimizing the bad or good behavior of your children, or magnifying or minimizing a bad situation for the peace of your children. Therefore, parents, it is time for you to evaluate what side of the hand lens your children are seeing and adapting to.

Either way, your positioning in the life of your children will confirm your intimacy because intimacy is the foundation for building trust and confidence. When there is intimacy between parents and their children, there is room for communication, which makes the parent the first person the child runs to in a crisis, all because the foundation has been laid by the parents.

Parents of bullies

It is disheartening to know that some parents of bullies even support their children when teachers tell them the behavior and character their children are exhibiting at school. This behavior is even noticed in children in nursery or primary schools. Some parents ignore the observation, which eventually leads to the grooming of a bully. Some parents are raising their children to be a queen bee but fail to realize that there is a difference between teaching a child a leadership skill and raising a tyrant. When a child in elementary or primary school dominates fellow students and decides who belongs to a group and who should be an outcast in the class, he or she is not a leader but a dictator. A leader tries to carry everyone along and does not make it his or her agenda to hurt or make another person in the group an outcast.

Bullying tendencies can be eliminated in a child at an early age just as the shapes of glassware are determined and defined when they are still in a liquid form and not when they have gone through fire. Also, parents will have to decide if they want to raise a bully or a leader who will impact his or her world positively, because the actions of bullies are impacting their environment, but in a negative and disheartening way.

Parents of victims

Parents of victims program the course of their children's lives by the words they speak in their children's ears and over them. How you communicate with a child who is being bullied will determine the effect the actions of a bully and his or her followers will have on your child. When a child comes home and tells his or her parents what is going on with him or her, the parents tell the child that he or she is being bullied because he or she is weak. In this case, the parents have succeeded in aggravating the situation just like adding fuel to a fire, and we all know the implications of such action.

Parents are the authority figure over their children, and they are in the life of their child to weed or uproot whatever a bully has already planted—not water it. Even when the child is weak, it is not your duty to use it against him or her as a weapon but identify the weakness and support the child by working on the weakness in a positive way. Using all the necessary tools and right words will boost the child's confidence and self-esteem, and it will empower him or her to overcome whatever has been thrown to him or her by bullies and their followers.

Let your children know that they can sleep because you will not sleep or slumber until any attack from a bully is addressed by any legal means available. You are there to support him or her all the way. This will create an intimacy that will build the trust and confidence that your child needs to run to you in a crisis instead of bearing the attack of a bully alone.

Communication and Connectivity

In order to avert the tragedy that is associated with both cyber and physical bullying, there should be a communication line between all parties involved to bring about connectivity, which will enable everyone to be sensitive to the pain of the other person. This includes the following groups of people:

- Parents
- Children
- Schools

Most cyberbullying in school is unknown to the school authorities and sometimes the parents are not aware of what is happening as well. When all parties involved communicate properly, the tragedy that is associated with bullying in whatever form it is being executed will be contained, especially when the victims realize that their parents and teachers are for them and not against them. Armed with this confidence, the victims can then connect with both parents and teachers, which will help the victims to relate and easily communicate the issues confronting them.

It is crucial for parents and teachers to win the confidence of any child who is being bullied in order for the child to come forward to talk about what he or she is experiencing. When parents and teachers are on the same page with the victim, even the bullies, as a result of connecting with them on a level of *"I am for you and not against you,"* then the battle of bullying is half won. Since parents and teachers play a prominent role in the lives of children, it is mandatory for parents and teachers to work together for the benefit of the children.

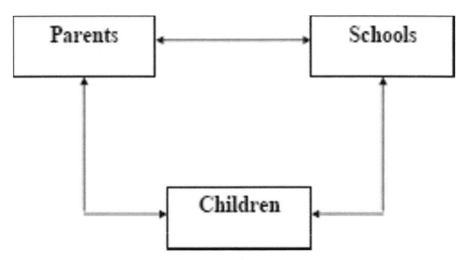

Figure 4. Diagram showing how parents and teachers can work together

The communication lines must flow between all the parties involved. The link or connection between parents and schools is the children. It is high time parents and schools put aside their differences and correctness in order to achieve the aim of both parties, which is the safety of the children. There is a need for proper communication between parents and schools.

Also, schools must put aside their bureaucracy when necessary for the betterment of the students, which is the reason for their existence, because if there are no students, schools will not exist.

Communication between parents and children

There is a great gulf between some children and their parents when it comes to communication. Children believe that their parents are not listening because they are too busy supplying their material needs, and this material supply has replaced one of the basic needs of a child, which is a listening ear and attention. Parents should try as much as possible to communicate more with their children. Most parents are tired after a hard day's work and, in the process of trying to provide for the needs of their children, have missed out on other vital needs. Connecting with them in order to build a foundation of trust is what eventually propels their children to come to them in difficult times.

Trust is the channel through which communication is transported. Trust can be built when children know that they have the uninterrupted attention of their parents, and no matter what might be going on with them, their parents' love for them will protect them, in spite of the consequences of their wrong choices. This trust builds confidence in a child, which becomes the baseline for building a strong communication channel between parents and children. When there is a solid communication line between children and their parents (especially mothers), stability and security in the relationship prevail, which will enable children to always come home to give an account of all the choices they made, whether good or bad.

Communication is the baseline for connectivity. It is vital for parents to have a means of communication with their children in order to connect with them, because communication is the opening or channel through which connectivity is established. No child comes to his or her parents with a problem without having confidence that the parents will be listening to him or her and connecting with him or her no matter the frequency the child is operating from or the child's emotions. Children will always come to their parents when they are confident of their parents' ability to connect with their emotions when they need them as an anchor to help overcome the storms of bullying confronting them.

When a child is struggling, because of the confidence and connectivity he or she has with his or her parents, parents will be the 112 or 911 emergency number the child will dial. In the face of turbulence, children will know the right alarm number to call because their parents have positioned themselves in their lives as a source of refuge and strength. But in a situation where children do not have the confidence to talk to their parents during crises, disaster is inevitable.

When trust is built on the foundation of love and care, no matter what a child may be going through, it is likely the child will go to the parents to talk about his or her trouble, especially when he or she realizes that the parents are listening. All a child wants in the time of a bullying campaign in school is a listening ear and not a judgmental speech.

When parents express their love in words and actions, their children will be at peace, and the security they felt from home will destroy or overshadow any form of tension or stress of bullying. When a child is confident that his or her parent is there for him or her as a refuge and a source of strength in good or bad times, then the child will be secured and equipped to confront the impossible situations, and even shoot for the stars. But if parents are not there consciously because they are busy with other things, they will not know what is confronting their child or what their children are battling in school.

Parents are the bridge over troubled waters in the lives of their children. They are the shield that covers them from the storms of life, and the compass that redirects them on the right path whenever they miss their way in the journey of life.

Communication between teachers and students

Communication between teachers and students can be addressed from two different angles: between the bully and the teacher or between the teacher and the victim. However, the flow of communication depends on the positioning of the teacher and the ability of the teacher to connect or relate with the student, and this will help teachers to take ownership of their classes.

The positioning of teachers will confirm who is in charge in a classroom. It is very important for teachers to take ownership of their classes, especially in a classroom where a bullying activity is dominating. The voice of the teacher should not be drowned out by the voice of the bully. But the reality today is that there are classes where the voices of bullies have drowned out the voice of the teachers; hence, the ability of the teacher to take charge is forgone. It is vital, then, for teachers to be well equipped so that they do not lose their authority in their classrooms.

Teachers should be equipped to handle situation that is undermining their authority in their classes and also have a support system to help those who are being victimized in their classes. Victims of bullying should have the confidence that their teachers will be there to support them and not pretend that it is not happening in their classes.

Parents should know that they are not the authority in schools, so they must stop promoting and supporting their children's bad behavior. Otherwise, they will send a conflicting signal to students when a school is carrying out any disciplinary actions against a bully, especially when the teachers are working within the ethics of their profession.

There is power in turning to each other for support instead of turning against each other. Two people cannot walk together except they agree on the direction.

Communication between parents and teachers

Most times parents and teachers are not on the same page when it comes to the issues and behaviors of the children in school. There are cases where teachers punish a student because of bullying, and when the child's parents find out about it, they contact the school and tell them the reason why their child will not be punished, or they will try to defend their child for what he or she did. Such actions from the parents send the wrong vibe to all parties involved.

When parents react in an unfriendly way to a teacher who is trying to execute his or her job within the code and ethics governing the profession, the hands of the teacher are automatically tied, and there is little the teacher can do because two people cannot walk together except when they agree on the direction.

Most times the students are aware of these differences in opinion between the parents and teachers; such situations will only empower the child to misbehave more in school because the child knows that he or she has the backing of his or her parents. Of course it is the duty of parents to protect the interest of their children, but parents should not support any misconduct of their child because not all teachers are biased in their dealings. There is power in turning to each other for support instead of turning against each other. Eradicating bullying in school may seem impossible, but it is doable when parents and schools work together as a team. It is very important for parents to know that teachers are not against them but for them and the betterment of their children.

Parents, Ask for Help

There are two types of parents:

- Parents who are or were victims
- Parents who want to help or bring a change but don't know what to do

Parents who are or were victims

There are some cases where parents are also victims of bullying at their place of work, or they were victimized in the past, and when their children come home to tell them of the ordeal in school, they are confused. Hence, they cannot provide the proper support their children need; they are powerless and have nothing to offer in such a situation to help their children.

These parents sink into despair and depression because there is no one to share their pain and experiences with, maybe because of the shame of being a victim, or because there is no official help line they can call.

Parents who want to help or bring a change but don't know what to do

While there are other groups of parents willing to help or make a difference, they do not know what to do. They do not know how to handle their children, whether bullies or victims. They want to do something but do not know where to go to seek the help they need to support their children.

In both cases, teachers are most times aware, and they can easily identify these groups of parents because they have more close contact with the parents and the students than any other person. Such a group should not be abandoned to fight alone; they need all the support they can get, especially the students in school. Thus, the role of the teachers becomes very important in order to bring about change.

Teachers, Support or Adopt a Child Today

After the parents, teachers are the special group that can influence a child; teachers know every child in their class and their parents. They know the capability of their students and, to some extent, the strength of the parents. Some groups of parents do not have the capacity and capability to help or support their children, and these students are the vulnerable group that needs the help of the school and teachers. They need a place where they can find help and support. These students are easily identified by their teachers; hence, they have more inside information to support and help them and not to judge them. Teachers need the appropriate tools and extra support to help these students.

If a teacher notices a child being bullied, and they can assess the strength of the parents of the child, it will make a great difference in the life of that child if the teacher will adopt such a student by providing extra support for the child to gain self-confidence and the trust they need to come out of the box of depression, pain, and low self-esteem.

Questions for teachers:

- Can you be a light that will guide your students through the dark tunnels of bully attacks and be the first glimpse of light after a dark night?
- Can you be the hand that will hold them when they are falling while walking on the slippery ice of bullying?
- Can you be the voice that will calm the storm of bullies when the parents do not have the ability to support their child?

Teachers, adopt a child in your class by being there in the child's time of need and through the storm of bullying. Lighten the world of those who are in the dark grip of bullies. Teachers, endeavor to be the refuge where those bullied in your class can run to for safety and draw strength. When a teacher stands up with the victim, it reduces the number of children being bullied. Just imagine, if every teacher contributed by empowering a victimized child, the strength of bullies would weaken drastically.

A good listener, an encourager, is a rare gem in the midst of life's challenges.

17

The Keys-Observations and Guidance

We all have a blueprint for our lives, and the mind of humankind is the drawing board of these blueprints; thus, the sketches of a person's destiny are being drawn, altered, and perfected by the transactions that go on in the mind of every individual. Therefore, it is your responsibility to ensure that this blueprint of your life is not being altered or tampered with by external influences and circumstances.

It is the major responsibility of parents to help their children identify or recognize the blueprints of their lives in order for them not to be derailed by external negative influences. The response of any child or adult in any bullying battle depends on the mental picture they have about themselves. Therefore, let us come to the place where we help those around us have a blueprint that will strengthen them in the midst of a bullying battle.

For those who are not aware of or do not have a blueprint, we should assist them to discover it by working on their sketches in order to make it a reality in their lives. There is a niche waiting for them to discover. Help them draw a blueprint of hope covered with colors that will bring beauty and honor to their lives. Let it be a blueprint that will help them see their future because without a blueprint, there cannot be a bright or fulfilled future. There is something to look forward to when the blueprint of a person is vivid in the mind of the person, even amid bullying battles. Thus, the blueprint in the mind of a person determines his or her performance and response amid life's challenges, and so the mind is the ground where the blueprint of a person's life is drawn and blossoms. So, let us take care in guarding the transactions that transpire in the minds of those being bullied because victory or defeat begins from the mind.

Guard the Mind

The activity that takes places in the mind determines the transactions that transpire externally; hence, the mind is the ground where actions are being processed before execution. Therefore, guarding the mind diligently determines the issues of life that flow through us to those around us, and guarding our minds means to detox, renew, and upgrade the mind in the appropriate area.

How successful we are in detoxing, renewing, and upgrading our minds depends on what surrounds us in our environment. In any bullying battle, victory begins internally and extends externally. According to an African proverb, if your mind has not been conquered, you cannot be conquered externally.

We all know that as a man thinks, so he is; therefore, it is crucial to address the state of the mind of any child being bullied in order to remove any limiting or defeating thoughts about himself or herself. This is possible by sieving the environment to remove all limiting triggers that are creating a defeating mind-set. The truth about the mentality of a person is that his or her thinking or mind-set is always fueled by his or her surroundings and who he or she chooses to believe. Therefore, this thing that fuels the thinking of a person is usually found in his or her surroundings; hence, the external environment has the capacity to influence the internal environment—the mind. However, the mind is the garden where whatever has been inculcated externally incubates and blossoms, which is later transported externally.

The word *guard* means to protect. Children should be taught how to guard their mind in order to protect themselves because anything that can access their mind can access their lives. The minds of children are treasures that need maximum security because the condition of a person's mind will determine what transpires in his or her life, even in the midst of battle. Most victims have been defeated in their minds even before the bullies launch their attacks. Parents must help their children filter all defeating thoughts that are being bred in their minds, while in the process helping them to find themselves by using their strength as an anchor.

Guarding the mind helps a person, whether a victim or a bully, to detox, renew, and upgrade his or her thinking process by removing those negative triggers responsible for his or her mind-set and replacing them with positive triggers for empowerment.

A mind that is not engaged positively will be engaged negatively.

Parents and Society

Bullying is a gray area that has not been given prominent attention in our world despite the effects and chaos associated with it. It is happening everywhere, and society is paying little attention to this epidemic that is so active and aggressive in our schools and workplaces. Bullying is predominant in schools, so it is vital to contain this behavior in a child when it is discovered at a tender age; otherwise, it will spill over into adulthood, and which will lead to too many atrocities.

Today, bullying is a worldwide epidemic that needs to be addressed by looking at the reasons behind the behavior. Therefore, the foundation of bullies must be addressed in order to avert the process of breeding more bullies in the future. As bullies increase their quest and desires to bully others, society needs to increase its pressure to eradicate this deadly disease called bullying by identifying the reasons and actions behind it; then we will gain the understanding we need to solve the problem.

According to Newton's law of motion, an object remains at rest or continues to move at a constant velocity unless acted upon by an external force. Also, in the case of bullying, until parents and society step in to stop bullying, it will continue to move at a high velocity in our schools and workplace. In order to avert more bullying atrocities in society, parents and society should come together as a team to address bullying issues. When parents and society decide to make bullying a problem that needs to be tackled, there is hope of finding a long-lasting solution.

We should not allow ourselves to turn away when bullying is taking place, and neither should we keep silent when another person is bullied, especially after reading this book, because when one child is bullied, a whole family and community is bullied. Thus, we all directly or indirectly feel the heat radiations that emit from the bullying attack. You can make a difference by not only speaking about bullying but by addressing bullying in your environment.

Observation Triggers Action

There are groups of children being bullied who do not tell their parents about their bullying attacks, and most times parents become aware of it only after the havoc. There are also cases when it is sometimes too late for any help to be rendered. The needs and challenges of life have put a lot of parents under pressure to the extent that their parental antenna of sensitivity has become inactive, which leaves some children drowning in the sea of bullies, while well-groomed children are being corrupted and initiated into aiding and abetting in all forms of bullying of other children.

The authority of parents is being undermined, and most parents are not even aware of what their children are involved in because schools have become a breeding ground where children are being influenced by negative association into bullying, and others are being targeted as the victims. The majority of parents are oblivious to all these transactions taking place in their children's lives. It is extremely vital for parents to be observant of what is happening around their children and on school premises. Parents should consciously choose to look around at what is going on in their children's schools, and they will see more than they bargained for. It will blow their minds how bullying activities are raging in schools.

BULLYING

There are societies where parents are permitted to walk with their children to the classroom, and there are cases where children are dropped off in the school parking lot or brought in by school buses. Take the time to observe the atmosphere in your child's school, whether from the parking lot or from within the school building, and you will see that there is an urgent need for parents to rise up and put an end to bullying.

At different points in history, a lot of discussion has being going on about making our schools bully-free. But talking about stopping bullying will be a mere desire or discussion when actions are not taken to enforce it. Actions can be taken when people are enlightened about the havoc bullying causes; then people become more observant and careful to pick up on any form of bullying escapade. When people are aware of the danger associated with bullying, their willingness to put an end to such a threat becomes a top priority, because what you choose to see will command your attention. Thus, observation triggers action. But there are cases where parents are not in a position to observe what is going on within and outside the school premises, and in such cases, parents should deploy their senses, especially the listening sense. The conversation that your child raises when he or she gets back from school is not just a mere chanting; sometimes there is a message that you might need to acknowledge. In some cases, it might not necessarily be about your child or that your child is being bullied; it might be about another child. Then it becomes crucial for you to take note and not let it slip because you can empower your child on how to support someone who is being bullied.

At one point or another, lifesaving opportunities have slipped past parents because of the busyness of life. Parents, do not be too busy to lose your child, and do not be too far to hear his or her cry. The ability to hear the cry of your child or other children around you is the genesis of finding a solution to his or her problem. That is why it is vital for parents to employ/deploy/activate their senses to hear, feel, see, and speak in order not to let anything slip past their attention. It is better to learn by deploying our senses than to learn through disastrous situations or happenings, which can sometimes be irrevocable and irreplaceable. Decide right now to be observant of what transpires around you because someone's life might be depending on you; consciously observe your environment today and identify those who need your help to conquer the bullying battle that is confronting them. In the end, you will be touching someone's life positively through the medium of being more observant, which will give you a satisfaction that you might not get elsewhere, because true satisfaction comes from touching lives positively.

> *A good listener, an encourager, is a rare gem in the midst of life's challenges.*

Listening is a Pathway of Guidance

Some children who are fiercely involved in a bullying battle are crying, and there is no one listening, no one to guide them out of the battlefield of bullies. There are some bullying pitfalls that could be averted, but because there is no listening ear for some children being bullied, many have not only fallen into the bullying pit but have sunk deep inside without hope of coming out.

Let us be more sensitive to the cry of those around us who are involved in a bullying battle. Let us rescue them from falling into the bullying snares, because listening to them will help them to avoid pitfalls. The place of listening is the pathway of guidance, where the listener connects and stays in touch with the pain of the victim and, in the process, helps the victim to find solutions to his or her problems. It is a place of bearing others' burdens in times of their battles, pain, sorrow, and joy. It is a place of encouraging others in times of need.

The ability to listen empowers you to stay connected, to be in the frequency where you are able to provide the right words of encouragement for those in need. Listening to the cry of children being bullied will make you an anchor in their lives, which will help them to sail safely through the troubled waters of bullies. Therefore, consciously choose today to be sensitive to the cry of those being bullied by being a good listener, an encourager, and a rare gem in the midst of life's needs. Be a map that will direct and teach those in a bullying battle how to make use of life's door signs in order to exit the battlefield without becoming a casualty.

The reality of life is that there is always a point of entry and a point of exit. There will arise a time in every person's life where these signs become the source of safety, especially for those who are conversant and fully utilizing these signs in their life's journey.

Make Use of the Entry, Exit, and Emergency Signs

In everything we do, there is always a point of entry and exit, while in some cases there are emergency points of exit. These doors can be found in major buildings such as schools, hotels, hospitals, homes, and even on aircrafts. Yet, there is always a control measure in place to permit access or entry to any of these buildings or aircrafts. But there comes a time when the need arises to exit or disembark, especially when the expected goal or destination has been reached. There are also times when it becomes crucial to disembark at a location using the emergency exit door for safety purposes, especially when it pertains to saving lives and the destinies of people or nations.

There will arise a time in every person's life where these signs become the source of safety, especially for those who are conversant and fully utilizing these signs in their life's journey. It is crucial to recognize and activate these door signs in our lives, but most times we fail to activate them or make use of them when needed. Such failure to recognize the usefulness of these signs has led to the derailing of some people's lives and dreams. Some have lost valuable opportunities and even their lives in the process of not recognizing the value of these signs.

At some point, these door signs will be needed to either gain access that will make you or break you. But wherever you might find yourself in life, when using this entry door, it is never too late to make use of the exit door when necessary, because the exit door is there to make an escape route for you. In case you have ignored the need to make use of the exit sign, it is never too late to make use of the emergency door sign, especially when the alarm bells and lights are beckoning you. Whether you are a grown bully, a victim, a follower, or whoever, ensure you make use of these signs. Your destiny and those around you depend on it.

To the parents of young children, teach them early on in life how to place these door signs and appropriate these doors effectively as they journey through life. To the parents of children being victimized, teach them the usefulness of these door signs, because their ability to recognize these door signs will help them save themselves from any threatening situations. In particular, the entry sign is vital because if there is no entry, there will be no need to make use of the exit or emergency exit. So, let your children know that they are in charge and not the bully because they control who or what gains entry (access) into their lives. Thus, parents equip your children with tools and resources that will secure the borders of their lives. In a situation where there is already an entry, tell them it is never too late because that is what the exit and emergency exit doors were meant for. Help them to make use of the exit or the emergency exit doors, depending on which door suits their situation. To each of us, do not ignore these door signs in your life; apply them today to escape any casualties or calamities that would have happened. Thus, let these door signs be active in your daily endeavor.

You are the driver of your life.

18

It is in Your Hands

Your life is like a vehicle, and you are the driver of that vehicle; you are the one who decides the destination of that vehicle and not the manufacturer. There might be a manufacturer's guide and instruction manual, but the decision to comply is in your hands.

You are the driver of your life.

Therefore, how you drive the vehicle of your life might be influenced by certain factors, such as your behaviors, attitudes, actions, exposures, and handling of the vehicle, which will eventually confirm how far you will reach, considering the duration and the route you decide to take to get to your destination.

All these factors determine if you will arrive at your destination, but be sure the vehicle is moving, it is not static, and you are either in the right direction or the wrong direction. Always remember that, you are in motion and this motion is on a highway. But you cannot guarantee the behavior of other drivers; hence, it is for your own good not to stand still in the middle of life's highway; there are drivers who are bullies looking for someone to hurt or harm, which can end your journey in life or distract or derail you and bring you to the destination *they* have decided for you.

In life's journey, your focus is the fuel for your victory—so remember, you are not a victim until a bully controls your focus; hence, whatever controls your focus controls your life.

Do not stand still on the highway of life because standing still in the middle of a highway will only result in disaster. Any time you are wallowing in self-pity as a result of a bully or bullying situation, you are exposing yourself to be crushed by other reckless drivers on the highway of life. In order to prevent that from happening, keep on driving and do not allow another person to distract or derail you in your vision and purpose. Whatever controls your focus controls your mind and your emotions, which will eventually enslave you. Remember that you are the driver of your life, and what controls the focus of the driver determines the destination of the driver. In life's journey, your focus is the fuel for your victory—so remember, you are not a victim until a bully controls your focus; hence, whatever controls your focus controls your life.

Be a Vanguard and a Rear Guard

In schools, teachers and authority figures are pressured to complete the school syllabus. In businesses, accountants are pressured at the end of the month and year to accurately report their figures. Also, in the journey of life, there are syllabi that need to be covered, but most of the time people fail to make an attempt to implement or cover their life syllabus. Until parents come to the place of ensuring that bullying is one of the life syllabi they need to address, there will be no change or prospect of ending bullying in schools because you can never change what you do not acknowledge. Parents should consciously decide to be the vanguard in ensuring our schools are bully-free and a rear guard to those who have been a victim in order to prevent them from sinking into despair. Too many children who are being bullied have no one to watch their back for them.

Parents should unite to put an end to bullying. Whether you are the parents of the bully, victim, follower, bystander, or the voice, let us all come together and stop pointing fingers, because we have been pointing fingers for too long, and it has taken us nowhere. An effective and long-lasting change can be achieved when all parents come together to become a vanguard and a rear guard in ending bullying. Being a vanguard or rear guard is a choice, a choice that will attract a huge responsibility and impact our world far more than you will ever imagine. Let parents come to a place where they will make a difference by becoming the vanguard in bringing bullying to an end in our schools and changing the calendar in our school system concerning bullying. Let parents take it as a responsibility that is greater than "I want to make a difference" and come to a place of "I have to make a difference."

I Want To and I Have To

There are major phases that amplify the power of choice and responsibility, such as "I want to" and "I have to."

"I want to" is a choice. Meaning, there are options available for you to choose from. There is room for negotiations that certainly attract consequences, which can be beneficial or detrimental, depending on what you have chosen. Choices are the trigger for responsibility and irresponsibility. When you choose responsibility, you come to the realm of "I have to," which is taking ownership of the situation.

"I have to" is a responsibility. Here no option is provided; necessity made it impossible to transfer one's duty, which eliminates excuses and compromises. "I have to" can be of great benefit if it is for a good purpose but can also have a negative outcome when the reason behind it is evil.

Hence, the highlights of life's journey are a compilation of choices we make every second, consciously or subconsciously. It is crucial to think carefully whenever you use the phrases "I want to" and "I have to" because they come with consequences that can be profitable or harmful. It is in your hands to make choices that will bring you to the realm of being responsible because you are the custodian of your actions.

The choices we make in life show what we are committed to because our choices are a reflection of our commitment.

Responsibility is a Choice

Responsibility or irresponsibility is a choice. Responsibility is a choice that can become a mandate when you choose the pathway of being responsible. When you decide to follow the path of responsibility, discipline becomes your watchword because it takes responsibility to instill discipline. In every area of life, it takes discipline to establish order, and order is the birthplace to bring structure to all of life's endeavors; hence, parents are order-keeping disciplinarians in the lives of their children.

In any area of life in which parents choose responsibility as a mandate, discipline becomes the foundation to bring order and structure; therefore, in bringing order and structure to our classrooms in schools, parents and school authorities have to collaborate as an order-keeping force so that there will be a lasting change in our schools. Your response to the bullying of a child who is not yours is a confirmation, if you have taken it as a responsibility, to ensure that our schools and work floor are bully-free. Taking responsibility gives you the ability to act and make a difference in any given situation, including bullying, but being indifferent to the bullying attack of another child only aggravates the situation, which might endanger the life of the person being bullied.

Note that your indifference to the bullying of others might be a catalyst for the depression, isolation, or death of an innocent child. Hence, eradicating bullying is a choice that parents have to make, and this choice comes with a huge responsibility that will save the lives of innocent children. I believe that it is a responsibility worth taking. Whatever you decide to do after reading this book is a choice, and any choice you make concerning bullying attracts consequences. The choices we make in life show what we are committed to because our choices reflect our commitment. When you choose consistently to make it your responsibility that no child will be bullied to depression, isolation, or even an early grave, that choice becomes a mandate that will empower you to make a difference. Making your environment bully-free because you are consistently speaking and acting against bullying will be like a persistent drop of water that will gradually erode granite; hence, your decision to stand up against bullying can even break a stonyhearted bully. Thus, in consistency lies the power to make a difference in our schools and workplaces. Remember, your decision today will not only affect your generation but generations to come; your decision will become your legacy for posterity.

> *"In consistency lies the power."*
> *—Gloria Copeland*

Acceptance of Responsibility

In every phase of life, we only respond to what we have accepted responsibility for, and most of the time we become nonchalant to those things or situations that we believe are not our responsibility. But there comes a time in life when certain issues do not affect us directly, yet we decide to correct what has been corrupted in order to avert the pain and heartache of others.

> ***Bullying is an endless nightmare when there is no acceptance of responsibility and intervention by society.***

Some of you reading this book might not have experienced the agony of bullying personally but will choose to make it your responsibility to advocate against bullying in our schools and workplaces. The group of people and parents who accept this responsibility are responding to the cry of those in the tunnels of bullies by being the light that shines at the end of the tunnel, giving hope and strength to those who are held in the web of bullies.

In acceptance of responsibility lies the power to tackle the bullying problem that is confronting so many people. Until every one of us becomes our brother's keeper by speaking against bullying, there will be no solution, because responsibility births solutions. Dodging responsibility, on the other hand, only escalates problems. Accepting responsibility to stand with and for a person being bullied makes you an extinguisher that will put out the bullying fire in the victim's life. Whoever chooses be an extinguisher in putting out the bullying fire in another person's life has distinguished him- or herself from the crowd.

Parents should be the vanguard by acting as the extinguishers for others to emulate. When all parents accept this responsibility, they will reign, and when parents are reigning that means they are in charge of correcting what has been corrupted in our schools.

Parenting with Positive Passion

Parenting with positive passion will bring a tremendous change to the lives of children while making parenting much easier and less challenging. Passion brings enthusiasm and positive energy, and it is the flame that keeps love aglow in whatever you do. When parents, especially mothers, put their passion into the upbringing of their children, it will certainly rub off on their child, because the child will attract that aura of passion, which will build confidence in the child and help him or her to conquer any obstacle.

When the passion of the parents is fueled by love, there will be no room for a bullying mentality in a child because where there is no bully, there will be no bullying. Parental passion gives access to parents to connect with their children in a way that is so powerful and effective, impacting them in a more positive way. When parents take it as a responsibility today to wholeheartedly come together to put an end to bullying in our schools, there will be no force that can stop them, especially when they put their passion into it to ensure that our schools are safe for learning. A clear message will be sent to the bullies that their actions are unacceptable, and there is no hiding place for them to operate.

One of the most crucial ways to end bullying is when parents, especially mothers, put their passion into ensuring that no one's child will be a victim of any bully. Then, there will be a glimpse of light at the end of the tunnel. The passion of parents will be the fuel that will influence the atmosphere in our school environments by setting in motion the necessary steps needed to communicate to children that bullying is not an acceptable norm, no matter who they are or what background they are coming from. This will be possible when parents take it upon themselves to be the vanguards in ensuring that no child, not even one, will be bullied to obscurity. It will amaze you what impact parents can have in making our schools bully-free zones.

Until mothers kindle that passionate part that made them mothers, the hope of stopping bullying in our schools will be a mere wish. Mothers have the capacity to bring a change to situations that seem hopeless because of their passionate nature as women and mothers. Thus, I appeal to all mothers to be a mother to all children. Be other children's keepers and have zero tolerance for any form of bullying.

Parents, especially mothers, putting their positive passion to work will help eliminate bullying atrocities and will transform children which will eventually affect the entire school atmosphere. Thus, when parents with passion make it their vision to have bully-free schools, they are on a mission of saving lives. Vision determines mission. Parents, make it your vision that no child is bullied to obscurity, and then you are on a mission. Parents, with your passion, you can make a difference by making it your vision to stop bullying in school. Then, you are on the mission that will feature a safe learning environment for future generations. Indeed, this vision is worth pursuing because it is a vision of saving lives and destinies.

> *No child should be left behind on the sidelines of life because of bullying.*

Passion: Pass it On

Passion is the birthplace of mandate, and a mandate is fulfilled by the frequency of passion, which is Pass It On. When parents come together, especially mothers, to awaken their passion to speak against any form of bullying in schools, it will become a mandate, which will be fueled by their passion.

When mothers put their motherly passion positively into ensuring no child is left behind on the sidelines of life because of bullying, it becomes a mandate with a message that is fueled by passion for others in our society to emulate. A mandate becomes successful when it has the ability to invoke a change and influence others to become a part of the mandate, which will impact a change; thus, the passion of parents for their children will be the trigger to influence others to join forces with schools in creating a conducive environment for learning for all children. The passion of parents, which will fuel this mandate, will create opportunities for schoolchildren to exploit and express their hidden treasures.

To all parents, will you, as you walk the streets of life today, create an atmosphere where opportunity is given to someone to exploit and express his or her hidden treasure, where he or she can become confident in his or her abilities? If your answer is yes, then you are saving and impacting lives.

Atmospheres are created and opportunities are given. As you walk the streets of life today, create an atmosphere where opportunity is given to someone to exploit and express his or her hidden potential by creating an atmosphere where people can become confident in their abilities.

The Streets of Life

It is not enough to be aware of the atrocities caused by bullying activities; it is crucial to be sensitive to the havoc that bullying is causing in our schools and society. Never walk the streets of life with your eyes closed to the needs and hurts of others. As you step out to your daily endeavor, let your eyes be opened to see those who are being bullied around you; be sensitive to their cry and pain. Be a source of strength and encouragement to rescue and save a life from the grip of bullies.

IT IS IN YOUR HANDS

Extend a hand of support to someone today, be the shining light in the pathway of those you come into contact with, and let them know there is always an exit point in every tunnel—and hope for the hopeless. So, be the light that shines on those being pushed by bullies into a dark corner, and endeavor to let your light shine brighter every day. It is in your hands to make an impact in someone's life by walking through the streets of life with your eyes open to see the bullying fire that is raging in the lives of others. Please walk the streets of life with your eyes open to see beyond the realm of "I want to," and arrive in the realm of "I have to."

Attitude Counts

Every new day is a fertile day that is being cultivated by your attitude; how productive your day is or was is proportional to the attitude you exhibit or take into each day. Hence, wherever you are today is at the mercy of your attitude. Your attitude transmits information about who you are, which can be accessed by people with or without your consent; your attitude is like the Internet that can be accessed by being connected. Those around you can easily access who you are based on what you are transmitting with your attitude.

With the rising and setting of the sun, opportunity is given to you to speak against bullying in your school, workplace, or neighborhood, and whatever pathway you choose is being transmitted by your attitude; thus, your attitude toward bullying is either abasing or amplifying bullying in your schools and workplaces. Every day you have the opportunity to put an end to bullying in our society, and your ability to do it is being cultivated by your attitude. How productive and effective you are in ending bullying in your environment is proportional to the attitude you exhibit in any bullying environment.

Whatever path we choose regarding bullying in our environment, we should always remember that our lives are like a blank open book, and we have been given the opportunity to write whatever we desire on those pages. Every day a new page is waiting for us to write, and we are writing on those pages with our attitude and actions. Whatever you choose to write on these pages of your life's book is a choice with consequences, either positive or negative. But you must remember that this book you are writing is an open book that is opened to the world to read with or without your consent. Whatever is the content of those pages of the book of your life is your legacy, which becomes the pages in history that will not be forgotten, depending on how impactful you were in the world.

Your responses and attitudes toward bullying in your environment are being seen and read by those around you; it does not only affect those being bullied around you, but it also affects your productivity each day, whether we accept it or not. Directly or indirectly, we are making an investment and deposit into our tomorrow with our attitude toward bullying in our society, and certainly we are making withdrawals, which set in motion our harvest in our different endeavors.

Expression is a Snapshot

Every day, every minute, we as human beings are on a journey. It is a journey where we travel through the streets of life, which become our transit hall, where we meet with other travelers and, likewise, go to our connecting flights to our various destinations.

It is a journey where there are continuous interactions where people meet for different periods—some short term, some long term, and others a lifetime. All these connections take place in various settings, which are mostly our transit halls where people connect with their next flight in life. This transit hall can be a work floor, school, station, mall, or even the street, and at the end, what is left behind is an impression—a memory.

There is always a contact transaction going on. It is crucial for you to express yourself in a way that will benefit you and those you meet in the streets of life, because your expression is a snapshot you leave behind. It is the picture or impression drawn on the lives of those you meet, which determines their response to you. Since your expression is a snapshot of who you are, then your expression is your will, which is communicated to those you come into contact with when you form an impression on them; hence, in life, never communicate what is not your will via the agency of your expression. What you do not want or mean, do not express, because your expression determines your impression on others and the response you get from them. Whether you are a bully or victim, there is never a second chance to make a first impression; therefore, do not give a signal that will be detrimental to you and others.

Your Life is a Seed

Your life is a seed that is being sown into the lives of others in the form of relationships and associations, but the uniqueness of this seed is that you are the farmer that will sow the seed of your life. Since there are different types of soil, as a farmer you decide the type of soil in which you will sow the seed of your life. Believe it or not, directly or indirectly, you are sowing your life seed already into one of these soils. Whatever soil you choose will determine the fruit you produce.

Our decision about bullying should be made with the future in mind because the consequences of our decision today will tell on the future generation.

Sponsored

Everything that takes place in any sphere of life is being sponsored in order for its actualization. Directly and indirectly, we are actively involved in sponsoring activities going on in our lives and in the lives of those we meet. Your sponsorship can have a positive or negative impact on your life and on those around you; thus, sponsorship is responsible for every transaction that takes place in our activities in the streets of life. The place of sponsorship is the place of promotions, where lives are being impacted and influenced. Here are some sponsorship examples:

- Output is sponsored by input.
- Reaping is sponsored by sowing.
- Success is sponsored at the place of time investment and working at your goals or dreams.
- Honor is sponsored at the place of respect.
- Character is sponsored by content.
- Relationships are sponsored at the place of investing time to nurture, groom, build, and maintain.
- Accountability is sponsored at the place of willingness to be a disciple and disciplined.
- Acceptance or rejection is sponsored by actions.
- Actions are sponsored by decisions.
- Decisions are sponsored by input, which affects the state of the mind.
- State of the mind or mind-set is sponsored by the transactions in the mind via the agency of influence of the environments.
- Depression is sponsored at the place of loneliness.
- Unity is sponsored at the place of solidarity.
- Solidarity is sponsored at the place of acceptance.
- Disunity is sponsored at the place of rejection.
- Bullying is sponsored at the place of mingling with the wrong company and by upbringing.
- Victims are sponsored at the place of low self-esteem, low self-confidence, and who they choose to believe for their self-description.
- Ending bullying is sponsored by our decisions and actions today.

Therefore, it is in your hands to end bullying. Whatever is your perception concerning bullying, it is directly sponsoring bullying or stopping bullying in your environment. Let us come to a place where we will consciously choose to stop bullying in our environment.

It is in Your Hands

The damage bullying leaves in the lives of parents, family members, friends, colleagues, and loved ones is irrevocable, irreparable, and a reality that these

IT IS IN YOUR HANDS

families are living daily. Therefore, whatever you choose to do in any bullying situation will confirm whether you are endorsing bullying, but either way, you are doing something, and it is in your hands to make a change.

Remember, nothing changes on its own and situations change when people decide to do something about it. Bullying will not stop in our schools or workplaces until something is done about it; we have been talking about bullying, but it is time for each of us to start addressing bullying in our environments because change takes place when a situation is being addressed, not merely talked about. As a parent, what you do not want to happen to your child, you should not want it to happen to other people's children.

We all have a role to play, and most things in life begin with the actions of one person. Consider this, for example:

- Walking starts with one step.
- Talking begins with one word.
- Numbers start with one.
- Writing starts with a number or an alphabet or a word.
- Building a skyscraper begins with one brick.
- Drinking begins with a sip from a cup at a time.
- Eating begins with one spoonful at a time.
- Sleeping happens in one bed at a time.
- Breathing happens one breath at a time.

Ending bullying begins with one person deciding not to be a contributor

- as a bully,
- as a follower,
- as a bystander, or
- as a victim.

Remember the following advice:

- It's not about them but *you*.
- There is no them but *you*.

- Change starts with *you*.
- Choice starts with *you*.
- Victory starts with *you*.

Ending bullying in your environment and our world begins with *you*. It is all about *you* making a positive difference in our world by saying no to bullying. Your voice counts in stopping bullying. It is all about *you*, and *now* is the time to make a difference.

It is in your hands.

Food for thought

- People feel compelled to tag or label others; however, it is your decision to accept or reject whatever tag or label they want to give you. But remember that the mental picture you have of yourself will determine the response.
- Endeavor to extend a hand of support to someone today by being the shining light in their pathway. So, be the vanguard in putting an end to bullying in your environment.
- Each of us can lighten the darkness of another. Do not allow anyone to quench your light because there is someone your light will guide today.
- Extend a hand of support to someone today; be the shining light in the pathway of those you encounter; let them know that there is always an exit point in every tunnel, and there is hope for the hopeless. Be that light that shines on those being pushed by bullies into a dark corner, and endeavor to let your light shine brighter every day.
- Every day a new page is being opened to us in our life's book; therefore, whatever we decide to write in the blank pages of our life's book will determine the reactions we get from others. Whether you are a bully or a victim, remember that each day you are writing a story with your life that is open to the world to read, with or without your consent. What story are you writing with your life today?
- We cannot turn back the clock but *can* set it forward, just as bullies cannot undo what they did in the past; however, they can choose to be a better person today by deciding not to be a bully.
- People are being victimized and bullied into obscurity and silence. Do not take their silence to mean they do not need help because in their silence they are crying, reaching out, and waiting for you to rescue them. Are you willing to be the person who illuminates the way for someone being bullied? Stop the bullying activities that are happening all around us.

For further inquiries or support on the subject,
Visit my website: www.evelynekhator.com

Food for thought

- Reflect on your strengths; it will generate the confidence you need to achieve your goal.
- The positive empowerment of a child is the equipment for victory in life's journey, irrespective of the challenges he or she might encounter.
- No one has your interest at heart more than you do. For your own good, it is vital for you to exit the company of those who underrate or have no confidence in you. Avoid any association who uses words to kill your dreams; run away from those who do not believe anything good will come out of you; and stop fraternizing with those who pull you down; instead, seek out those who will propel the hidden treasures in you to be birthed, and mingle with those who will help you to maximize your potential.
- Ask yourself why you are in this person's life today. Your ability to discover why you are in someone's life gives purpose to the relationship; thus, in any relationship that is not defined, abuse is inevitable.
- The picture you have of yourself is the picture you present to others, and their response to you is determined by your presentation.
- Any society that does not make the youth a priority has no future because the future you spoke about yesterday is today. Investing in our youth is an investment for a bright future, and the future is tomorrow.
- Consciously choose your words today, for your words have the power to impact positively or derail others you meet. So, choose your words carefully, and stop bullying with your words.
- Most of the time, a bully cannot operate without followers and bystanders who directly or indirectly endorse the bully's operations. Whatever is your stand regarding bullying, we all are signing our signature consciously or subconsciously to either stop bullying or promote bullying activities.

- In life, every moment counts. Utilize every moment and the opportunities that come with it because life's issues are always factored in. Do not allow anyone to isolate or deprive you from enjoying your moment.
- Bystanders should be the Good Samaritan who will rescue a victim from the isolated alleys of bullying. Impact a life today by standing with and for a person who is being bullied.
- Take advantage of every moment today because life transformation occurs in a moment. Life's journey is a compilation of these moments. The responsibility is on us to make our society bully-free, so stop bullying as every moment counts in your life's journey.
- Smiling will cost you nothing, but it will reflect on those with whom you come into contact and brighten their day. So, be the rainbow that will add color to someone's world, someone surrounded by the cloud of bullies.

Made in the USA
Charleston, SC
19 October 2015